PONTE VEDRA BEACH

A HISTORY

MAURICE J. ROBINSON

THE History PRESS

Published by The History Press
Charleston, SC 29403
www.historypress.net

Cover image: "Shoreline Dunes." *Courtesy of Ellen Diamond and Fairfax Publishing, www.ellendiamond.com.*

First published 2008
Second printing 2008

Manufactured in the United States

ISBN 978.1.59629.441.7

Library of Congress Cataloging-in-Publication Data

Robinson, Maurice (Maurice J.)
Ponte Vedra Beach : a history / Maurice Robinson.
p. cm.
Includes bibliographical references.
ISBN 978-1-59629-441-7
1. Ponte Vedra Beach (Fla.)--History. 2. Ponte Vedra Beach (Fla.)--Social life and customs. 3. Ponte Vedra Beach (Fla.)--Economic conditions. 4. Ponte Vedra Beach (Fla.)--Biography. 5. Ponte Vedra Beach Region (Fla.)--History, Local. I. Title.
F319.P68R63 2008
975.9'18--dc22
2008015020

To Helen,
whose optimistic outlook and encouragement made this possible.

If I should go to heaven, which I much doubt, when St. Peter lets me walk through the Pearly Gates, I'm sure that I will look around and say, "St Peter, I'm disappointed. I used to live in Ponte Vedra."

—Harry Johnston

CONTENTS

PREFACE

I began studying the history of Ponte Vedra back in 1995 when I moved to Ponte Vedra from Virginia. My youngest daughter was in the St. Johns public school system and chose to write a paper on Ponte Vedra. The printed information that we could find was very sketchy to say the least. Eventually, we did find newspaper and magazine articles, but found nothing definitive.

I began to prepare myself to undertake the project of researching and writing a more comprehensive history of the Ponte Vedra/Palm Valley area. With the help of Dr. Shafer at the University of North Florida, and the cooperation of organizations, colleges, historical societies and friends, I have organized and written this book and compiled illustrations inclusive of the most significant events in the history of the Ponte Vedra area.

Though Ponte Vedra may seem insignificant when compared to our historic "First Coast" neighbors, St. Augustine and Jacksonville, I think we have an important and equally interesting history to relay here in this small but unique area of St. Johns County, Florida.

Please enjoy this chronicle of the many events that have occurred in our small town, unique to both Florida and the United States.

Acknowledgements

First of all, I would mainly like to thank the staff at The History Press, especially Magan Lyons, senior commissioning editor/publisher, and Jaime Muehl, project editor.

This book would never have been completed without the assistance of Dr. Daniel L. Shafer, history professor at the University of North Florida (UNF). Dr. Shafer's encouragement and his thoughtfulness sent me back to college to learn how to interpret history more professionally.

Many have helped me gather and present the historical information that is necessary to express and accurately recapture most of the historical events in the Ponte Vedra Beach area.

Thanks go to Taryn Rodriguez-Boette, archivist, Beaches Area Historical Society (BAHS); Charles A. Tinsley, St. Augustine Historical Society; Dwight Wilson, director, BAHS; Dr. Dale Clifford, chair of the History Department at the University of North Florida; Jerome Fletcher, Fletcher Land Corporation; Sid and Jo Mickler, Palm Valley; Phil and Julianna Howe, Jacksonville Beach; University of Florida Archives; Sharon Laird, archivist, Jacksonville Historical Society Archives; Robin Moore, archaeologist, St. Johns County; Marsha A. Chance and Greg C. Smith, senior archaeologists, Environmental Services, Inc.; James R. "Jimmy" Stockton Jr., Ponte Vedra; Robert "Bob" Kroner, son of Elaine Koehl, Ponte Vedra; Fred Cosby, certified hotel administrator, Ponte Vedra Inn and Club; Kirt Kaunath, Ponte Vedra; Steve Sciotto, Palm Valley; Irma Heilman, South Ponte Vedra; Don Staley, Neptune Beach; Ponte Vedra Public Library; St. Augustine Public Library; University of North Florida Archives; Susan R. Parker, PhD, State of Florida; Christine L. Newman, archaeologist II, State of Florida; Jennifer Lynch, researcher, U.S. Post Office, Washington, D.C.; Bruce A. Chappell, archivist, University of Florida, Smathers Library, just to name a few.

INTRODUCTION
WHERE IS PONTE VEDRA LOCATED?

The counties of Baker, Clay, Duval, Flagler, Nassau and St. Johns are known historically as the "First Coast" of the New World to be explored by the Spanish. Of these, Ponte Vedra Beach can truly boast of being "first on the First Coast" because it is believed that Ponce de León landed on its shores at Guana State Park in 1513.

The unincorporated area of northeast St. Johns County, Florida, includes Ponte Vedra Beach, Ponte Vedra, South Ponte Vedra Beach and Palm Valley and encompasses fifty-one square miles along the Atlantic Ocean from below J. Turner Butler Boulevard, south to and including Guana River State Park and South Ponte Vedra Beach and farther south to Vilano Beach. The twenty-eight miles of beaches are on the barrier island that extends from Mayport to the north and St. Augustine (Vilano Beach) to the south.

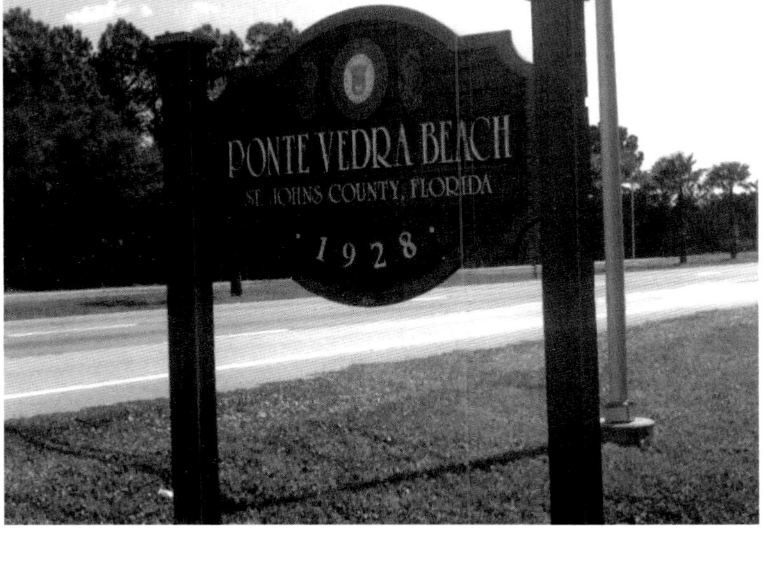

The welcome sign at Ponte Vedra Beach in the most northern portion of St. Johns County on A1A. The sign recalls the community's establishment in 1928. *M. Robinson photograph, 2004.*

Part I

Pre- and Post-Columbian History Through the Twentieth Century

1. Florida's Geographic Coastline Changes and Prehistoric Civilizations

Before the White Man

Paleo-Indian Period (15,000 to 8000 BC)

Little is known of the Paleolithic Period along the coast and in the east and central Lake District cultural area, which includes St. Johns County. Theories about the paleo-man's existence are based primarily upon site size and the uniformity of the known stone tool kit of the period. It is thought that these early populations lived a nomadic life based on hunting and gathering, and it appears that they clustered near certain waterways, springs and cenotes (water-filled limestone sinkholes) throughout the peninsula. This information is based upon research conducted and published by the U.S. Army Corps of Engineers when surveying the Palm Valley Bridge vicinity.

About fourteen thousand years ago, people first entered the Florida peninsula. Known as Paleo-Indians, these original Floridians survived by hunting mastodons, camels, mammoths, bison and horses. At the time, much of the world's water was frozen in glaciers, sea level was much lower than it is today and Florida was a large, dry, grassy prairie. The North Florida coastline extended into the Atlantic and the Gulf of Mexico at double its present size.

Discoveries of stone spears and animal bones have been found, insinuating that there has been human travel in Florida since 12,400 BC.

Paleo-Indian Sites

According to Elizabeth Purdum in *Florida Waters* (2002), the accompanying map indicates the changes to the coastline of the First Coast and the number of years it took to change. The map indicates that Paleo-Indian sites have been recorded in Florida, but because many may be underwater and will never be located, it has been difficult to determine the extent of Florida's Paleo-Indian culture.

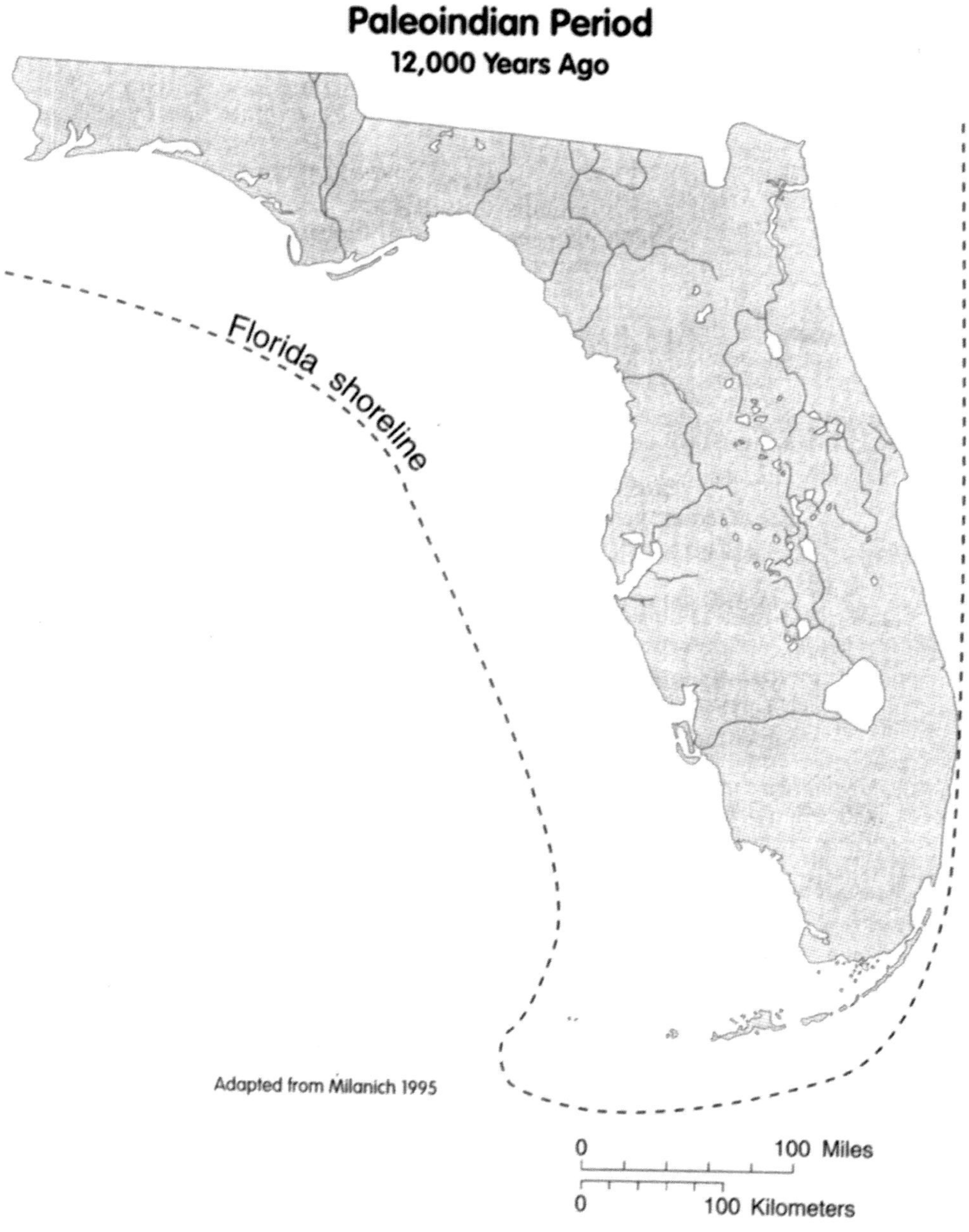

A map of the Florida shoreline in the Paleo-Indian Period, twelve thousand years ago. Many Paleo-Indian sites are now underwater. *From Elizabeth D. Purdum,* Florida Waters *(Florida State University, 2002).*

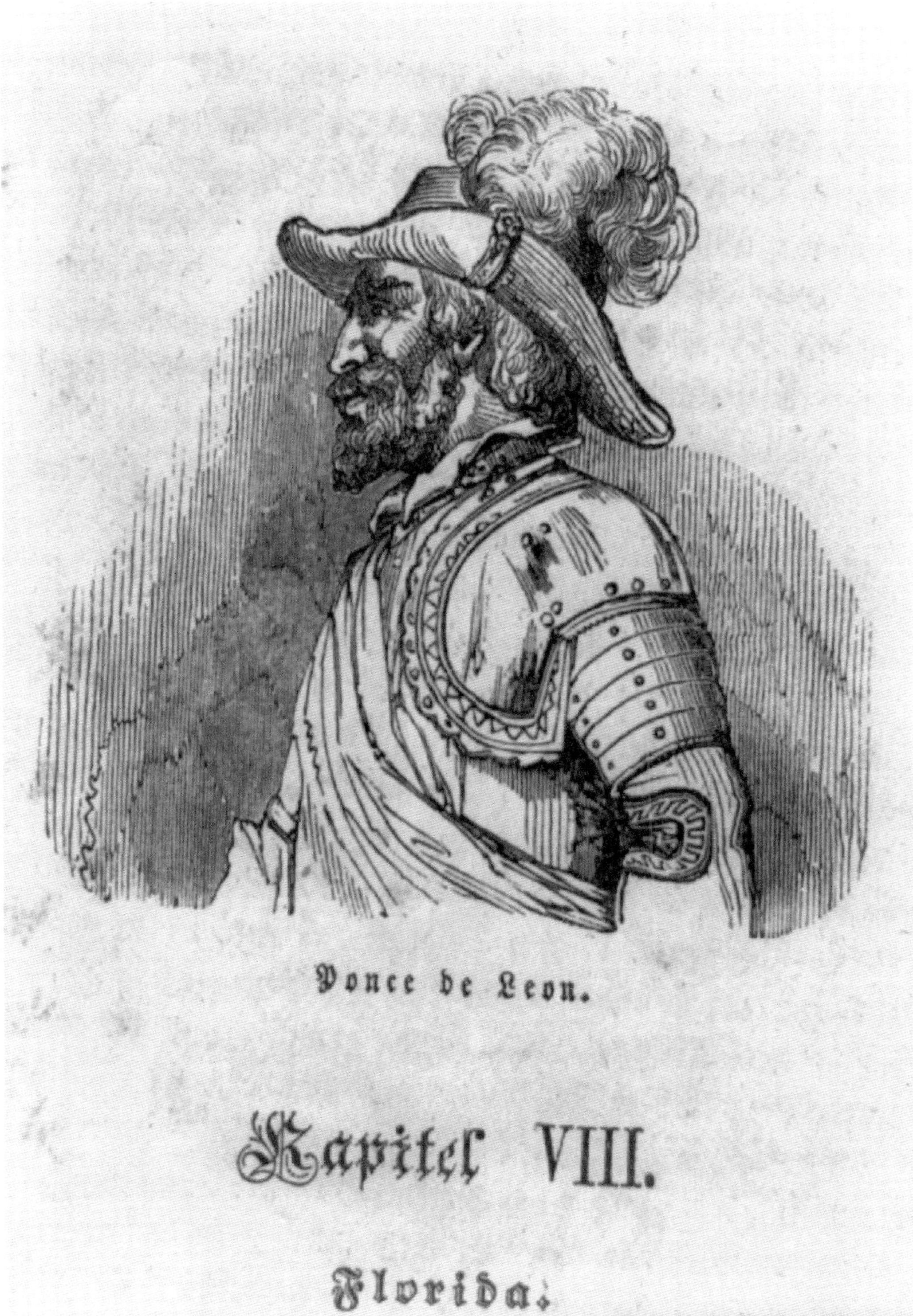

Juan Ponce de León, from John Ledyard Denison, ed., Die Illustrierte Neue Welt (1858). *Courtesy of Library of Congress Prints and Photographs Division.*

The term "Paleo-Indians" refers to the small bands of nomadic people who first populated North America. After crossing the large expanse of land that appeared between Alaska and Siberia during the last glacial period, they kept traveling until some of them had reached as far as the southern tip of South America. Currently, however, we know very little about the everyday life of these people. The Paleo-Indians were the first human residents recorded in Florida, according to archaeologist Jerald Milanich.

After about 9000 BC, as glaciers melted and sea levels rose, Florida's climate generally become wetter than it had been, providing more water sources around which the Paleo-Indians could camp. But as the sea rose, coastal areas were flooded and the Florida landmass was reduced.

CLOVIS CULTURE (11,500–10,500 BC)

The Paleo-Indian people of the Clovis culture colonized North America, including Gulf Coast areas of Florida, after crossing the Bering Strait from Siberia. The first material evidence of Clovis culture dates back to 11,500 BC. Although no Clovis sites have yet been found in St. Johns County, future undersea archaeology may discover evidence of Clovis culture under the Atlantic Ocean along Florida's coast.

THE ARCHAIC PERIOD

The Archaic tradition (8000–500 BC) is divided into three parts: Early Archaic (7500–5000 BC), Middle Archaic (5000–3000 BC) and Late Archaic (3000–500 BC). Milanich states that these divisions are based largely on stylistic changes in stemmed projectile points and fiber-tempered pottery dating from the Late Archaic Period.

Throughout the Archaic Period, natives are thought to have been dependent on fishing, hunting and gathering, but with increasing sedentariness from the early to late periods and an egalitarian form of social organization.

Approximately fifteen hundred archaic sites are recorded throughout Florida. In several Florida counties, there are over a hundred sites recorded. In St. Johns County, there are nine archaic sites recorded. Because sea levels continued to rise during the Archaic Period, many more archaic sites are undoubtedly located on the continental shelf off the coast of Florida.

There are several written records from the time when the first humans were in the North Florida area. Archaeological digs in Jefferson County (which was the county seat before President Jefferson separated it from Leon County in 1827) on Florida's Gulf Coast unearthed tusks with stone tool–cut marks, indicating that humans existed here in approximately 10,300 BC.

The Timucuan Indians of the Saturiwa tribe arrived in Florida from the North between 8000 and 1000 BC.

The Mount Taylor People (6000 to 4000 BC)

The record of the first (or any semipermanent) settlement of the Florida Indians indicates that it probably occurred around 5000 BC.

The climate of the earth began to warm in about 6000 BC and the sea level rose. The Ice Age had come and gone. Archaeological evidence of mounds of freshwater snails is attributed to the Mount Taylor people. One site was Cootnie Island at the south end of St. Augustine on the Intracoastal Waterway. This was the first known site in St. Johns County and the first evidence of the Mount Taylor people living along the Intracoastal Waterway.

The Mount Taylor name comes from a site along the St. Johns River in Volusia County that was dug a century ago. The Mount Taylor people were the archaic hunters during this time.

The Orange Period (Circa 2000–1000 BC)

The beginning of the Orange Period is marked by a shift in population, the making of pottery and the use of oysters—all occurring at the same time. Mount Taylor people moved from the river's intracoastal area to the coast. They were the first to use pottery in the New World made from the sandy clay found in the marshes. When fired, it produced a coarse, orange-colored pottery with plant-fiber impressions throughout.

They overharvested the freshwater snails during this period for making pottery and began the use of oysters. Abundances of oyster shells have been found and are called shell middens (most likely the village trash heaps). In 1000 BC, the Orange pottery began to disappear and was replaced by ceramic known as St. Johns pottery.

Only ten sites from the Orange Period are known in St. Johns County. One site is in North Ponte Vedra Beach and two are in South Ponte Vedra Beach in the canal area. However, it was not until about 2000 BC that any large settlements of Native Americans first appeared, especially near the water in northeast Florida.

Florida Transitional Period (Circa 1200–500 BC)

During this period, changes in technology and lifestyle occurred in Florida to mark the beginning of the Formative Period. Sand-tempered and limestone-tempered pottery began to replace pottery that was created with plant fiber. A nomadic lifestyle was no longer required as prehistoric peoples refined their subsistence strategies in order to more efficiently exploit their resources, and pottery began to change.

THE ST. JOHNS CULTURE (500 BC–AD 1565)

St. Johns I Culture (500 BC to AD 800)
St. Johns II Culture (AD 800 to 1565)

St. Johns pottery took over the Orange Period pottery in about 1000 BC. This was a new type of pottery that today we call "ceramic." Only a very small portion of St. Johns County was suitable for the type of farming used by the St. Johns people. This kept the number of St. Johns residents relatively low.

But by about AD 1300, the St. Johns II culture exhibited the greatest degree of social complexity in northeast Florida. Sites from this period contain pottery and other goods brought in from throughout Florida and elsewhere in the Southeast.

Jerald Milanich also noted that these were probably the first natives of North America to make any contact with the exploring Europeans at the beginning of the sixteenth century. At this time, there were no more than 250,000 recorded Native Americans throughout the state. Upon white man's arrival in Florida, the Timucuas were the most populous native tribe.

2.
St. Johns Timucuan Indians—Saturiwa Tribe

The First Americans

By the year 1500, the Native Americans who "discovered" Florida and began to occupy the entire peninsula and the Florida Keys had reached a population estimated at 250,000, according to historian Charlton Tebeau in his *A History of Florida* (1971).

When the Europeans arrived in Florida, the St. Johns people were known as the Timucuan Indians. We know that the activities of the Native Americans, which span eight thousand years, occurred in less than 5 percent of the county, within a stone's throw of the Intracoastal Waterway or the St. Johns River.

The Timucuas were likely the first Native Americans living in what is now the Southeastern United States to come in contact with people from the western hemisphere following Columbus's 1492 voyage. The first documented instance of such contact was the expedition of the Spaniard Juan Ponce de León, who landed on the Atlantic coast of northern Florida in 1513.

Where did the name "Timucua" come from? One story is that the major chief on the East Coast, Saturiwa ("saltwater"), gave a silver ingot to the Frenchman René Goulaine de Laudonnière (of the French Hugenots), who founded Jacksonville's Fort Caroline in 1564. The soldier asked the chief where the silver had come from, and Saturiwa pointed to the southwest and said, with great anger, that he had captured it from Thimagona. This word is generally believed to mean "terrible enemy," rather than a specific person or people.

Another story is that the word "Timucua" comes from the word *atimoqua*, which means "lord" or "chiefs" in their native language. It was allegedly mistaken by the Spanish for the name of one of their chiefs. Other names for the Timucuas include Atimuca, Thimapoa, Tomoca and Utina. The Spanish began using the name "Timucua" for all the native peoples who occupied North Florida east of the territory of the Apalachee. They would have pronounced it "Tee-moo-qua."

The Timucuas comprised a number of autonomous provinces that were hostile to one another when the first Europeans arrived. During the time the French were in

Florida (1564), the three head chiefs were Saturiwa (east and north of the St. Johns River), Outina (west and south of the St. Johns River) and Potano (west and northwest of Outana). These three chiefs were generally at war with one another. Wars were not fought in the European fashion (i.e., killing all enemies and taking their land). Rather, battles were ended when one or two men were killed. After the battle, the natives went back to their tribes and land was never taken.

The Timucuan Population

Jerald Milanich's research suggests that prior to Ponce de León discovering the new world, there may have been two hundred thousand Timucua-speaking Native Americans in Florida and southern Georgia. The total region occupied by the Timucuas was about 19,200 square miles, of which 12,000 square miles are in present-day Florida and 7,200 in Georgia. In AD 1513, at the beginning of the historic period, it is conservatively estimated that there were about two hundred thousand Native Americans living in Florida.

The Timucuas were described as tall and healthy. The first chief that the Spanish encountered was about seven feet tall. The Timucuas lived in villages, often with log walls surrounding the village. The chief's house, which was the largest dwelling, was often on an elevated mound. Some villages had mounds that served either ceremonial or burial purposes, and kitchen mounds with shells heaped very high were common. This describes the village at Guana Park, which we will discuss later.

The Timucuas of the St. Johns culture created many shell piles. At one time, these shell middens literally blanketed portions of the East Coast from Cape Canaveral north. The shell middens for the St. Johns culture were so immense that nineteenth-century observers had a hard time believing they resulted from human activities.

The Timucuan tribes whose names appear in Spanish documents were the direct descendants of the St. Johns people. The archaeological evidence of the St. Johns culture can be traced in a direct line from the Late Archaic/Orange culture into the sixteenth and seventeenth centuries.

Settlements Near the Water

The Timucuas looked to the water for sustenance, settling along rivers or near the coast. Their prehistoric ancestors were called "People of the Shell Mounds." Besides collecting shellfish and fishing, they hunted and gathered in the forests and swamps and planted maize, squash and beans. Often, in their palisade villages, they lived in circular dwellings with conical, palm-thatched roofs and walls of woven vines caulked with clay. Ceremonial squares in the larger villages were the scenes of festivals, dances and religious ceremonies.

The Timucuan Warriors

The Timucuas were a warrior people who engaged in chronic but episodic warfare with their neighbors. The men wore their long hair piled on the tops of their heads with buns at the very top. In warfare, they put arrows in their hair to facilitate rapid fire. The women wore their hair down their backs and wore skirts made of Spanish moss. Both the French and the Spanish described them as a handsome people. The upper classes identified themselves with tattoos. Very wealthy chiefs had tattoos all over their bodies.

Their approach to warfare was simple and direct: surprise. The rule of thumb seems to have been that if your clan had more warriors and the advantage of surprise, then planning an attack was imminent. Retreating was quite acceptable. The rumor that Europeans introduced scalping was just that. Evidence suggests that the Timucuas took scalps. Displaying them played a major role in victory celebrations that could last up to three days.

The Black Drink

The Timucuan people had a drink called the "black drink." It came from a plant called yaupon holly—or in Latin, *Ilex vomitoria*—a relative of the tree used for yerba maté among natives of South America's Plata Basin. Yaupon holly is one of the few plants native to North America that contains the ingredient caffeine, concentrated in the leaves when they first sprout in the spring. The Timucuas collected these leaves and roasted them to increase the caffeine's solubility in hot water (like coffee today). Yaupon holly usually grows in coastal areas, so local Timucuas probably traded the leaves inland for valuables including chart, raw material for projectile points, and clay, raw material for pottery.

Something more than yaupon holly may have been used for the ceremonial draft. It was noted that "*cassinet* is made from composite of herbs and looks like the beer of our country." The chief was the first to drink in this ceremonial use, employing a vessel (vase) that held about a quart by Paris measure.[1]

Yaupon holly provided more than just trade value. Due to its chemical properties, it served an important cultural role. Caffeine is a diuretic that helps one sweat. By Timucuan belief, this sweating allowed the drinker to remove physical and spiritual impurities from his system. Only adult men could partake of the black drink. These men sipped the black drink in morning gatherings while they discussed things of importance. The Timucuas used this as an extreme form of purification and it served a valuable cultural role for Native Americans throughout the Southeast.

> *When you drink cassina and look into the cup, you see many reflections of your face in the bubbles, even though there is only one of you. So it is with God, although he is only one, he is everywhere.*[2]

The Missionizing of the Timucuas

By the late 1570s, few from the two Timucuan villages closest to St. Augustine—Nombre de Dios (on the northern outskirts of old St Augustine) to the north and San Sebastian to the south and west on the river of that name—had sufficiently relinquished their attachment to their ancestral religion to begin to become Christians.

Establishing missions among the Timucuas and other native peoples of Florida in order to convert them to Catholicism was one of the requirements of the contract negotiated between Pedro Menéndez and the Spanish Crown. This included teaching doctrine and bringing aspects of the Hispanic society to the Timucuas in order to make them loyal subjects of the Spanish monarchy.

The establishment of a system of missions was an important part of Menéndez's plan for his colony. Missions provided a means of pacifying the Timucuas and other native groups and a means of organizing the native population for administrative and other purposes, including labor. According to Milanich's research, free or lowly paid labor was necessary for the colony to profit and to ensure a reasonably comfortable lifestyle for Menéndez, his family and the other colonists.

The End of the Timucuan People

The European colonization brought with it disease, causing epidemics that cut like a scythe through the Timucuas. By the second quarter of the eighteenth century, the native population of Florida and southern Georgia was so reduced that the few native settlements that existed consisted of only small numbers of people.

By the early third quarter of the eighteenth century, there literally were only handfuls of Timucuan refugees still surviving. In the end, the European conquest of Florida proved to be totally catastrophic for the Timucuas. The Timucuas were among the many American Indian groups who did not survive the European conquest of North America. Later, in 1763 and 1764, those few Timucuan people who had been living under the auspices of the Spaniards in St. Augustine would be taken to Cuba. Other groups in the Eastern United States did survive the colonial era, and their descendants continue to live in that region and in Oklahoma.

The exiles' departure to Cuba ended the Timucuan experience in Florida. The émigrés did not fare well in Cuba, as lack of subsistence, disease or old age took their tolls. By 1766, the Timucuan population had shrunk to fifty-three.[3]

University of Florida Professor Michael Gannon writes in his book, *The New History of Florida*, that by 1759, only two missions—Tolomato and Nombre de Dios—were left serving ninety-five Native Americans, which included the Timucuan and Guale Indians. These natives left St. Augustine with the Spaniards and were resettled in the Cuban town of Guanabacoa.[4]

Approximately 250 years after the landing of Juan Ponce de León, only one Timucua remained—Juan Alonso Cabale, born in 1709 at the mission Nuestra Señora de la Leche, Florida. He died on November 14, 1767, in Guanabacoa, Cuba.[5]

Today, there are no known Native Americans who call themselves Timucuan. All we have left in Ponte Vedra to remind us of the Timucuas are the shell mounds in Guana Park.

3.
AMERICA'S EARLY EXPLORERS, 1492–1526

ARRIVAL IN NORTH AMERICA IN THE FIFTEENTH CENTURY

In 1492, Christopher Columbus was the first European to land in the Americas on the island that he named San Salvador for Spain. In 1497, the English sent a Florentine, John Cabot, who supposedly traveled from Canada to Florida but left no permanent record of his explorations. Americus Vespucius (Amerigo Vespucci), whose first name was later given to the New World, could have explored the Florida coast around 1497, but no historical records were maintained.

EXPLORATION OF THE SPANISH IN NORTH AMERICA BEFORE PONCE DE LEÓN—1500S

In 1500, the oldest map of the New World by Juan de la Cosa shows a depiction of Florida. In 1502, the first Spanish map by Alberto Cantino depicted a peninsula, like Florida. The Nicolo Caveri (Canerio) world chart of 1504–05 and Martin Waldseemuller's world map of 1507 also showed the Florida peninsula. It appears that the Spanish explorers may have seen the area as early as 1482, but they never landed on the Florida shores according to written records.

However, according to George Fairbanks's research into the history of St. Augustine, there appeared in 1508 some written records of a Florida coastal area. In 1511, Peter Martyr published *Decades*, which included crude maps showing what appeared to be the coast of Florida. Martyr was a friend of Columbus and was the most significant chronicler of the initial stages of the discovery of the New World.

Furthermore, Peter Martyr affirmed his belief in his second *Decade*, addressed to the pope:

> *Among the islands on the north side of Hispaniola, there is one about three hundred and twenty-five leagues distant, as they say which have searched the same, in which there is a continual spring of running water, of such marvelous virtue that the water thereof being drunk, perhaps with some diet, maketh old men young again. And here I must make protestation to your Holiness not to think this to be said lightly, or rashly; for they have so spread this rumor for a truth throughout all the court, that not only all the people, but also many of them whom wisdom or fortune hath divided from the common sort, think it to be true.*[6]

THE ABORIGINAL FLORIDIANS

In the 1500s, there may have been as many as a hundred thousand aboriginal people living in what is today Florida. By 1800, all aboriginal Floridians were gone. Educator Charles Blanchard states:

> *The loss of their wisdom and knowledge stopped 12,000 years of tradition in his tracks, causing an informational implosion, a thunderous silence that continues to echo through the Native American world today. There is simply no one left to ask for first-hand answers to the questions of who our predecessors in this corner of the planet really were, or how they lived, or what their take on the Cosmos really was.*

Accounts written by early European explorers give us only glimpses of aboriginal Florida people. Our real knowledge of the past twelve thousand years of continuous human occupation comes from the archaeological records and the research of archaeologists such as Robin Brown, who published her findings in *Florida's First People: 12,000 Years of Human History* in 1994.

DON JUAN PONCE DE LEÓN'S LIFE AND RECORDED DISCOVERY IN 1513

PONCE DE LEÓN'S LIFE (1460–JULY 1521)

Don Juan Ponce de León was born into a noble family around 1460 at San Servas in the province of Campos, Spain. There is little record of his birth, his parents' names or his earlier years. As a lad, Ponce de León served as a page to Pedro Núñez de Guzmán, who later tutored the brother of Charles V, the Infante Don Fernando. In his younger years, Ponce de León also served as a squire and earned the nickname "poor knight." From that day forward, he trained himself in the arts of war and survival to prepare himself for a future of daring and unimaginable adventures to the unknown. As a teenager, he joined Spanish forces that eventually defeated the Moors of Canada.

In 1493, Ponce de León joined Christopher Columbus on his second voyage to the Americas. After that time spent on Hispaniola (Espanola), Columbus became a military commander and a deputy governor.

In 1502, Ponce de León married the daughter, Leonor, of a Santo Domingo innkeeper in what now is the Dominican Republic. Together they had three daughters, Juana, Isabel and Maria, and one son, Luis. Maria and Luis were born in Salvaleón (Ponce de León's settlement in the Dominican Republic).

According to historian Robert Fuson in his book, *Juan Ponce de León and the Spanish Discovery of Puerto Rico and Florida*, Christopher Columbus died in 1506, but two governors had served in Santo Domingo before his death. The governors were in violation of the agreement between Columbus and the Catholic sovereigns, allowing that Ponce de León alone would govern the island. Almost immediately after Columbus's death, his elder son, Diego, contested the violation of his father's rights and, temporarily at least, won. Thus the first admiral's rights and privileges passed to Diego, who became the second admiral. This one decision affected Ponce de León in a material way, altered the course of Puerto Rican history and probably accelerated the discovery of Florida.

In 1506, Ponce de León discovered a nearby island named Boriguen, which was later renamed Puerto Rico. Ponce de León helped crush Native American revolts on the island of Espanola and was rewarded in 1508 with a commission to explore Boriguen. He became the island's first governor in 1509 and founded Puerto Rico's first European settlement, Caparra.

Although Ponce de León was under constant pressure from Diego Columbus throughout 1512, he was somewhat protected because he remained military captain of the island and King Ferdinand V held him in the highest esteem. In fact, it was Ferdinand who suggested to Ponce de León that he move onward and search for new land

In 1512, King Ferdinand V (Ferdinand V of Castilla; also became Ferdinand II of Castilla) granted Ponce de León a patent to discover and settle the "island of Beimeni (also Bimini, Benimyu, Bimene)." Ponce de León never found Bimini (not officially recorded) or the Fountain of Youth. Until the completion of his voyage in 1523, however, Bimini and Florida were perceived as one and the same. The formal contract between the Spanish crown and Ponce de León for the discovery and settlement of the island of Bimini was dispatched from Burgos (Spain) on February 23, 1512.

Eleven months were to pass before Ponce de León was able to secure the necessary ships, crews and supplies for the expedition authorized by Ferdinand. During that time, despite constant support from the Spanish crown, Ponce de León was harassed, condemned and intimidated by Spanish officials in San Juan Bautista (Puerto Rico).

The three ships for Ponce de León's voyage were the *Santiago*, *Santa Maria de la Consolacion* and the *San Cristobal*. This fleet departed San German on the afternoon of March 3, 1513, a Thursday, and sailed to Aguada on the coast of San Juan Bautista, the same site used by Columbus in 1493. The three ships (and about two hundred men) sailed from Aguada on the evening of March 3, 1513, bound for Bimini.

Ponce de León's departure from Puerto Rico was with two caravels (the caravel, also spelled "carvel," is a light sailing ship that was developed by the Portuguese in the late

1400s and was used for the next three hundred years) and a bergantina (a smaller ship for exploring shallow inlets and harbors). The Portuguese developed these ships to help them explore the African coast. Ponce de León's pilot was Anton de Alaminos, the most experienced pilot in the islands. Two women, Beatriz and Juana Jimenez, who were probably related; two African freemen, Juan Garrido and Juan Gonzalez (Ponce) de León; and two unnamed native Taino seafarer guides from Puerto Rico were also onboard.[7]

Ponce de León was given the right to find and take the island of Bimini (in the Bahamas) since he was searching for riches and the Fountain of Youth (a legendary spring believed to grant people eternal life and health).

This expedition took him sailing at stops to Grand Turk Island and San Salvador before he finally reached the east coast of Florida. Finally, disappointed but not disheartened, he extended his researches in a northwesterly direction. As he approached the wooded shore, Ponce de León saw beautiful trees (magnolias) with marvelous blossoms that lined the forest and gave off a delicate fragrance. He was approaching the First Coast.

Discovery of the First Coast

The Ponce de León expedition reached the east coast of Florida (St. Johns County) in April 1513. Ponce de León named the land "Pascua de Florida" (feast of flowers) because he first spotted land on April 2, 1513, Palm Sunday, and claimed it for Spain.

Ponce de León's trip to Florida was an exhaustive one. It is reported that at sunrise, at latitude 30° 8' north, a landing party went ashore (at a site in Ponte Vedra Beach). This was eleven miles south of the old pier at Pablo Beach (now Jacksonville Beach). His view of the land in this area overlooked "the Guana." However, the location did not provide a suitable harbor for his three ships. On April 8, 1513, he left the Guana area, sailed farther down the coast and landed at the present site of St. Augustine. Even though Ponce de León was only in Ponte Vedra for eight days, he was the first to land on what we now call the First Coast, according to L.D. Scisco's 1913 article, "The Track of Ponce de Leon in 1513."[8]

In 1949, Julien C. Yonge, director of the University of Florida Libraries, stated, "The best authorities believe that Ponce de León landed on the beach somewhere in the Ponte Vedra region. He made no mention of entering a harbor." T. Frederick Davis, in the *Florida Historical Quarterly* of July 1935, placed the first landing of Ponce de León in the region of what is now Ponte Vedra. The source of his reasoning was the writing of Antonio de Herrera, who was appointed by King Philip II of Spain as the official historiographer in 1592 and gave a detailed account of the voyage of Ponce de León in his writings.

Ponce de León continued traveling south through the Gulf Stream, around Miami and along the west coast of Florida to Tampa Bay. He made a return trip through Cuba, Miami and back up the east coast of Florida. Then he traveled through the Bahama Islands and back to Puerto Rico, where he ended his five-month trip in October 1513.

In 1514, Ponce de León received a royal commission to colonize the "inland of Florida," but he did not return to Florida until July 1, 1521.

It has been recorded that no one on the Ponce de León expedition suspected that Florida was part of the North American mainland. On the contrary, Florida was thought to be a large island, and the nature of the Florida peninsula was not understood until after 1519—many, including Ponce de León himself, did not even understand it then.[9]

During the voyage to Florida, Ponce de León also found the Gulf Stream—perhaps the most important Castilian discovery since the first voyage of Christopher Columbus in 1492. This vast river within the ocean moves as much as four billion tons of water a minute at speeds up to five miles per hour near Palm Beach, Florida. The volume of its flow is a thousand times greater than that of the Mississippi River.

Ponce de León went to Castilla, Spain, in the spring of 1514. There he was knighted by the king, becoming Don Juan Ponce de León, and he was given a personal coat of arms.

In 1517, Ponce de León returned to St. Augustine. On his return, the Native Americans lined the shore to meet him. But the greeting was far from cordial, as Charles Gallagher notes in his book, *Cross & Crozier: The History of the Diocese of Saint Augustine*.

> *"Suspicion and Hostility," the historian Robert Wooster has remarked, "stemming from technological and cultural differences, as well as mutual feelings of superiority, have permeated relations between Indians and non-Indians in North America."*[10]

Unfortunately, Ponce de León's greatest personal loss occurred during the first week of July 1521: he died at the age of forty-seven, probably from an infection in his thigh brought on by a Calusa arrow.[11]

There is nothing of significance dedicated to Don Juan Ponce de León in the city where he once lived and whose soldiers he once commanded.

The First Black (African) Settlers

Well in advance of the time when permanent black settlers arrived in Florida, other persons of African origin had passed through this sometimes punishing land. Significantly, not all of them were slaves. Free Africans Juan Garrido and Juan Gonzalez (Ponce) de León (conquistadors) accompanied Juan Ponce de León in 1513 on his voyages of discovery to the American Southeast. By 1526, the first known enslaved Africans arrived among the six hundred Spanish settlers brought to North American shores by the Lucas Vázquez de Ayllón expedition.

Historian Larry Rivers adds, in his book *Slavery in Florida: Territorial Days to Emancipation*, that the word "slave" could have been misleading in the case of these individuals. In addition to performing the hard labor commonly associated with slavery, these Africans were also considered by Spanish officials to be "skilled artisans" and domestics from Spain.

The Spanish regulated slavery in East Florida by a complex set of codes that largely protected the rights of the enslaved persons living in and near St. Augustine. Many enslaved persons could own property and sue owners and others in the courts. During the first Spanish period, which ended in 1763, enslaved Africans could win or earn their freedom with relative ease—a condition necessitated by the relative ease of escape. With the fortified settlement at Fort Mose shining like a beacon of freedom for most of the period from 1738 to 1763, many blacks—including runaways from the English colonies to the north—found freedom in Florida. Other blacks won their freedom by serving in the militia and protecting St. Augustine against intruders.

Ponce de León's Legacy

Although other explorers may have come before him, Ponce de León was the first to claim the land for the Spanish king. As history tells us, the landing of the British at Jamestown, Virginia, did not happen until 1607, and the landing of the Pilgrims at Plymouth Rock, Massachusetts, did not occur until 1620. As we understand from our history, Ponce de León in Florida did not celebrate the first Thanksgiving. However, the first Thanksgiving observed in this country took place at St. Augustine on September 8, 1565. Florida's first Thanksgiving was widely overlooked, according to Dr. Michael Gannon, professor emeritus of the University of Florida.[12]

As for the first Thanksgiving meal, no menu was described. It was probably "*cocido*, a stew made from salted pork and garbanzo beans, laced with garlic seasoning, and accompanied by hard sea biscuits and red wine," writes Dr. Michael Gannon.[13]

According to Patricia Griffin in *Life on the Plantations of East Florida 1763–1848*,"the model for Florida was Virginia and the Carolinas, and also the West Indies, where extensive plantation agriculture already existed."[14]

The legislature and governor of Florida declared that April 2 would be celebrated each year as State Day for the Ponce de León discovery of Florida. Ponce de León had not found for himself the water of immortal youth, but he had been immortally honored as the discoverer of the First Coast of Florida, the Gulf Stream and the Calusa Indians on Florida's west coast at Charlotte Harbor.

4. Spain's Control of and Contributions to North Florida, 1565–1763

La Florida's Territory in 1565

According to James Cusic, curator of the P.K. Yonge Library of Florida History, when Spain first established La Florida in 1565, the colony had nebulous and far-reaching borders, stretching northward into today's Virginia and Carolinas and westward toward the Mississippi River. By 1763, when Spain surrendered its Florida territory to Great Britain, the province's borders were much smaller. The colony consisted of the Florida peninsula south of Georgia and a long strip of land along the west coast that included about half of today's Alabama and Mississippi. The British decided that this area was too large to govern as a single entity. They divided it at the Apalachicola River. The western portion became British West Florida with its capital at Pensacola. The peninsula became British East Florida with its capital at St. Augustine.

Catholic Spanish Pioneers

Jason Grimary Shes wrote in 1899 that the Spanish were the most influential in colonizing Florida. Ponce de León named Florida to commemorate its discovery on the Feast of the Resurrection. Not only were Catholics the first explorers, but they were also the first geologists and botanists of the territory within the limits of the present United States. Catholic priests came with Columbus and his followers (Ponce de León) on their transatlantic voyages. Missionaries came with Ponce de León in 1521 to minister to the intended settlements in Florida and to labor for the conversion of the Native Americans.

In 1597, four Franciscans were slain in Florida. The labors of these missionaries were not without fruit for the time being, but the results were not permanent. The natives associated with the religion preached by these missionaries spoke about the greed and cruelty of the Spanish invaders. During the sixteenth century, as in later

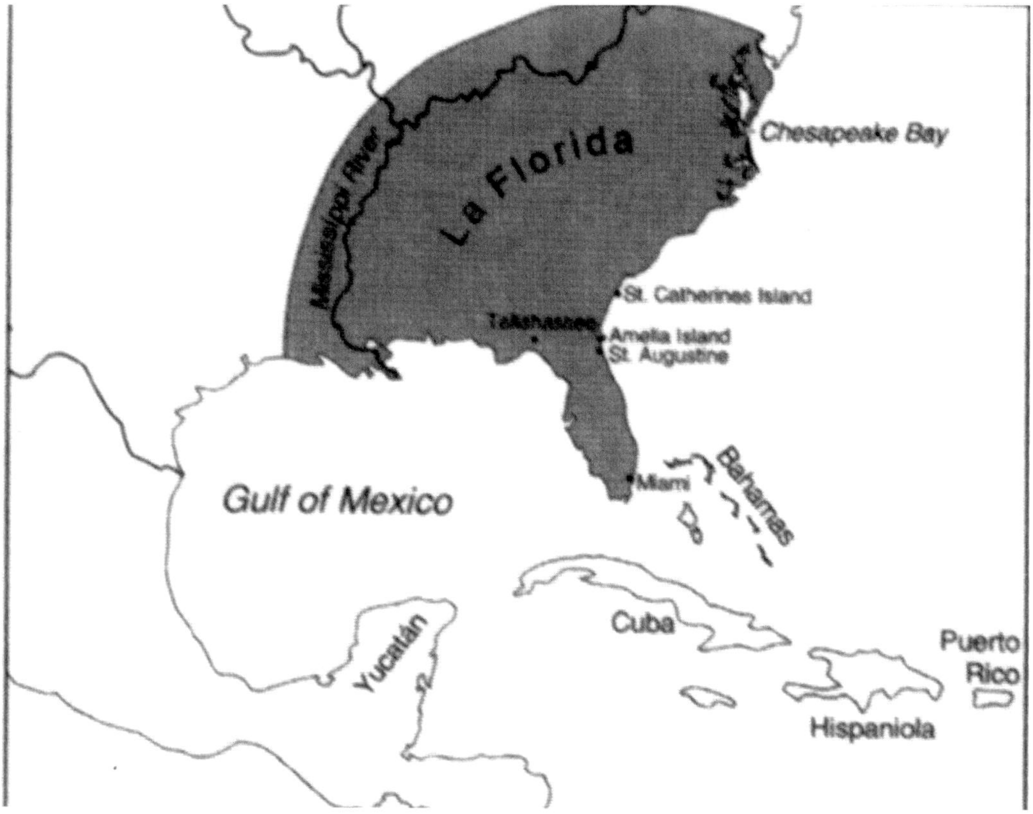

An early sixteenth-century map of La Florida, which encompassed the entire southeast portion of the United States. (Some modern place names are noted.) *From Jerald T. Milanich,* Laboring in the Fields of the Lord: Spanish Missions and Southeastern Indians *(Smithsonian Institution Press, 1999).*

times, the Christians themselves were the obstacle to the success of the missions among the Native Americans.

The church has not been untrue to its mission of teaching nations, nor has it at any time failed to find apostles ready to answer its call. But Christian peoples and governments, instead of seconding the church's efforts, have put obstacles in its way. They seem to be more intent on selfish aims than on the spread of truth and the salvation of souls. On them, not on the church, rests the responsibility of failure in gaining to Christianity the aborigines of this continent. Future generations will count our Indian wars and our Indian policies as sad commentary on our Christian civilization.

Naturally, those discoverers, founders of colonies, explorers and missionaries must have left behind them a very large amount of literature concerning the areas and American people that now make up the United States.

Spanish Missions and Religious Life

Members of the Society of Jesus (Jesuits), who made the first missionary efforts in Florida, uniformly met resistance even though soldiers accompanied them. Jesuits are members of a religious society founded in 1534 and devoted to missionary and educational work.

During the 138 years of Florida's mission era (1567–1705), missions were attempted or established among at least eleven distinct Native American populations, with about eighty mission centers serving a far greater number of individual villages and hamlets. Almost all of this was the work of Spanish Franciscans. According to John Hann's essay "The Missions of Spanish Florida" in *The New History of Florida*, Franciscan friars of St. Augustine were the first schoolteachers, beginning in 1605.

Historian William Coker adds that most of the missions in Florida were established between the years 1606 and 1695. More than a hundred locations in Spanish Florida were devoted to religious purposes. These included: mission centers (*doctrinas*), subsidiary missions (*visitas*), native villages with a resident priest and other settlements visited by the Native Americans for religious purposes.

Three Spanish missions in Ponte Vedra—La Natividad (1620), Santa Cruz (1690) and Tolomato (1717)—were located in the Guana area. The Spanish Franciscan mission was La Natividad de Nuestra Señora de Guadalupe de Tolomato (1620–1720). This mission was located just three leagues north of St. Augustine.

Establishing La Florida Missions

Establishing missions—first Jesuit, then Franciscan—accomplished several goals. First, the indigenous peoples of La Florida could be brought to Catholicism, and it was hoped that they would abandon their native "pagan" beliefs that were thought by the priests to be associated with the devil.

Second, missionizing the native peoples transformed them from possible military opponents into allies. It was more expedient to use missionaries to control the people of La Florida than to establish forts and try to accomplish the task by military might. That rebellions did occur indicates that conversion did not always make for lifelong allies with the Native Americans.

Lastly, the mission system was intertwined with Spanish ranches on which missionized natives could serve as laborers and transporters of food and goods to St. Augustine for use there or for export. La Florida was a relatively poor colony, and one way a profit could be turned was through the ranches.

In the earliest years of Spanish settlement, Jesuit missions were established in southern Florida, along the Georgia coast and as far north as present-day Virginia. All of these early efforts met with resistance and failure, and the discouraged Jesuits withdrew in 1572. While the first Franciscans arrived the following year, it was not until 1595, more than twenty years later, that the Order of Friars Minor launched the

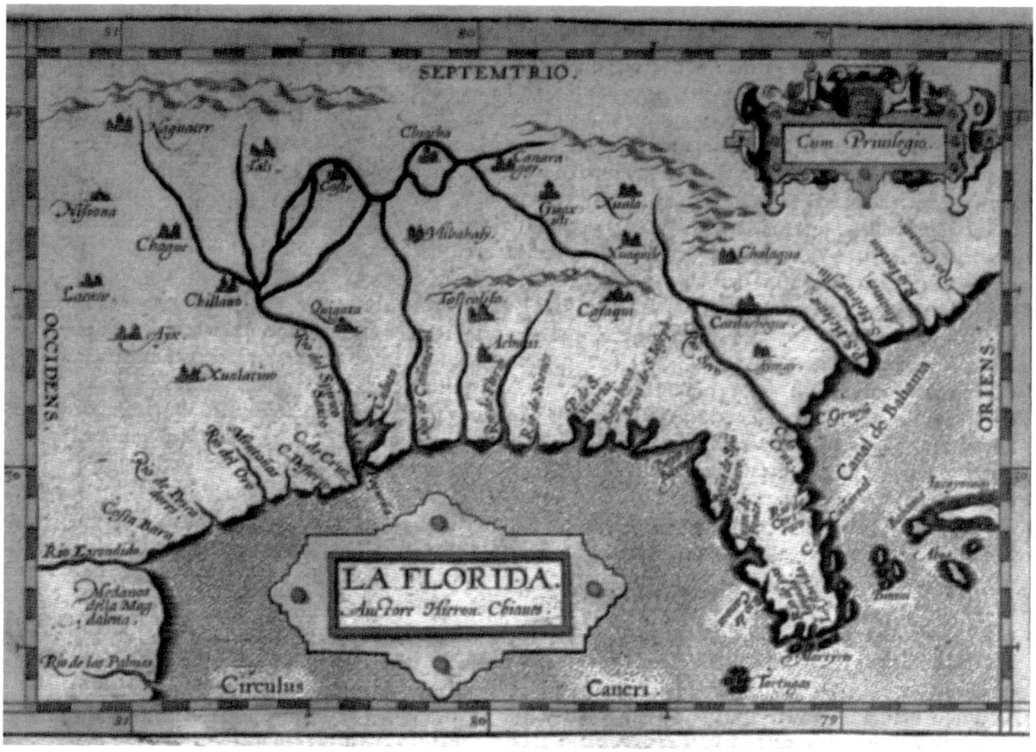

A map drawn of Florida in 1584. The area shown extends throughout the present-day Southeastern United States. *Special Collections Department, University of South Florida.*

large-scale, intensive missionary effort that resulted in the seventeenth-century mission chain of La Florida.

During the sixteenth and seventeenth centuries, 128 places that were missions, *visitas* or Spanish towns visited by the natives were mentioned by name in the documentary sources of Spanish Florida. Obviously, these were not all occupied at the same time, and many missions were short-lived, but the number alone does dramatize the magnitude of mission activity.

While the missionaries sought to turn the Native Americans into good Spaniards in many ways, it was the field of religion that concerned them most as many of the customs and practices to which they objected were indeed in the realm of sacred beliefs for the Native Americans. These folklore ways had to be subdued if the Native Americans were to be recognized as Christians.

SPANISH MISSIONS IN THE GUANA AREA

The location and physical features of most of the missions within St. Johns County are still undocumented. It must be remembered that mission buildings were fragile structures, constructed generally of palm or wattle and daub with thatched roofs. Given the harsh climate of Florida, the general absence of masonry building materials, the periodic rebellions and wars and the duration of their existence, it is clear that mission buildings were routinely destroyed or replaced and that the missions themselves were frequently relocated. Much research, both historical and archaeological, remains to be done before the character of the missions located within St. Johns County can be fully understood.[15]

Until the middle of the 1600s, the Tolomato people inhabited the area around St. Catherine's Island on the Georgia coast. Spanish St. Augustine resident Alonso de las Alas spoke of visiting the villages of Yoa and Tolomato along Sapelo and St. Catherine's Sounds in his testimony of September 12, 1600. Some researchers have suggested that the village was located at the site where Fort King George (now reconstructed) was built in the 1720s. A Catholic mission was also established at the Tolomato village.

In 1689, there were some one hundred Timucuas living at Nombre de Dios (St. Augustine), with some 125 Guales living about eight miles north of St. Augustine at Tolomato (Guana). The raids by James Moore brought an end to the Spanish mission system outside of St. Augustine and refugee Native Americans from many tribes and areas were relocated to the town. These events—taking place largely on the mission frontier—dramatically affected the population composition of St. Augustine after 1700.

In 1703, just after James Moore's first raid on Florida, there were reported to be eight missions and refugee towns, including Tolomato, near St. Augustine. Later, Governor James Moore of South Carolina and Colonel Robert Daniel destroyed the Tolomato mission at Guana. By July 1724, Governor Moore had burned all of the Florida missions.

The mission era of Spanish Florida ended abruptly between 1702 and 1704 after a series of military strikes by the British and their Creek allies. During these devastating raids, virtually all of the missions, except those confined to the immediate vicinity of St. Augustine, were abandoned or destroyed.[16]

It was not until 1717 that another Tolomato mission would reemerge in the Guana area. However, very little is known about the exact location of this mission.

5.
Settlement of Diego Plains (Palm Valley), 1700s

Fort San Diego

During the 1700s, a dozen local families rose to prominence in Florida by acquiring land and raising black cattle. Among them was the Diego Espinosa family, whose lands lay north of St. Augustine in Diego Plains.

The early Spanish settled in the Diego Plains area (now Palm Valley) in 1703, and in 1736, Espinosa built Fort San Diego, which was attacked by General Oglethorpe's troops in 1736 and again in 1740. Diego Espinosa was married to Josefa Torres, and they had two children—a son, Sebastian, and a daughter, Josefa. Josefa inherited the plantation called "Fuerte de San Diego" (Fort Diego).

Research in the *Spanish Land Grants of Florida*[17] indicates that the Sanchez, Espinosa and Zavalia families initiated Fort San Diego in order to protect themselves from hostile Native Americans and other enemies. The fort was actually a house that was fortified, and it was located in the vicinity of Diego Plains near the road that formerly went to San Mateo.[18]

James Oglethorpe's Attack

Trouble was again brewing for the inhabitants of Diego Plains. By 1739, Great Britain and Spain were at war. General James Oglethorpe, leader of the English colony of Georgia, was commissioned to harass the Spanish settlements, especially that of Don Diego Espinosa. In 1740, the British General James Oglethorpe again invaded Florida from Georgia, seizing outlying forts. He laid siege to St. Augustine for twenty-seven days until a lack of fresh water and provisions, combined with the July sun and hordes of insects, caused him to turn away. He did, however, free the fifteen hundred soldiers and townspeople crowded in the Castillo de San Marcos.

Oglethorpe next organized a large force of Native Americans and colonists to invade Florida in December 1739. After navigating up the St. Johns River, he sent before him a party of Native American scouts, who fell upon a small fort of Spaniards at daylight and burned it to the ground. Farther upriver, another fort was attacked and captured. This gave Oglethorpe possession of the St. Johns River and cut off the Spaniards in St. Augustine from their native allies.

On their second journey to Fort San Diego in 1740, Oglethorpe stopped at Los Cañuelos, which was halfway between St. Augustine and the St. Johns River inlet, before attacking Fort San Diego.[19] Oglethorpe made up his mind to attack St. Augustine itself. In May 1740, he left Frederica with nine hundred men and eleven hundred Native Americans. He captured Fort San Diego (Diego Plains, now Palm Valley), located twenty miles from St. Augustine, with fifty-seven men and nine cannons, and made Fort San Diego his field headquarters. The Spaniards abandoned Fort Mose, located two miles north of the city of St. Augustine, when they heard of the approach of Oglethorpe, and the garrison retreated to the city.

6. Arrival and Influence of the British in Florida, 1763–1783

British Control

The British period and their control of Florida began in 1763, when England received Florida as its territory through the terms of the Treaty of Paris, which formally ended the French and Indian/Seven Years' War (1756–1763). The British exchanged Havana and Cuba for Florida, and Spain evacuated Florida, leaving the province virtually empty. St. Augustine, during this time, was only a garrison community with fewer than five hundred homes, and Pensacola was only a very small military town.

Great Britain emerged from the war as the world's most powerful empire. In Florida, unlike during the recently terminated centuries of Spanish rule, the British did not have to concern themselves with hostilities and attacks from nearby enemy colonies. The entire Atlantic Coast of North America was in British possession after 1763.[20]

Although the Spanish Indians living near St. Augustine left Florida with the Spaniards at the end of the first Spanish period, a new group soon took their place. This new group was predominantly Creek, although there were also others who left the Northern areas of North America after the Revolutionary War. More than three hundred Native Americans apparently relocated to the St. Augustine vicinity, where trade was the major form of Indian-European interaction.

Only the Sanchez, Solana and Herrera families in the St. Augustine/Diego area actually lived there during all three periods.

The British had a very ambitious agenda for the newly acquired Florida territory. They divided Florida into East Florida, their fourteenth colony, with St. Augustine as its capital; and West Florida, their fifteenth colony, with Pensacola as its capital. The British developed a relationship with a group of Native American people who came into the area from the North. These people were the Creek Indians, who were descended from the Seminoles.

In East Florida the economy turned principally to agriculture. Vast tracts of land were cleared along the St. Johns River and the seacoast, and aside from St. Augustine, the plantations were the centers of life in the colony. Many indentured servants helped to run the plantations. It was, reported Governor Grant, "the largest importation of white inhabitants that was ever brought into America at a time."

Most numerous (in Florida during this period) were blacks, of whom the great majority were slaves. Not only did they till the fields and operate the mills, but they also sailed as crew members of naval and merchant ships, where they frequently outnumbered whites.

The more talented (British) newcomers produced plays and books and published Florida's first newspaper, the *East Florida Gazette*. Numerous Patriot leaders also came to St. Augustine as prisoners, including three signers of the Declaration of Independence: Arthur Middleton, Thomas Heward Jr. and Edward Rutledge.[21]

GOVERNOR JAMES GRANT

In 1763, the British Crown appointed James Grant as governor of East Florida. St. Augustine became the provincial capital of East Florida. The British invalidated the earlier Spanish land grants and implemented a liberal land grant system. Within several years, Grant's Villa, the governor's plantation (at Guana), became a model plantation, growing indigo plants and functioning like a modern agricultural experiment station.[22]

Grant (bachelor governor) arrived in St. Augustine on August 29, 1764, determined to transform Britain's new East Florida colony into a plantation province through the labor of African slaves. Earlier experiences in South Carolina had convinced Grant that plantations could only develop in warm-climate colonies with the hiring of black workers.

Some of the first plantations attempted in East Florida by British absentee owners employed white indentures, but the results were so unsuccessful that Grant warned others against using that type of laborer. Grant advised the absentee owners to start plantations with "country born" Negroes, available in South Carolina, who were familiar with the planting practices and the language of their owners.[23]

The governor was convinced that the key to profitability was a stable labor force, which could be obtained by relying on enslaved Africans. The governor sent a consistent message to the absentee grantees: "Africans are the only people to go to work in warm climates."

In 1768, Grant opened an indigo plantation a few miles north of St. Augustine. Intending to spur on absentee grantees and to speed up development, Grant's Villa became a training school for the province's inexperienced overseers. Daniel Schafer notes, in *The Oldest City: St. Augustine Saga of Survival*, that "for several years 'the Villa' served as an agricultural 'college' to train the overseers of the province."

In July 1770, Grant inherited title to Ballindalloch Castle and all of its associated properties and became the Laird of Ballindalloch. Grant was afflicted by a "bilious disorder," a serious stomach ailment that his doctor felt merited a return to England.

When Grant departed East Florida on May 9, 1771, he intended to return within twelve months, but he would never return.

Alexander Skinner was given full authority to manage Grant's Villa, although he would work in cooperation with David Yeats, agent for Grant's overlap business activities. Income from Grant's Villa would continue to arrive at Ballindalloch even after the province reverted to Spain in 1783. In March 1779, while traveling to Savannah on government business, Alexander Skinner was killed by Native Americans.

David Yeats—physician, planter, official secretary of East Florida and business agent to Grant—assumed more supervisory authority of Grant's plantation affairs.

Slaves During the British Period

Most slaves in Florida were either criollos born in other parts of the Southeast or the Caribbean, or Ladinos, persons of mixed descent. Toward the end of the first Spanish period, however, planters began to introduce more bozals, or African-born slaves, into Florida.

As Daniel L. Schafer has shown, the Africanization of Florida increased while the British were in possession of Florida. "New Negroes" made up 66 percent of the fifty-one laborers who initiated "the Villa." Grant boasted that his first indigo crop brought a modest profit, and that he expected his second crop to

> *clear a good 15 percent for all the money I have laid out…all my expenses was upon Negroes who are walking about, no white face belonging to the plantation but an overseer.*

Toward the end of the American Revolution, Loyalists fled Charles Town (now Charleston) and Savannah to resettle in Florida with over eight thousand slaves, an influx that brought the black population to three times that of the white population.[24] Sales of slaves to East Florida were arranged primarily by two colonial merchants, Henry Laurens of Charles Town and John Graham of Savannah.

Late in January 1769, Graham sent Grant four

> *black ladies…* [including] *two very strong and able wenches, and will do as much work as any man, and are also young…* [and] *a very likely, young smart girl goes by her country name Sulundie. Your tom speaks her language.*

Look for the ship, Graham told Grant, and for "your four wenches…[marked] with yellow silk ferret [ribbon] tied round their wrists."

Occasionally, a snippet of nonbusiness good news passed through the list of problems reported by the overseers. One report of a happy celebration was penned by Alexander Skinner (the overseer at Grant's Villa) in December 1772.

The Christmas feast was an annual ritual at Grant's Villa, as it was generally at plantations of the Lowcountry. Skinner also described the 1774 festivities: "A carcass of beef with all its appurtenances was sent them [the slaves] yesterday with some rum for their Christmas." Perhaps it was the Christmas celebrations that Grant had in mind when he wrote in 1784:

> *They served me well and faithfully. Some of them I remember very well, others* [grew] *up upon the plantation since I left the Province of East Florida, and I dare say there are no better slaves anywhere. They have always been well fed and well-clothed.*[25]

There were hints of conflicts among the slaves, perhaps prompted by interethnic jealousies and by something resembling class antagonism. The poisoning of two of Grant's slaves, for instance, may have been the work of "new" Africans brought to his indigo plantation. Grant's agent, Dr. David Yeats, informed him on June 5, 1780, of a most shocking affair that had lately happened at his plantation. Leander, one of Grant's best Negroes, and Jack, his brother—old Carolina's sons—had both been poisoned and were dead. They died suddenly within two days of one another in great agony, exhibiting all the symptoms of poison.

What helped to make this matter worse, Yeats indicated, was that

> *three of your won Negroes have been accused of it. Two fellows and a wench and one of the fellows (Walley), has since shot himself...I should be happy to have this fellow punished as he deserves for so atrocious a deed and to deter others from the like, if we can fix it upon him, but* [it is] *a difficult matter to come at the truth where none but Negroes are concerned.*

The planters believed that balancing sex ratios was an effective way to control the behavior of their male slaves. Some owners believed that the way they treated their slaves made a difference in how they behaved and worked. Grant described the work routine at his estate as "very strict" and regular as "clockwork."[26]

Grant's slaves went briefly to the Bahamas and were later sold to a consortium of Santee River rice planters—at prices almost double their cost to Grant in the 1760s. Not until eight decades later would their descendants be emancipated under the Thirteenth Amendment to the Constitution, free to start their own estates.[27]

BRITISH LAND GRANTS

British authorities at home and in the colonies were anxious to attract settlers to occupy, defend and eventually sustain the governments of the newly established provinces. Two types of land grants became available. The privy council in England created grants of up to twenty thousand acres to be settled at the owner's expense by white Protestant families with at least one person to each one hundred acres. The governor and council in the colonies granted family or head rights—one hundred acres for the head of the family and fifty acres for each additional person, white or Negro, and an option to buy up to one thousand additional acres at five shillings per each five acres.

Between 1764 and 1770, the Crown, in East Florida alone, issued approximately three million acres of grants, but only sixteen of those were settled by the outbreak of the American Revolution.[28]

The complete plantation system became an important segment of northeast Florida's economy during this twenty-year rule of the British. Massive land grants were soon distributed to influential British subjects to encourage the system's development. Many grants were given to land speculators who hoped to profit from inflated property prices.

Before the end of 1784, Schafer adds, all planting efforts at the Villa and Mount Pleasant Plantation had ended. The 1783 map of the Mount Pleasant site shows thirty-seven "Negro Houses" on alternate sides of what are today Neck and Mickler Roads. The thirty-seven slave cabins that once straddled the road were dismantled in 1784 and the boards were transported to New Providence Island along with the inhabitants.

The Minorcan Residents

When the British evacuation began in 1783, the Minorcans were in an opportune position to acquire farmland at minimal prices. Juan and Thomas Andreu were the first to began cultivating small tracts at Grant's Villa. The Spanish census of 1786 lists Juan Andreu occupying the six acres he previously rented from Yeats. A water well lined with coquina stone constructed during Andreu's time still stands on the shell bank (at Guana).

So many Minorcan families established settlements along the North and Guana Rivers that a special section of the 1797 Spanish census was dubbed the "North River Settlements." In 1804, Andreu received royal title to 160 acres that he named "White Oyster Shell Bank Plantation."

Just south of this was a 367-acre piece owned by Jose Peso de Burgo, a native of Corsica, who moved to this tract in 1786, calling the northern section San Genaro and the southern part El Burgos. Like most of the Minorcans of St. Augustine, Burgo, his wife Maria Mabrity de Burgo and a daughter lived in the Minorcan Quarter of town and traveled by day to the farm at North River or the estate on the San Sebastian River. By the time Burgo died in 1818, he had become a merchant, the owner of substantial rural acreage and the owner of twelve slaves.

Burgo's widow, Maria, married Juan Andreu II and combined the acreage they each had inherited to create the most significant landholding on the former site of Grant's Villa.

Antonio Andreu, another brother of Juan Andreu, purchased a homestead, known as Santa Catalina Plantation, at the former site of Grant's Villa from Lorenzo Capella in 1804.

Miguel and Jose, sons of Antonio, received a 103-acre service grant, "the Chimneys of Governor Grant," for their military contributions. In 1829, Miguel Andreu purchased San Ignacio, which had originally been granted to Lazaro Ortega, from Juan Segui. San Ignacio stayed in Miguel Andreu's hands for only three years and then he sold it to Ramon Sabate on February 17, 1832. Sabate retained ownership throughout the remainder of the century.

The land south of "the Chimneys," where Grant's overseers had resided, was also divided into small tracts and granted to Minorcan settlers. Mariano Fontan, Antonio Caballero and Jose Hernandez Carmona claimed ownership of the tract immediately south of the Chimneys, and they fought each other in court for years to gain clear title. Eventually, part of a hundred-acre tract was awarded to Fontan.[29]

James R. Hanham, a former captain in the United States Army, was one of the few non-Minorcans who bought property in the area. Soon after the purchase, however, Hanham experienced economic hardship and let the land lay fallow until it was acquired by Charles Seton in May 1826. Phillip R. Yong bought the tract in 1832. Following Yong's death in 1853, the El Burgo property was retained by successive generations of the Yong family until the 1920s.

PLANTATION CROPS

The first main cash crops in this period were indigo, rice and timber. There were also attempts at producing sugar, cotton and silk. Other food crops were grown, such as corn, carrots, watermelon, lettuce, broccoli, cauliflower, spinach, butter beans, herbs and parsnips. However, indigo was the most highly valued crop. It was one of the oldest and most durable of dyes with its use dating back to ancient times in India, Persia, Egypt and Peru. Indigo was an intense blue dye derived from the indigo plant through a time-consuming process. Indigo production began in East Florida during this period and was both the colony's most important crop and a profitable export.

OLD KING'S ROAD (ROUTE 1)

The Old King's Road was Florida's first highway, beginning in St. Augustine in about 1765 and eventually connecting to Colerain, Georgia, on the St. Mary's River, passing through the settlement of Cowford (Jacksonville) and along Ponte Vedra, adjacent to where Route 1 is located today. It was once one of the most important roadways in America.

> *Establishing a network of roads became a top priority of Colonel James Grant, the first governor of British East Florida, after he arrived in St. Augustine on August 29, 1764.*[30]

A road of sorts ran from St. Augustine to Savannah, Georgia, but Grant became

> *uneasy upon finding that some* [settlers who]...*had attempted to come here were obliged to return, on account of bad roads and difficulties they met with passing rivers, as no ferry boats were established.*

By the summer of 1765 Georgia planter Jonathon Bryan searched for a route for the northern segment of the road between St. Augustine and the St. Mary's River. Riding on horseback for eleven hours, Bryan recorded a distance of thirty-eight miles from St. Augustine to the narrows of the St. Johns River.

Bryan predicted the "road must be a causeway almost the whole way" with several short bridges, a project of "great difficulty." However, work proceeded slowly, and it was not until 1775, only months before the American Revolution, that the northern route was finally completed.

British engineers, following the established trails of indigenous people, using crushed coquina shell as the surfacing material, constructed the road. Most of the highway has disappeared under pavement; however, traces remain. Aerial photography of Florida, taken from 1943 on, reveals small segments of the original road.[31]

Late in the war years, refugees from the southeastern colonies who remained loyal to the Crown followed the route to Loyalist East Florida with their families, slaves and what they had retained of their personal belongings until the area was ceded back to Spain in 1783, prompting evacuations, followed by an influx of new settlers seeking land grants from the Spanish government. Many would follow the route that James Grant planned in the early 1770s—a route they could call the King's Road, a name that persists today.[32]

7.

Three Spanish Citizens Remained Through the British Period

During the first Spanish period, a dozen local families dominated the Diego Plains area, and they have been documented by historian Jane Landers in her book, *Colonial Plantations and Economy in Florida* (2000). Among the families was that of Diego Espinosa, whose lands lay north of St. Augustine on the Diego Plains. The original homestead, the San Diego, consisted of five additional pieces on the Diego Plains, including the Laurel de Sanchez, the Swamp, the Consejero and the San Francisco Afuiqui (three hundred acres), all of which Francisco Sanchez acquired at later dates.[33]

Another Sanchez property in Diego Plains was a nearby hundred-acre plot bearing the appropriate name of Monte de Puercos, or "Hog Mount"—a hammock plentifully stocked with the native razorback hogs.[34]

The Sanchez family was linked with the Diego Espinosa family when Francisco's brother, Jose Sanchez de Ortigosa y Perez, married Diego Espinosa's daughter, Antonia Petronila Espinosa, in 1756.[35]

The Espinosa and Sanchez holdings had escaped the early damage wrought by the Moor invasions. The families converted the Espinosa ranch into a fortified strong house known as Fort San Diego, but General Oglethorpe overran Fort San Diego in 1740. Over the next years, the Espinosa and Sanchez families slowly rebuilt their Diego Plains estates, but British-inspired Native American raids continued to be a problem throughout the 1750s.

Francisco Xavier Sanchez, Manuel Solana and Luciano de Herrera were still alive and residing in St. Augustine in 1786 and remained there until the Spanish regained control.

Sanchez and Solana had prospered under British rule, especially in the final days when they had acquired valuable properties at bargain prices from departing British residents. Herrera had remained in St. Augustine in 1763 under British rule, but he later fled to Havana when Governor Tonyn discovered he had been spying for Spain (only to return to St. Augustine later).[36]

Don Francisco Xavier Sanchez (1736–1807)

Don Francisco Xavier Sanchez de Ortigosa was one of North Florida's most successful planters, and his career and life spanned three separate colonial regimes (only two others are known to have lived through the three regimes, namely, Don Manuel Lorenzo Solana and Luciano de Herrera). In the late 1700s, Francisco, the Florida planter and merchant, inherited plantations and produced great wealth.[37]

Francisco was born in 1736, the son of Jose Sanchez and Juana Perez of St. Augustine. Francisco's original homestead (empire) was the thousand-acre San Diego on the Diego Plains, now Palm Valley, which he acquired from Diego Espinosa, to whom he was related by marriage.

In 1763, when Francisco was seventeen, Spain ceded Florida to Britain, and young Francisco chose to remain in the British colony of East Florida. He lived in the colony of Saint Augustine (Diego/Palm Valley) until his death in 1807. During those unstable years, he became one of the richest and most influential men in East Florida. He was a merchant, a farmer and an affluent businessman, as well as one of the banditti.

Sanchez owned three separate plantations. The Sanchez empire stretched along the Diego Plains, north of St. Augustine almost to the St. Mary's River and west to the St. Johns River. Sanchez's original homestead, the San Diego, was located to the east on the Diego Plains. Sanchez's main plantation on the east bank of the St. Johns River was called the San Jose, comprising over eleven hundred acres. The Ashley, a plantation of five hundred acres, was just south of the San Jose. His plantations not only traded agricultural products, herds of cattle and timber products, but they were also involved in the trade of human beings.[38]

In the sixteenth century, the Sanchez family migrated to Cuba from Ronda, Spain, and in the eighteenth century, Francisco's father, Jose (Joseph) Sanchez de Ortigosa, and Juana Theodera Perez of St. Augustine, who relocated (from Cuba) to St. Augustine, were married. Joseph had a sizable family of eight children—the youngest was Francisco in Diego Plains.

Francisco's Slave Trade

Historian Jane Landers wrote in *Colonial Plantations and Economy in Florida* that by the beginning of the second Spanish period, local planter/merchants like Francisco carried on a slave trade between Havana and St. Augustine. That trade derived from the turmoil of the political transition and consisted primarily of stolen *criollo* slaves shipped out from Florida for sale in Havana or across Cuba's northern boundary with the United States.[39]

Governor Guerard charged that Francisco stole more than one hundred slaves from South Carolina and Georgia and sold them in Havana in June 1783.[40]

Francisco paid 650 pesos to acquire one slave seized from George Knolls and three who once belonged to William Jones. The four had originally been appraised at 780 pesos, so Sanchez received a good bargain.[41]

In 1784, the San Diego comprised over a thousand acres, on which Sanchez kept a herd of eight hundred to nine hundred cattle, thirty to forty horses and pigs and thirty-four slaves. When Sanchez was away on business, his trusted Guinea-born slave and the skilled butcher of his cattle and pigs, Felipe Edimborough, became acting overseer of the San Diego. It was much to oversee.[42]

The San Diego encompassed the main dwelling and assorted ranch buildings, such as a cookhouse, stables, granaries, storehouses, houses for the overseer and slave hands, carpentry and ironworking shops, a millhouse and a slaughterhouse. Slaves tended the horses, oxen and cattle and prepared dried meat, hides and tallow for sale to markets in St. Augustine and beyond. Slaves also raised and processed corn, cotton and other garden crops. Like most other contemporary plantations, Sanchez's was a largely self-sufficient operation.[43] Sanchez also had a small retail outlet on the Diego Plains.[44]

In the late 1700s, Sanchez was facing civil and criminal charges. This was directly related, in part, to Sanchez's close relationship with the noted bandit chief Daniel McGirtt.[45]

Sanchez dealt directly with Daniel McGirtt, a South Carolinian formerly of Brown's Rangers. McGirtt was perhaps the most notorious of the banditti, and he owned a farm on the St. Johns River, where many of the Anglo renegades gathered.[46]

Francisco's Association with Daniel McGirtt, the Scottish Tory Outlaw

Daniel McGirtt was attached to General Augustine Provost's army when it devastated South Carolina in 1779. Plantations were laid to waste and robbed of all their valuables, including livestock, silver and even Negroes. After the war, McGirtt took his band of desperadoes to Florida, where they managed to sustain themselves.[47]

McGirtt was not an ordinary criminal, but was driven to outlaw status by an incident that occurred early in the American Revolution. In South Carolina, he had enlisted in the rebel cause, joining the South Carolina Rangers. McGirtt's loyalties changed abruptly, however, after his superior officer tried to take his fine horse and then sentenced him to flogging and jail for protesting in disrespectful language. McGirtt escaped and fled to British East Florida, where he initially joined the Loyalists and later became associated with John Cruden's project. Although he acquired a plantation on the St. Johns River and rented a house in St. Augustine, he soon became recognized as the leader of a band recruited from both Georgia and Florida to steal and sell livestock and slaves.[48]

Dan McGirtt, leader of the banditti, terrorized remote plantations and robbed travelers along the King's Road from St. Augustine to Cowford (on the Ortega River, once know as McGirtt's Creek). McGirtt found a partner in Francisco Sanchez, whose plantations he protected from his fellow banditti. McGirtt and Sanchez helped to make the valley of the two rivers a lively place two hundred years ago.[49]

The noted McGirtt was confined in the castle of St. Augustine for stealing, but he made his escape in the face of the guards. Later, a party of about thirty men, led by the notorious Colonel McGirtt, met with a party of men under the command of Colonel

Young. McGirtt immediately attacked and killed Colonel Young and his servant and took eight of his men, whom he disarmed and let go.[50] Eventually captured, McGirtt was banished to the Bahamas in 1785.

Francisco's Family

Sanchez's extensive landholdings and wealth made him a respected and influential member of the Spanish community. Sanchez lived with his common-law wife, Maria Beatriz de Piedra (also known as "Stone"), a free mulatto born in Charleston, for almost twenty years on the San Diego plantation.[51]

In 1787, at the age of fifty-one, Sanchez married Maria del Carmen Hill, the seventeen-year-old daughter of a wealthy South Carolina family.[52] In the first years of their marriage, the couple lived together on the Diego Plains with their children and the children from Sanchez's earlier union with Beatriz. In the 1790s, Francisco set up his mixed-blood children in houses in St. Augustine and provided for their day-to-day needs and their educations.[53]

Sanchez died testate on October 3, 1807, and was buried in the Dolomite Cemetery in St. Augustine. When Spanish officials probated Sanchez's estate, it comprised nine plantations including the San Diego.[54]

At the time of his death in 1807, Francisco had thirteen children. Eight children (born between 1787 and 1807) were from his marriage to Maria, and an additional five "natural" children were born (between 1776 and 1784) to Beatriz.[55]

After Francisco's death, the family was split by the Patriot War of 1812–13. The Patriot side of the family, headed by Francisco's nephew, Roman, moved much of the family's holdings to the newly opened Alachua region of central Florida, where the extended family continues to live. The Sanchez Diego Plains holdings remained in the family's possession into Florida's territorial period.[56]

Francisco's third son, Joseph Simeon Sanchez, was also a very important and colorful citizen of St. Augustine. Joseph's wife was Maria Lopez, whose mother was Maria Dolores Solana. This marriage was the first blending of the Sanchez and Solana families.[57]

The empire that Francisco built over the course of a lifetime was a cornerstone of colonial Florida's economic development.

Don Manuel Lorenzo Solana (1740–1821)

Manuel Solana was born in St. Augustine on April 7, 1740. His parents were native to the city. In 1763 Don Manuel was only one of eight men, "Mounted Dragoons" of the Spanish Army, remaining in St. Augustine when Spain traded Florida to the British. Don Manuel stayed in St. Augustine for twenty years during the British period, helping to settle Spanish property claims. He married Mary Mitchell, and they had a daughter and two sons. They later separated, and Don Manuel married Mary Mestre in 1781.

At the start of the second Spanish period, Don Manuel acquired the former Solana family properties along Aviles Street. He first owned the middle plot where the Casa de Solana is now located. Solana lived on Aviles Street (Hospital Street during the British occupation), when not on his plantation, until his death in 1821, the same year that the United States took over the territory.

The Don Manuel Solana House at 20 Charlotte Street was located on the site of much earlier houses, including a tabby house. Manuel Solana built the house after 1788. The house later became the home of Oliver Bronson Jr., who was a county commissioner after the Civil War. The house stands as a good example of Spanish colonial architecture of the second Spanish period. The main section of the house was constructed of coquina. This house had a loggia (an open-air room and entrance porch visible from Aviles Street) built on the rear. The flooring was all wood.

After ownership by the Solana family (the other Solana house was located at 21 Aviles Street, from its construction circa 1805 until 1867), this Spanish dwelling became the winter home of humanitarian Dr. Oliver Bronson. In 1883, Maine native Charles F. Hamblen bought the house, which was adjacent to his hardware company.

Solana had managed to acquire much of the former Solana family properties along Aviles frontage, thus extending his ownership to the entire south end of the block.

Luciano de Herrera (1736–1789)

Luciano de Herrera was a Spaniard who came to St. Augustine with his family in the first Spanish period and built a two-story, six-room house at 20 Charlotte Street in St. Augustine. Today, Herrera's original homeplace is now the site occupied by a building similar in size and shape to the Herrera home. The new, modern building was constructed in 1967 as office space and is now used as a restaurant.

Herrera was born in St. Augustine on December 12, 1736, as the eldest son of Sebastián Méndez de Herrera. Luciano would eventually have seven brothers and sisters in the tradition of the large families of the time. Although his father came to Florida from Spain, his mother, Dona Antonia, descended from a family that had resided in St. Augustine for at least four generations.[58]

When Governor Melchor Feliu closed the extensive and complicated operation of evacuating Spanish residents from St. Augustine on February 5, 1764, he reported that in order to provide for looking after certain properties and horses, he had left seven soldiers and an interpreter there. One of these was a militiaman, Luciano de Herrera.[59]

Herrera's luck and good fortune, however, did not last. Late in 1781, British Governor Patrick Tonyn apparently located letters from Herrera's correspondence with officials in Cuba that clearly showed Don Luciano to have been violating English law. Herrera escaped to Havana with his life.

With the return of Spanish rule, Herrera was able to return to his family home on Marine Street in St. Augustine, and he brought with him a reward from a grateful Spanish government. In early June 1784, two weeks before he left Havana for St.

Augustine, Governor Vizente Manuel de Zespedes appointed Herrera to the position of chief overseer of works in East Florida.

By early 1788, Herrera's health had begun to fail. Luciano Herrera lingered through much of the hot summer. His long and distinguished career had spanned one of the most colorful and traumatic periods of Florida's colonial history. First as an espionage agent and then as Indian commissary, Don Luciano de Herrera made signal contributions to the history of Spain's presence in St. Augustine. It is most fitting that, almost two centuries after his death, his name still evokes recognition from present-day residents of the city he loved so dearly.[60]

The British Evacuate Florida

In the early 1780s, refugees loyal to Great Britain fled to British Florida from the rebelling colonies of South Carolina and Georgia as American Revolutionary troops ousted British troops from the Southern colonies. Spain's support of the American revolutionaries was repaid at the peace talks in 1782 with the restoration of the Floridas to the Spanish empire. This time it was the British who would evacuate, although quite a few British subjects chose to remain in non-Spanish East Florida.[61]

8.
From Diego to Palm Valley, 1800s–1900s

During the Espinosa to DeGrove Era

In 1819, the Espinosa heirs granted to Philip Solano 245 acres for a cattle ranch at Two Sisters. The site became important in 1824 when the Solano house served as the dividing line between Duval and St. Johns Counties. Philip Solano in turn sold the land to Anna Pons. Andres Papy, through a land grant, acquired the 126-acre tract known as Fort San Diego. Antonio G. and Mary Jane Powers Mier were the last persons to acquire the property in the nineteenth century. Later, it was sold to Flavian Mickler in 1949.[62]

The valley, simply called Diego in the late 1800s, later became a place of small farms where sugar cane and cattle were raised along with some produce. It remained a cultural backwater (meaning a slow-developing area) until the first part of the twentieth century.

The old road that crossed the swamp about where the Palm Valley Road landing is now located was called Masters Ford, and branch roads led from Diego (Palm Valley) to what are now known as Bayard, Mandarin, Jacksonville Beach and Jacksonville.[63]

Wild cabbage, swamp cabbage and cabbage palmetto are pioneer names for the sabal palmetto or palm, Florida's state tree since 1953. It was from the abundance of these trees that the name Palm Valley was created in 1908.[64]

On the original Diego homeplace property, a man by the name of Twilligo once settled, and he built a dam across Diego Creek and erected a mill to grind his grain. He also operated one of the first sawmills in this area.[65]

The Mier family and the DeGroves had farms on Palm Valley Road. William DeGrove (whose wife was Mary Townsend) was the first mail carrier. The old DeGrove house stood on the corner of Canal Boulevard and Palm Valley Road. Built in 1910, the coquina blocks were made in Mayport and hauled out to Palm Valley.[66] The Red School House now stands on the Canal Boulevard site of the original DeGroves' home and farm.[67]

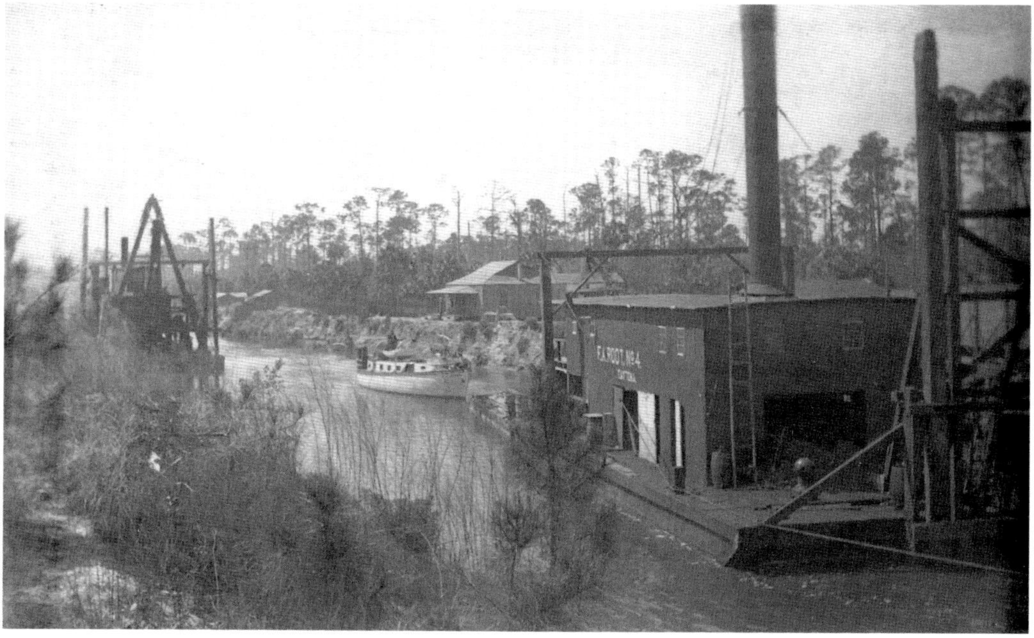

Equipment for dredging the canal around the area of Shore Sawmill at Cracker Landing on the Intracoastal Waterway, Palm Valley, Florida. The F.A. Root No. 4 dredge and pleasure boat is in the middle. Circa 1916. *From the collection of the Beaches Area Historical Society.*

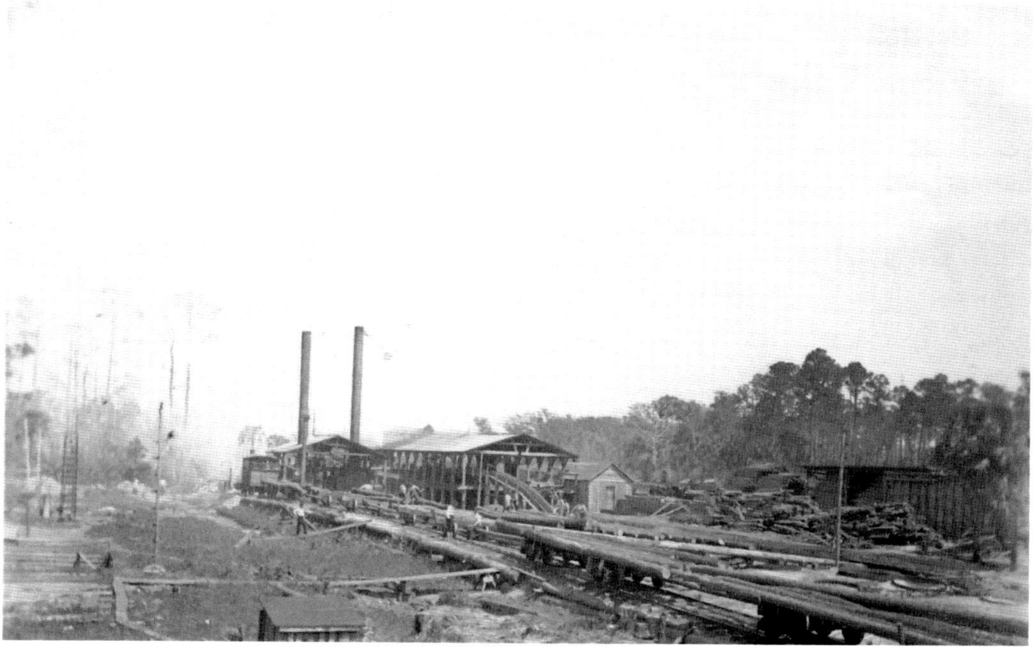

Shore Sawmill at Cracker Landing (early residents called it "Craddock Landing") on the west side of the Intracoastal Waterway (then Pablo Creek). The train is hauling the lumber to Jacksonville Beach. Circa 1916. *From the collection of the Beaches Area Historical Society.*

Twenty Mile Station or Halfway House

According to Mr. Baynard Kendrick of Leesburg, Florida, Juan Jimenez, a Spanish citizen of northeast Florida, was the innkeeper of La Posada Media during the period from 1800 to 1823.[68] "Twenty Mile Station" or "Halfway House" was located on Twenty Mile Road, and during the Spanish period, it was located just a mile North of Palm Valley Road (CR-210) west of the intracoastal canal area. This station was a halfway point for travelers between Jacksonville and St. Augustine.[69]

Twenty Mile House along the King's Road north of St. Augustine became an important communication hub and security post in East Florida. Although few physical remains are evident at Twenty Mile, the site remains an important place name in northern St. Johns County. Later called by historians "Florida's First Highway," the King's Road encouraged some British investors and settlers to organize plantations near its alignment.[70]

The Twenty Mile House served as a halfway station where messengers changed horses when traveling between St. Augustine and San Vicente Ferrer, the Spanish post at St. Johns Bluff. The exact date of construction of the complex is unknown. In 1787, Spanish engineer Mariano de La Rocque found the buildings there in such condition that he ordered them replaced. Their condition and the temporal proximity to 1784 indicated that the buildings at Twenty Mile Station probably dated from the British period. New buildings, described in detail in the *East Florida Paper*, were constructed in 1787 and remained in service through at least 1804.[71]

La Casa de Los Dragones

The Old Fields of the Dragoons were the plots of land where soldiers-turned-farmers raised vegetables and fruits or corralled the horses for the men stationed at La Casa de Los Dragones de Las Veinte Millas, or Twenty Mile House. It was here that messengers changed horses, their path leading them through much of Dee-Dot (Ranch) on its way north. Groups of cavalry might find a night's rest here, or the mounted mailman might find shelter before continuing on to the bluff or to Judge Fatio's on the San Pablo River.

Those soldiers who were stationed at Twenty Mile Station remained alert. The crack of a twig on a summer's night could mean a hostile Native American, a bear, a lost traveler or a friend.

Hidden away in early Spanish records are the details of the first house built at Twenty Mile. The date of its construction has not been uncovered. When Governor Zespedes toured East Florida, he found the buildings at the post dilapidated and ordered that they be repaired. In La Rocque's orders are found the construction specifications for the buildings. Trees were felled and lumber was "cut and shaped" at the site. The bunkhouse was built with three doors, a shingled roof and a masonry chimney. The separate kitchen was made of pales. The stable, which provided two bunks inside for those who tended

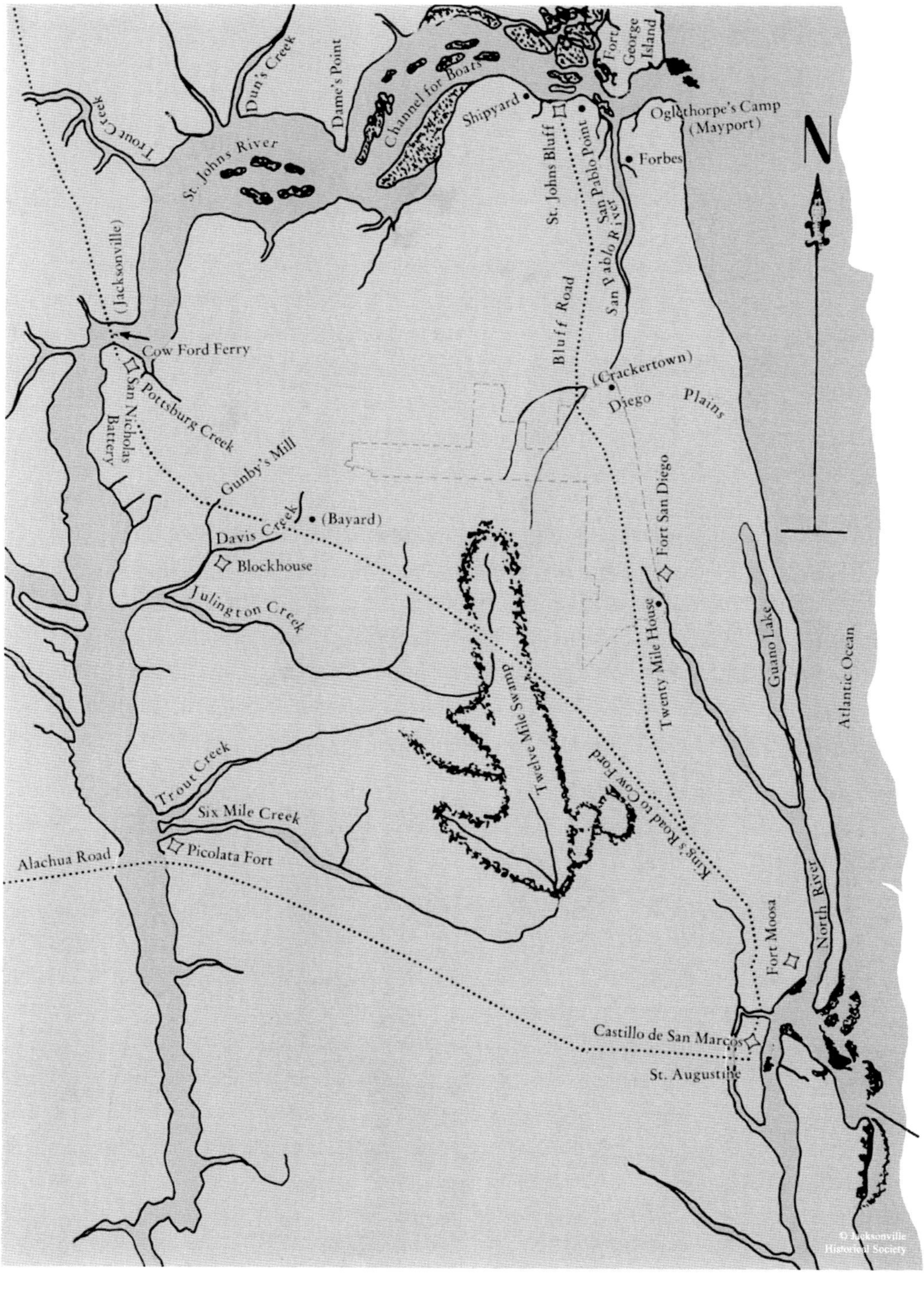

Northeast Florida in 1821. This map is an adaptation of one sent to General Andrew Jackson, Florida's first American governor. Places that did not exist in 1821are shown here in parentheses. The dotted outline in the center of the map indicates the approximate location of Dee-Dot Ranch and Fort Davis. *From Dena Snodgrass,* A History: Dee-Dot Ranch and Twenty Mile House *(Jacksonville Historical Society).*

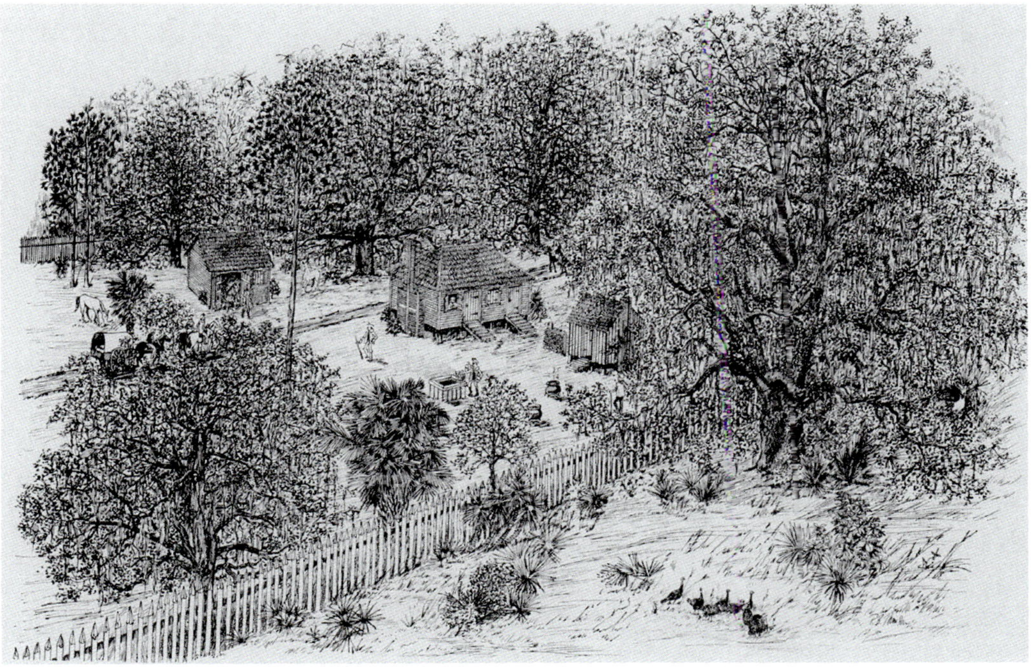

Twenty Mile House (*La Casa de Los Dragones de Las Veinte Millas*). This military outpost, twenty miles north of Spanish St. Augustine, was a way station on the trail to fortified St. Johns Bluff and was a part of the defense system of East Florida. Soldiers, mail carriers and travelers found food, rest and fresh horses here. This sketch is an artist's conception in 1787 based on detailed reports by Spanish military engineers, whose duties included the maintenance of the buildings at this post. The site is near the southernmost tip of Dee-Dot Ranch. *From Dena Snodgrass,* A History: Dee-Dot Ranch and Twenty Mile House *(Jacksonville Historical Society).*

the horses, was placed between the house and the road. A well with a wooden curb was in the yard, and the hole was enclosed within a picket fence.

The work on the Twenty Mile Post began on June 25, 1787, and was completed on November 10. Two years later, the chimney was enlarged. In 1796, general repairs were made, and in 1804, a September storm damaged the house. This entry is the last mention of the buildings at Twenty Mile yet uncovered in Spanish records. In the 1970s, the ruins of one small house, built by Robert Mier after 1900, still stood on the site near the southern tip of the Dee-Dot (Ranch).[72]

Also at the Twenty Mile Post was the station that housed the dragoons. The dragoons were members of a European military unit trained and armed to fight, mounted or on foot.[73]

Palm Valley Bridges[74]

There have been a total of four bridges over the Intracoastal Waterway in Palm Valley.

First, there was a turnstile sort of bridge owned by the Canal Company that was a toll bridge for boats. The bridge structure pivoted on a round pedestal in the center

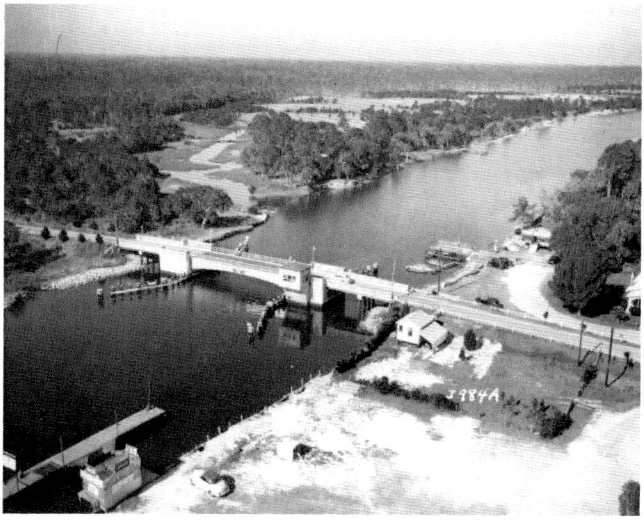

The Mickler Palm Valley Drawbridge over the Intracoastal Waterway in the 1940s, looking southeast. *State Library and Archives of Florida.*

of the waterway. When a boat approached, the bridge tender walked to the center of the bridge, manipulated a large crank and turned the bridge parallel to the waterway. The boats stopped as they passed through the resulting opening(s) and paid a toll to the bridge tender.[75]

The first two bridges were located directly in front of the Canal Bridge Camp. The third bridge was erected approximately 150 feet south of the camp, where portions of Palm Valley Road on each side of the waterway were consequently rerouted.[76]

The second was a barge bridge a bit north of the current location. In 1934, the U.S. Army Corps of Engineers constructed the barge bridge. The barge segment floated on the water and was connected to the banks by aprons, which flexed and could be opened by means of a counterweight system. Once the aprons were opened, the barge was then turned by a system of cables and pulleys. It pivoted on a piling at one corner to allow boats to pass by. This bridge was removed in 1936, after the drawbridge was built.

The third was a drawbridge. The Mickler Palm Valley Bridge was constructed in 1936 (by the Auchter Construction Company of Jacksonville) under the auspices of the U.S. Army Corps of Engineers. The bridge was known locally as the Palm Valley Bridge, but it was apparently designated the Mickler Palm Valley Bridge by Historic St. Augustine Preservation Board staff in 1985, when it was recorded as a historic structure.

Today, there is a new overhead bridge, which was built in 2002, replacing the old drawbridge.[77]

MOONSHINE

Michel Oesterreicher wrote in her 1996 memoir, *Pioneer Family: Life on Florida's Twentieth Century Frontier*, about the Prohibition era, which turned some of the valley residents to another source of income in the late 1920s and the early 1930s. The abundant water supply and the many places of concealment made the valley an ideal place for illegal whiskey distilling. During these Prohibition days, there were many stills hidden in the swamps and woods, and there was quite a lot of activity in that direction. The moonshine industry thrived even after the Volstead Act was repealed in 1933. The rising price of sugar finally brought the illegal whiskey industry to an end.

Hugie and Oleta Oesterreicher lived about two and a half miles north of St. Augustine on Twenty Mile Road (in the Diego Plains) in the 1930s. Because of the Depression, money was scarce, and making railroad crossties did not produce enough to feed their family. The second choice to make a living was to produce moonshine.

Michel wrote that, in the summer of 1932, Hugie Oesterreicher started making illegal whiskey. He did this on and off until the end of Prohibition in December 1933. During this time, he had to buy corn and rye and hundreds of pounds of sugar. In the beginning, he and Oleta could go to the wholesale house in Jacksonville and buy fifty- and hundred-pound bags of sugar. But later, when the government started cracking down and such large orders of sugar became suspect, the couple went from store to store in Duval and St. Johns Counties, buying five pounds of sugar here and ten pounds of sugar there.

When Hugie was finished, he would have five gallons of ninety-eight- to one-hundred-proof moonshine. In the early days of Prohibition, he could have sold a five-gallon jug of whiskey for fifty or sixty dollars, but in the early 1930s, when Hugie took up the business, there were so many competitors that the market was glutted, the price deflated and moonshine from his still only sold for fifty cents per gallon. Aged whiskey sold for about two dollars a gallon.

Michael wrote:

> *During the year and a half from the time he made his first batch of whiskey to the end of Prohibition, Hugie had several close calls with the law. One cold, damp fall day, he was out in Durbin Swamp running off a batch of whiskey. He heard a Model T, probably out on Old King's Road, approach the edge of the swamp.*
>
> *"Revenue men!" he gasped softly to himself as he pushed himself thought the under brush. Sheriff Boyce of St Johns County and Federal Government men were merely five feet from him. He crawled through the swamp back toward his home. Oleta heard the sound of ripping metal and heard an engine turn and move away into the woods. Shortly, Hugie came into sight. Hugie went back to see the damage they had done. They chopped it up and hauled the whole thing off and chopped up several barrels of whiskey aging.*

West of the Intracoastal

The family of William West from South Carolina was among the first known to have settled on the west side of the canal in Dewey and north of Pablo Creek, a turpentine settlement. West, "the Woods Rider," moved with his family to the east side of the canal around 1919.

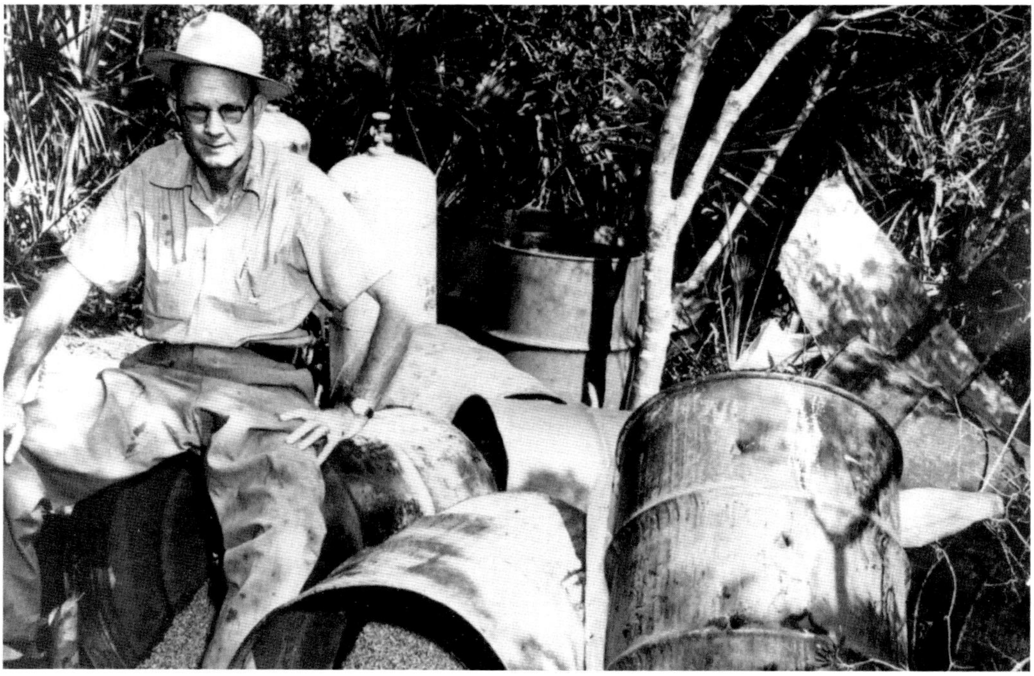

Sheriff Roy Landrum, after raiding and destroying a moonshine still in Palm Valley, circa 1950. *From the collection of the Beaches Area Historical Society.*

In those early days, West operated the turpentine still, where he employed fifty to seventy African Americans. He also ran a commissary in connection with the still. The only access to Diego was in "turpentine lighters" or other small boats.

After moving across to the east side of the canal in 1919, West ran a commissary on Roscoe Boulevard and later turned to farming by selling fruit and vegetables.

The W.R. Crain family home was also west of the swampy canal area, north of SR-210 (Palm Valley Road) and east of Twenty Mile Road. The Oesterreichers were another of the old families that lived along Twenty Mile Road, about two miles north of SR-210, and dabbled in the sale of palms and moonshine.

The Oesterreichers' homestead (actually over the line into Duval County) was originally built in 1873 with two rooms. In 1905, two more rooms were added. The house had no indoor plumbing, electricity or window screens until 1942. It is a rare example of Cracker-style architecture.[78] This original home still exists today.

In 1976, across the west side of the canal, there were the large ranches owned by Dr. Earl Roberts and the McCormick farm. Dr. J.A. Clements and Earl Pierce also had places over there.[79]

Among the homesteaders across the canal were William and Sarah Mickler, raising a large family in a rambling frame house that clung with a purpose to the road. Other families chose the more secluded and unbeaten paths where they nestled in primitive woodlands in and around Durbin Swamp.[80]

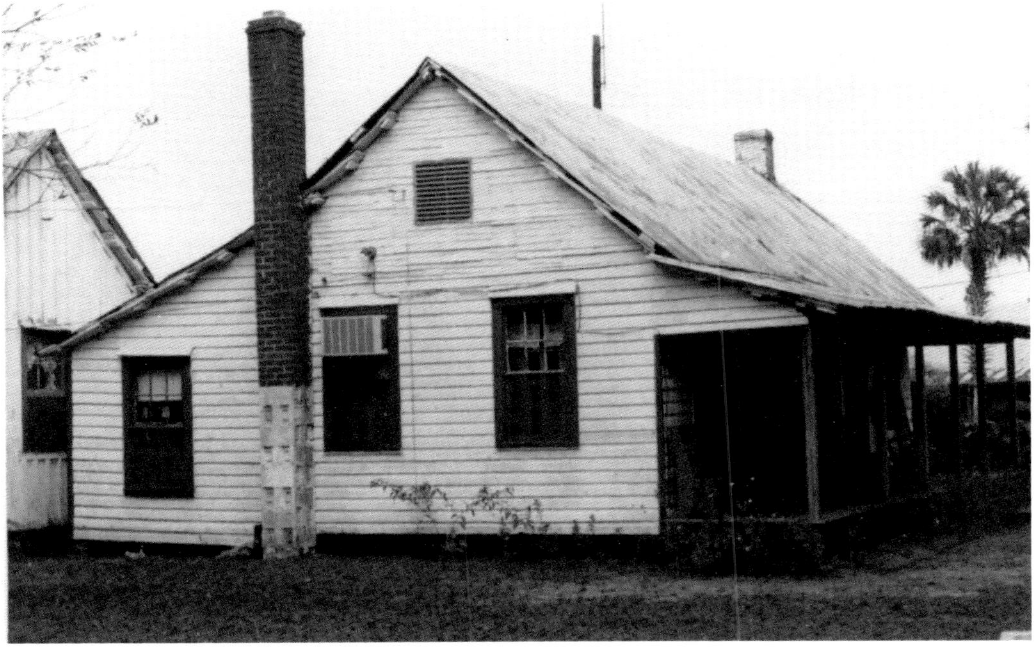

The 1800s Oesterreicher Homestead, built in 1873 at Diego (Palm Valley). The kitchen is located in the building at the left. *From the collection of the Beaches Area Historical Society.*

Durbin was a small town along King's Road that later became U.S. Route 1 and intersected with SR-210 at the western area of Palm Valley. English planters built the King's Road by subscription during the years 1765–75. It was considered one of the world's most outstanding engineering feats for its time, running as it did through swampy land and thus requiring the construction of causeways at the bridge crossings. It extended from St. Augustine north, crossing the St. Johns River at Cowford (present-day Jacksonville). There it met the connecting roads to Savannah and Charleston. Durbin was also one of the train stations that operated from South Jacksonville to St. Augustine.

The Jacksonville, St. Augustine and Halifax River Railway (JSAHRR), which began operating on February 28, 1881, ran excursion trains back in the early 1880s. The JSAHRR served the northeastern portion of the state and was the first railroad in what would eventually become the Florida East Coast Railway Company (September 13, 1885). The Durbin train stop gave Palm Valley residents another means of traveling to both St. Augustine and Jacksonville.[81]

In 1942 , Fort Davis was built near Pablo Creek by James Roosevelt Stockton Sr., who named it "the Haunt of the Hermit," as a gentleman's hideaway. It was the scene of many gatherings. Perhaps the most colorful of these was the debut of the Stocktons' daughter, Preston. The J.E. Davises (of Winn Dixie and Nocatee fame) bought the property in 1954 and built a house made of cypress logs chinked with concrete. The Davises' name for the ranch (Dee-Dot Ranch) is a contraction of the names of the Davises' son and daughter, Dano and Dorothy.

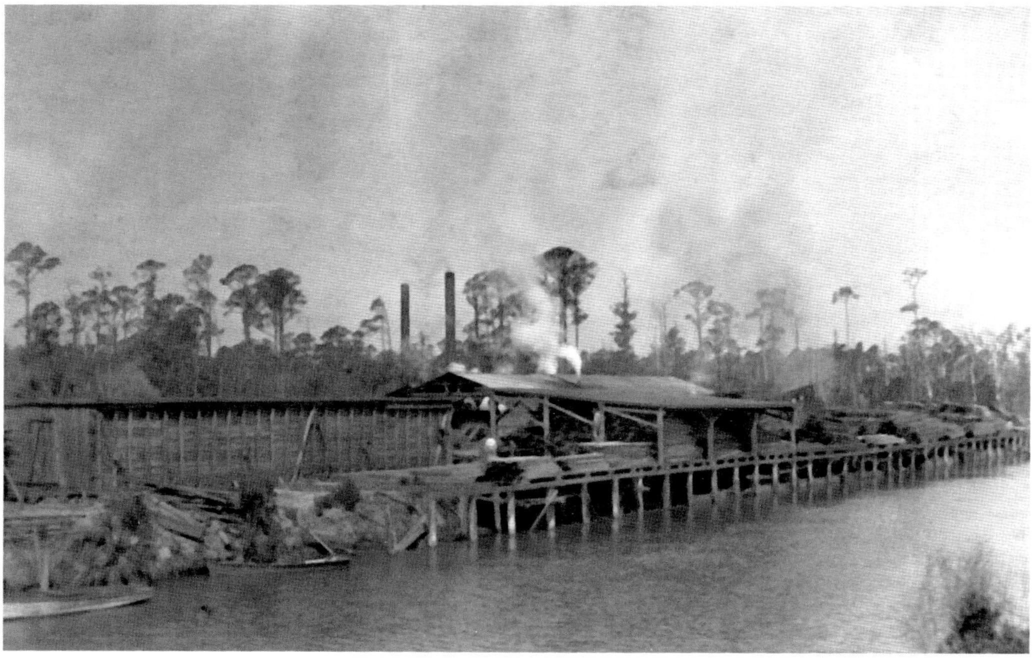

The Shore Sawmill at Cracker Landing. The canal is in the foreground with the lumber stored on the pier. Circa 1916. *From the collection of the Beaches Area Historical Society.*

In the early 1900s, there existed a local rail line of the Gress Company's tramway (operated by the action of the tides) from Crackertown, west of the San Pablo River to Bayard on U.S. 1. The last of the giant cypress was snaked out of the swamps by this company in about 1920. Much of this property, after removing the cypress, was planted with millions of pines, which thrived especially well on this once-cultivated land—the Fitch Old Fields, the Old Fields of the Dragoons.[82]

The Shore Sawmill (circa 1916) was in Palm Valley on the northwest side of the Intracoastal Waterway (then called Pablo Creek) at Cracker Landing. Old-timers called the area Craddock Landing.[83]

THE MICKLER FAMILY

The earliest account of the Micklers in America was in the mid-1700s. "Captain" Robert Mickler (pronounced Mi´-ke-ler) moved to Florida from St. Mary's, Georgia, and married Anna (Margarite de Ortagus) de Mier, the widow of Antonio (Jose Fernandez) de Mier, a native of Cadiz, Spain, around 1750. Later, in 1822, a cousin of Robert, Jacob Mickler, married Anna's daughter. It was from this early beginning that the settlement of Diego Plains (Palm Valley) by the Mickler family was to begin.

A lot of families settled in Diego Plains (Palm Valley) after the Civil War. The Micklers came in 1875 and lived in the Henson house, but the land was too low, so they built on the hill on Mickler's Road, right about where Raymond Mickler's log cabin was located. This ten-acre site was about a quarter mile from what now is A1A and Mickler's Landing in the area called Diego.[84]

Back in the nineteenth century, when the Micklers began living in the canal area, the various "valley" areas had many different names such as: Possum Trot, Diego Plains, the Canal, Carter's Run and Racetrack Island.[85]

It was in 1908 that Diego Plains residents decided to change the name of the area to Palm Valley. At this time, the road from CR-210 east to Mickler's Beach entrance was named for the Micklers. One of the first houses in Diego Plains (Palm Valley) was that of Yulee Raymond Mickler in 1875. In the 1970s, the Eston Barkoskie family occupied this same home.

Old Yulee Mickler used to tell his children that, when he was a boy, he used to go out to any of the ponds "'round about" with his young friends. When they shone a lantern, the eyes of the alligators would light up until there were so many that they looked like the electric lights of a city.[86]

Raymond Mickler was Sidney Mickler's grandfather and he had ten children. His wife died and he met and married Mrs. Barkoskie, who also had ten children and whose husband had also died.

In the 1920s, there were only about six or seven families in the Palm Valley area. When the Micklers married the Oesterreichers, all families were related either by birth or marriage. Up until the early 1940s, there were only fourteen Mickler families in the valley. And soon after, the first family unrelated by blood or marriage moved in.

Dancing on the Beach

In 1916–17, there was a pavilion built for dances down at Mickler's Beach. The social activities included dancing in a pavilion on the beach, as well as many beach picnics.

There was much talent available to provide music. Fiddlers included Bob Mier, Eddie DeGrove and Howard and Raymond Mickler. We are still able once in a while to get Bob Mier working on his fiddle (and he is really good at it). Many have had the pleasure of hearing him at various times and places.[87]

Fish Camps

The valley also had its fish camps built around 1930s (the George Oesterreicher family fish camp at the Intracoastal Waterway, and the Drayton and Desmond Oesterreicher family fish camp off Neck Road). The old Clam Shell, in 1940, was down near the bridge on the left before you went over the Intracoastal Waterway. Alfred and Edna Ray Mickler owned their first eating establishment. On that site, in 1947, was the Anchorage, a restaurant that was very popular with the locals.

MICKLER'S PIER

In 1935, Sidney "Sid" Mickler Sr. built a fishing pier at the end of Mickler Road—eventually named Mickler's Landing for Yulee Raymond Mickler. "It wasn't just a little pier, it went way out beyond the breakers," said Flavian Mickler.[88]

Mickler's Pier (admission twenty-five cents) extended three hundred feet into the ocean and was popular with fishermen (bait and tackle were available at the pier for surf fishing). The fishing pier on the ocean (indicating that its location at that time was in Palm Valley) was built by the Micklers. This Atlantic Ocean pier at Mickler's Cutoff was built with palm tree pilings and using live oak decks and railings. The pier had a windmill—the ocean breeze powered the pulleys that brought the ocean's salt water up to the top of the pier to keep the live fishing bait fresh.

Sid Mickler's father built Mickler's Landing and the ocean pier. The former six-hundred-foot pier, which survived a storm in the early 1940s, wasn't around long enough to become a historical landmark. The pier was torn down in the summer of 1945.[89]

Sid's family tended the kiosk[90] on the pier and assisted with the demanding tasks involved in running a pier. A dory originally used for long netting was situated beyond the kiosk. It held ocean water pumped from below.[91]

Although the pier was finally destroyed by a storm, Mickler's Landing, with its overhanging trees, high dunes and beautiful beach, has remained as "the place for teen-agers and young adults to swim and surf." It may have been the fishing pier that introduced people to the Palm Valley area and brought to it both people and progress.[92]

Mickler's Landing entrance to the beach by motorized traffic was closed in June 1978. Public access at Mickler's Landing was donated to the county by developers of the plantations at Ponte Vedra.

Today, at the Mickler's Landing or Crossroads location, one can see the old concrete pilings next to the now wooden walkway to the beach. The pilings and walkway were installed by the FEC railway for the purpose of keeping vehicles off the beach.

There are no Barkoskies and only a few Mickler families in the Palm Valley area today. Readers are thankful for the many stories and experiences written about the Mickler families—their lives and adventures still live with us in many ways.

THE MIER FAMILY

It was back in 1883 that two of the earliest Diego residents, Tulano and Naomi Mier, were having their fifth child, George. This Diego area was named after Diego Artegus, the first settler in the valley, according to George Mier. The Miers' original homestead was a hundred-acre plot of land, which they purchased for less than $200 and developed as a family truck garden.

Young George grew up on his father's land and was educated through the fifth McGuffey reader by a visiting teacher. It was George who followed up with his father's truck garden, just a mile away from the current Ponte Vedra–Palm Valley School. Their garden included crops of corn, potatoes and melons, to name a few, as well as the raising of beef, range cattle and horses.

Annually, George hitched his horse to his two-wheeled buggy for the five-hour ride to St. Augustine, twenty-five miles to the south, to pay the taxes on the hundred-acre family spread.

It wasn't long before George married Anita Braddock from Sampson, a small community just southeast of Bayard, and they soon had five children. George remembers the first appearance, in 1914, of a "tin lizzie." Up until that time, it was always trip by horse and buggy and later by train. In the early 1940s, George tore down the old two-story home and built a new one-story home piece by piece.[93]

The Henson Family

It was in 1906 that Robert Jesse Henson, with his wife Lottie and their five small children (they later had four more children), decided to leave his job with the Georgia Southern and Florida Railroad in Jacksonville and settle in Diego. They took the train from Jacksonville to Pablo Beach, where they transferred to a horse-drawn wagon and waited for the tide to go out. They had to cross two sand hills to get to the ridge where their house stood. The one-and-a-half-story house was old when the Hensons moved in, but it was built of heart pine, and they purchased it from Thomas Patten in 1906.

The earliest known owner of this home was Venaucio Mier Jr., who acquired the house and thirty acres from the Florida Land Improvement Co. of Jacksonville in 1883 for ninety-seven dollars. But Yulee Mickler, an early Palm Valley settler who once owned the house, told Henson in 1925 that he knew it was more than fifty years old then.

Robert Henson worked to clear the right of way for the highway, helped with the dredging of the Intracoastal Waterway, became postmaster for four years, ran a small store and petitioned the citizens to change the Diego name to Palm Valley.

Palm Valley Schools

The first public schoolhouse (School No. 26) was opened in 1882 and was located west of what is now the Intracoastal Waterway in a swampy area near the W.R. Crain home. It later burned, but it contained two rooms that each held four classes of children. The second wooden schoolhouse (School No. 27) was also located adjacent to the Crain home. This school building was used until about 1927. The third schoolhouse was located directly across from the Palm Valley Baptist Church on the late Flavian Mickler's land, and it was opened in 1928. It had two rooms, each of which held four classes.

In 1915, residents had built a school near Cracker Landing for twenty-five pupils. The Cracker Landing School was closed, and Mineral City pupils were reallocated to the Palm Valley School rather than attend school in Jacksonville Beach. For a temporary period, students attended school in the Diego Baptist Church.

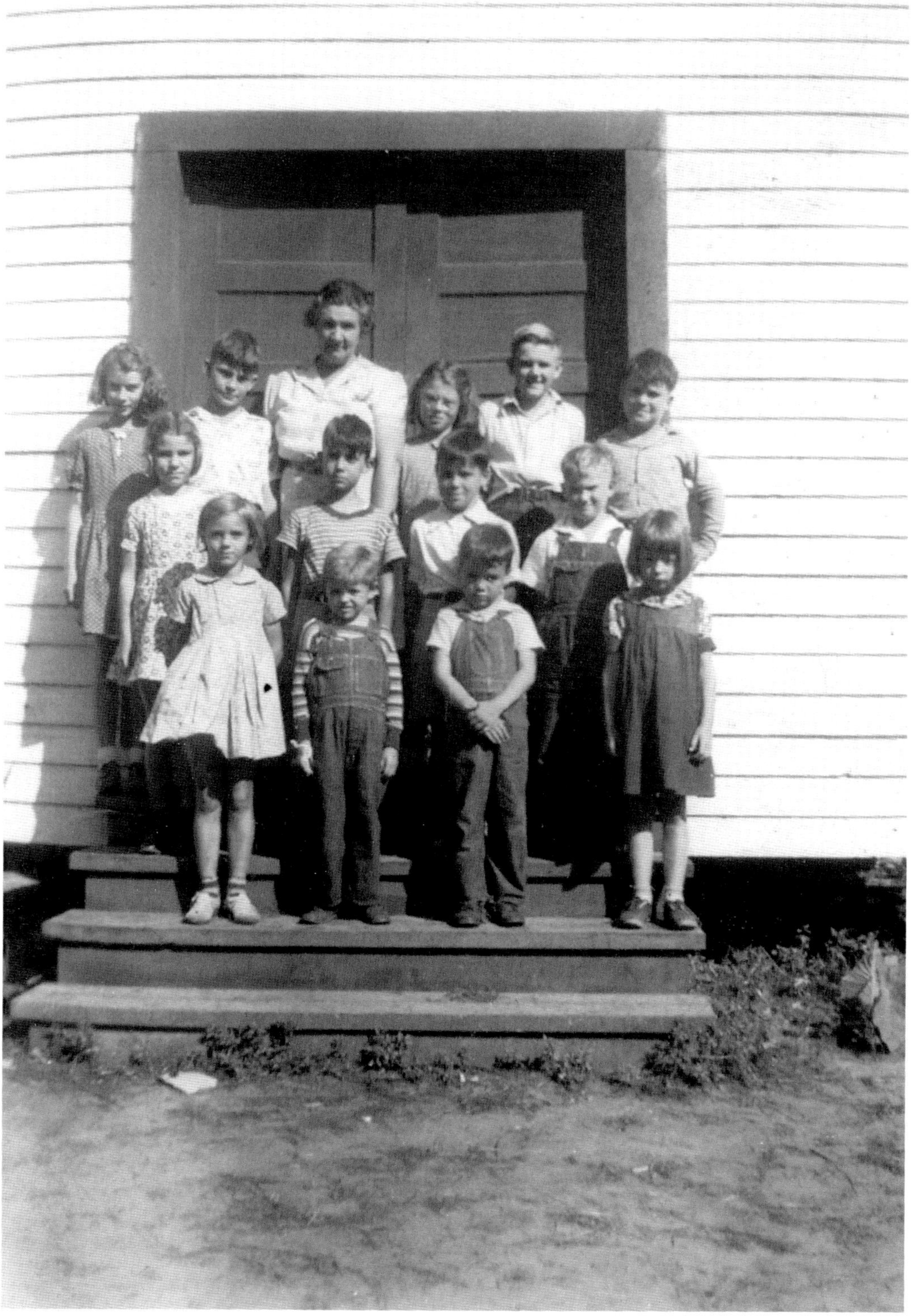

Palm Valley School House with teacher, Florence Hartsuff, and children on the steps. Circa 1900s. *From the collection of the Beaches Area Historical Society.*

The Palm Valley high school students were bussed over a dirt road to Route 1, then to St. Augustine, and Paul Henson drove that first school bus.

Sale of Palm Branches

The cutting and sale of palm branches, along with farming, were a primary support and livelihood in the 1940s. At least 400,000 palms were gathered each year and shipped to all parts of the United States, starting around the middle of February and continuing until Easter. They were wrapped in burlap and sewn with long needles by the women. Those participating were the Grove, Mickler, Mier and Oesterreicher families.

For the Oesterreichers, cutting palms in the late winter and early spring months added hundreds, sometimes thousands, of dollars a year to the family's income. Each winter, orders came from the nation's churches for fresh-cut palm buds for the celebration of Palm Sunday, one week before Easter Sunday. And each year, the Oesterreichers, along with other families from the area, cut palms, packed them in bunches of twenty-five or fifty and carried them to Durbin Station on the East Coast Railroad, where they were picked up by the train and shipped to churches all over the United States.

Later, after the Intracoastal Waterway was finished in 1912, the Oesterreichers carried the stacks of palms to a dock on the canal, where the *Navajo* or the *Alamo*, two packet boats that hauled freight between Miami and Jacksonville over the new waterway, picked up the stacks.[94]

Palm Valley Community Club House and Association

It was in 1948, at Mrs. Booker's home in Palm Valley Gardens, that the Palm Valley Gardens Women's Club began. A little later, the men's club was organized at the Palm Valley Landing. Both clubs needed a regular meeting place, and both clubs approached Jack Farr, who donated a large lot for a clubhouse on Canal Boulevard.

Joseph Roscoe suggested that Camp Blanding (a military building) be purchased for $2,000 and that the structure should be barged down the Intracoastal Waterway. Upon its final arrival, the entire community helped to reconstruct the building for use as a clubhouse.

Ocean Beach reporter Myrtle Stanley wrote in 1954 that

> *Palm Valley got its Center the hard way, but it has certainly been fun and has brought the members of the Community together for many, many happy times.*[95]

The two clubs eventually became what is now known as the Palm Valley Community Association, and it was the club to which almost all "valleyites" belonged in the 1950s. Its mission at that time was to draw together the residents in a spirit of fellowship and

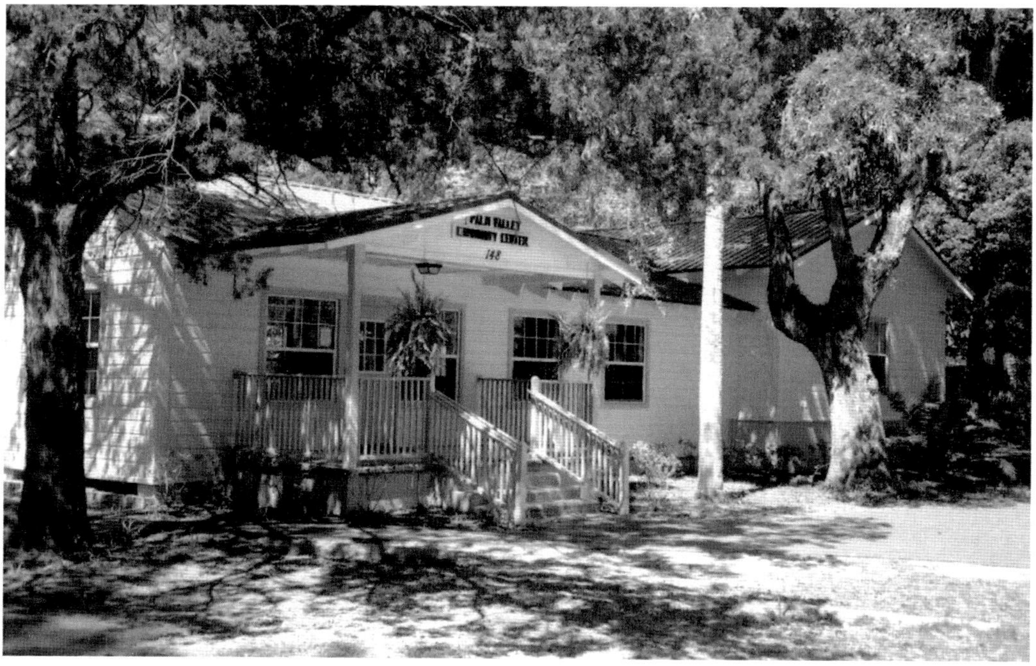

Palm Valley Community Center on Canal Road. Portions of the building were transported down the Intracoastal Waterway from Camp Blanding. *M. Robinson photograph, 2004.*

good neighborliness. The Palm Valley historical marker was recently sponsored by the St. Johns County board of commissioners.

THE INTRACOASTAL CANAL

The first dredging of the Intracoastal Waterway, also known as the East Coast Canal, was initially dug and operated through Diego/Palm Valley by the Florida Coast Line Canal and Transportation Company (FCLC&TC). This shallow canal operated around the period 1880–1908 and would only accommodate a limited number of shallow-bottom boats. Since this limited the shipping through Diego, it wasn't long before this initial attempt was dredged deeper through this area.

It was around 1908 that the Intracoastal Waterway's second dredging began, continuing over the course of two years. The canal through Diego Plains connected the San Pablo River to the north to the Tolomato River to the south. Organizing the first dredging of the canal were R.J. Henson Sr. and William Ketchell, who were in charge of digging the canal—which, at that time, was only a hundred feet wide. Deckhands on the dredge were paid twenty-five dollars per month; the mates were paid sixty dollars; and the levermen, ninety dollars.

The Intracoastal Waterway was completed in 1912.

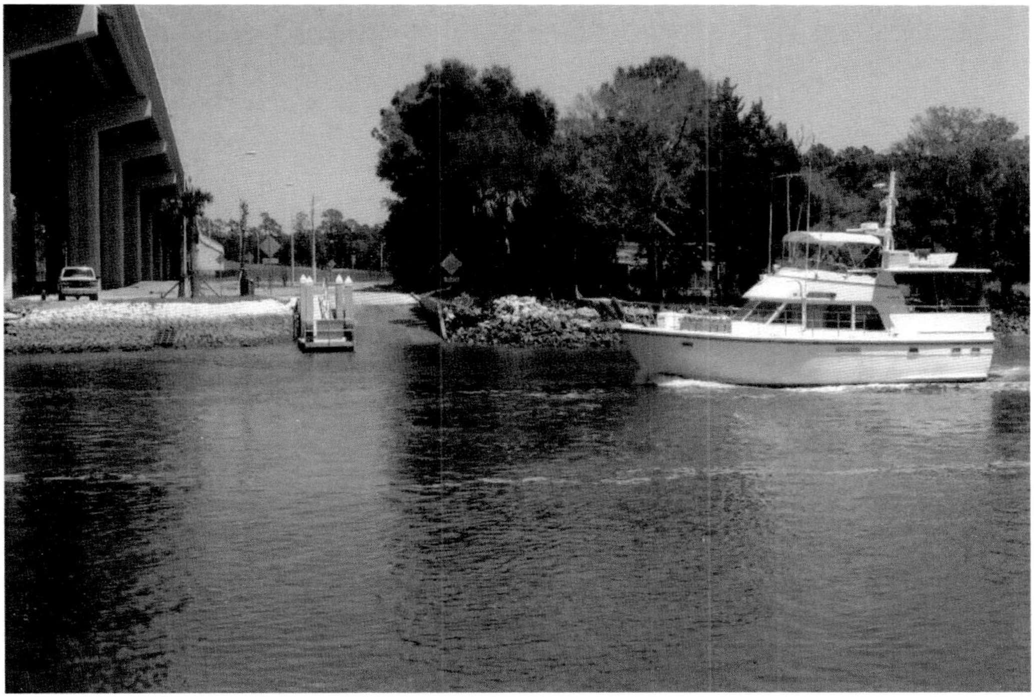

A yacht cruising northbound on the Intracoastal Waterway at Palm Valley public boat ramp under the overhead SR-210 bridge. *M. Robinson photograph, 2004.*

World War Army Training

Army training exercises held around Palm Valley and on Diego Plains for several weeks produced a war-zone atmosphere difficult for Palm Valley citizens to absorb. Servicemen swarmed across the parts of Diego Plains. A sentry stood guard at "the Pool," located off of Neck Road, and a password was required to pass in either direction.

Grahl Neitz wrote of the period, in *Cabbageberries, Dickfeathers and the Tides: A Collection of Palm Valley Memories*, that "the Blue army and the Yellow army raised a ruckus."[96]

Part II

Modern History—1900s to Present

9. Town of Mineral City—Mining for Minerals, 1914–1928

Early Beginning

Spreading along the shore of the Atlantic Ocean south of the Jacksonville Beaches, the area that would become Mineral City was opened for development in the 1880s by the San Pablo and Diego Beach Company. Platted in 1886, the plan of Diego Beach consisted of thirty blocks. But the company sold little of its property and most lots remained vacant. By 1917, the company had given up, and it conveyed most of its remaining property to Buckman and Pritchard, Inc., a Jacksonville real estate company.[97]

Mineral City's Beginning by Two Engineers

Mineral City had a most humble beginning. In the early 1900s, Mineral City, now Ponte Vedra Beach, was nothing more than a pristine wilderness of sand dunes, swamps, alligators and palmetto trees. This area, north of Diego Plains (now Palm Valley), first captured attention in 1912, when a vein that was rich in minerals was discovered running through the dunes on the beach.

George Anson Pritchard was a self-trained engineer who had chased gold in mines all over Central America and Colorado. In 1911, he met and partnered with Henry Holland Buckman in Indianapolis, where they were involved in a joint venture to develop an electric steel furnace that would withstand higher temperatures than those then used in making steel.

One of George's older sisters financed his education at the Colorado School of Mines. After he finished school, she sent him to Costa Rica to run the gold mine she owned. However, an earthquake closed the mine, and George then went to Indianapolis to visit another sister. It was in Indianapolis where he met Henry Holland Buckman.[98]

Buckman was born in Jacksonville to an aristocratic pioneer family. Shortly after the turn of the century, he went off to school in Buffalo, New York. He eventually graduated from Harvard and journeyed to Germany to study industrial engineering at the Universities of Berlin and Leipzig.[99]

Buckman had invented a device for measuring the moisture in silos, a very valuable measurement for farmers. He went to Indianapolis because that's where the company was making the device.[100] Buckman had also invented the first electric furnace, and ironically, he had written his thesis at Harvard on the "lack" of minerals on Florida's coast.

Buckman and Pritchard—"Buck" and "Prit," as they had begun to call each other—were mining engineers who combined resources to open a business in Indianapolis before 1914. They invented a machine to extract minerals through a patented washing process, and they used some of the research samples from Buckman's Harvard thesis, "The Sands of Florida," to analyze the Florida beach sand samples that had been sent to Buckman by his family in Jacksonville.

Search for Rare Chemicals

While examining each of the samples, Pritchard spotted little black specks of ilmenite, a very rare mineral. Pritchard knew of a company that could use thousands of tons of this material, but Buckman couldn't remember exactly where he had found the minerals.

The two of them headed to Florida to locate where the samples had been discovered. The sample container only read "Milepost 51." The two searched Milepost 51 at Spuds, near Hastings, but they did not find any of these samples along the tracks of the Florida East Coast Railway (FEC). Thinking the sample may have been gathered from Milepost 15 instead of 51, they searched Bayard (FEC), but the search was in vain. They asked if there were FEC branch tracks to the beach and they remembered the line to Mayport. They boarded the train from Jacksonville to Mayport that went through Ruby Beach (Pablo Beach, now Jacksonville Beach) and when they sighted the ocean, they saw Milepost 15.

Black "Gold"

They spotted the black specks in the sand, and the farther south they walked, it became more abundant. The heaviest concentration was in an area several miles south in Mineral City. Buckman and Pritchard had discovered another form of "black gold," and they didn't have to drill for it—it was right of top of the sand.

They set up their mining operation, consisting at first of a small mill. Mules hauled in the sand, and water and gravity were used to separate the minerals.

One day, Pritchard took a handful of the sand and threw it into the furnace during an experiment. Some of the darker particles in the sand stuck to his moist hand. Their curiosities aroused, they sent samples of the sand to the Pittsburgh Testing Laboratories. The firm's assay report read, "ilmenite (titanium), rutile, zircon and traces of many accessory minerals."

Pritchard said that he and Buckman, until then, had never heard of titanium, but they immediately started studying it to find out more. They learned that titanium in its ilmenite form was worth eighteen dollars a ton; rutile and monazite were quoted at eighty dollars a ton; and there was no known market for zircon of such small size.

Of the three recognizable minerals, titanium's use had the largest implications. "It was first used in building Big Bertha, the cannon used in World War I, to smooth out imperfections and strengthen the steel," said Pritchard's oldest daughter Patricia Pritchard Finley.[101] "All the rocket nose cones and airplanes as well." The titanium also had political importance:

> *At the time, the world-wide mines that produced titanium were controlled by the Axis, (Germany, Italy and Japan), this being the first found in the United States.*[102]

The partners found that there were fourteen minerals in the Florida sand and they mined four of these.[103]

Pritchard and Buckman roomed at Mrs. Perkins Bath and Boardinghouse in Pablo Beach. The men spent their days (in Mineral City) separating minerals from sand on

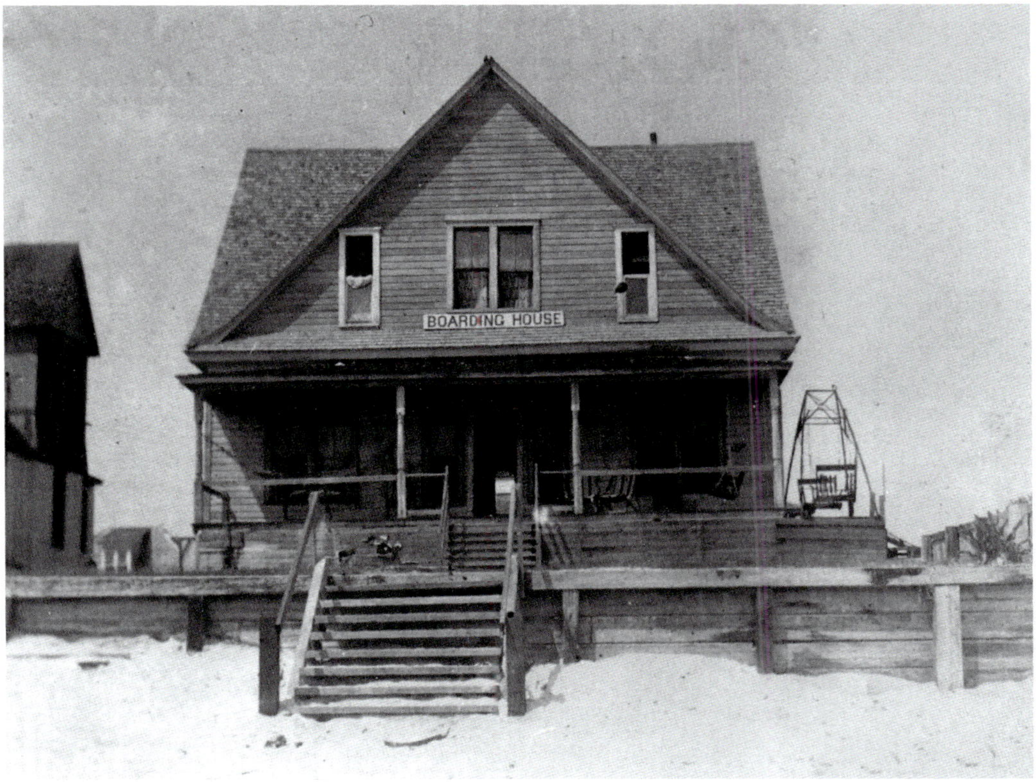

The Perkins Boardinghouse, Second Avenue and Boardwalk, Jacksonville Beach, where Buckman and Pritchard originally boarded before moving to Mineral City. Circa 1900s. *From the collection of the Beaches Area Historical Society.*

corrugated tables before sending them north on tramcars they invented. At the time, there were no roads south of Beach Boulevard. Finley said:

> *It was strictly a mining town. Unlike a typical western mining town, it was just the workers and a commissary. Their salaries varied from 25 cents an hour for a laborer to a $1.50 an hour for superintendents.*[104]

They finally bought a larger stretch of land at the northern end of St. Johns County. Today, it would be everything east of A1A for eighteen miles. Courtland Buckman, Mr. Buckman's uncle, decided that this particular stretch of land had the greatest number of minerals. He got the option to buy it for $500, and he later sold it to Pritchard for $1,100.

They mined the minerals right off the beach, carrying what they dug in tramcars up over the dunes to the plant, where the minerals were separated from the sand.[105]

They found an additional four-mile strip near what is now the Ponte Vedra Inn and attempted to buy it. But the owner was a Pittsburgh corporation (the National Lead Company), which refused to sell just the four miles. The National Lead Company (NLC) heard of the discovery, recommended immediate installation of a large-scale mining operation and offered to finance it. The partnership became the Titanium Pigment Company.

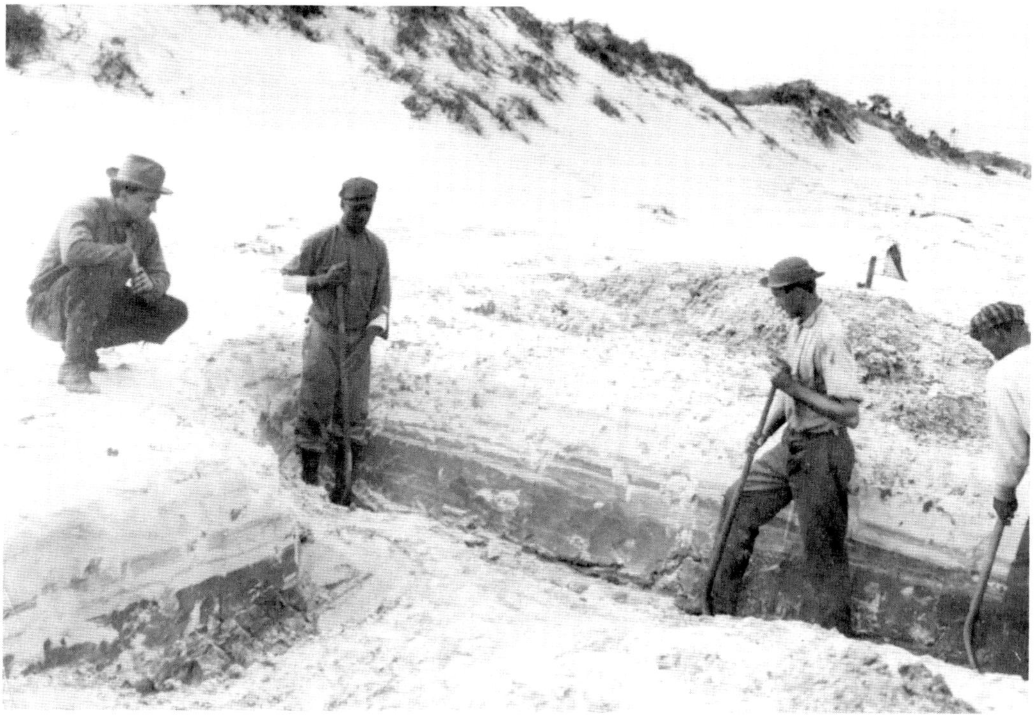

Buckman and Pritchard Sand Plant workers digging a test pit. The men dug holes along the beach to determine where the mineral veins were located. George Pritchard is pictured to left. Circa 1914. *From the collection of the Beaches area Historical Society.*

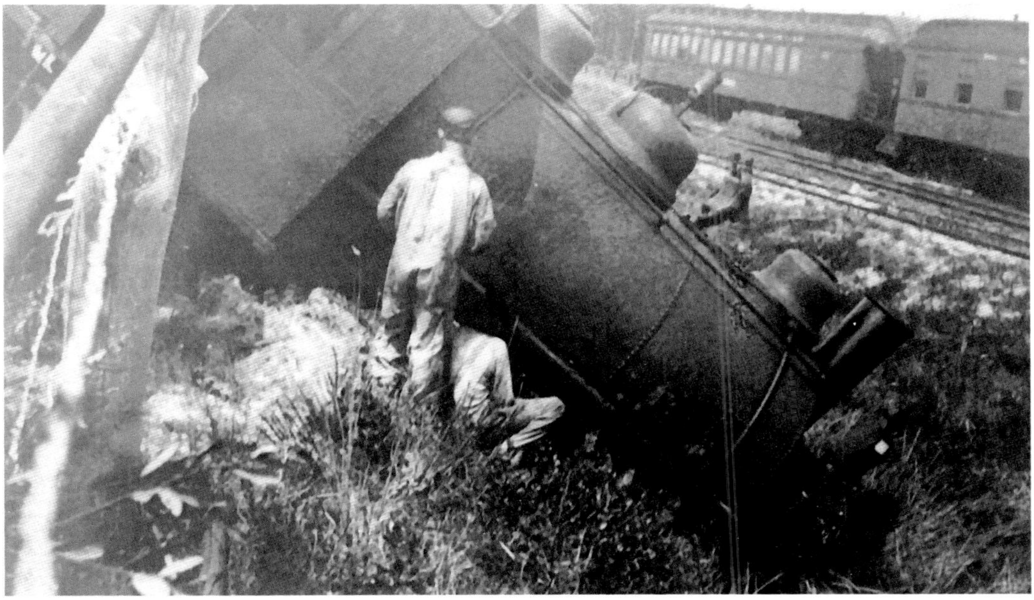

George Pritchard and Henry Holland Buckman Sr. (kneeling) working on a locomotive that had derailed. Railcars are in the background. This locomotive had to be assembled from scratch by Pritchard and Buckman. Circa 1922. *From the collection of the Beaches Area Historical Society.*

The Pritchards—First Family in Mineral City

The Pritchard family was the first family to live in Mineral City. Pritchard's son, Allen, was the first child born in Mineral City in 1920. Allen's older sister, Patricia, was born in New York, but the family moved to Mineral City before her brother was born.

Mineral City looked nothing like it does today. There was nothing there but the plant, Pritchard's house, Buckman's house and a few very small houses for the foremen. There were also small shacks in which the (African) workmen lived.

The only grocery store in town was the commissary used by the mineworkers, Mrs. Buckman and Mrs. Pritchard.

There were no roads, and A1A didn't exist. Everything had to be carried along the beach at low tide. Residents attest to a spot of quicksand that used to catch and damage the mining trucks, causing the company to lose valuable time and materials.

Nearly Broke

The partners also ran into money problems. They found that a large alloy company and its subsidiaries held patents, giving them the exclusive right to manufacture certain products containing titanium, mainly steel. The firm was the only real market for the partners' products.

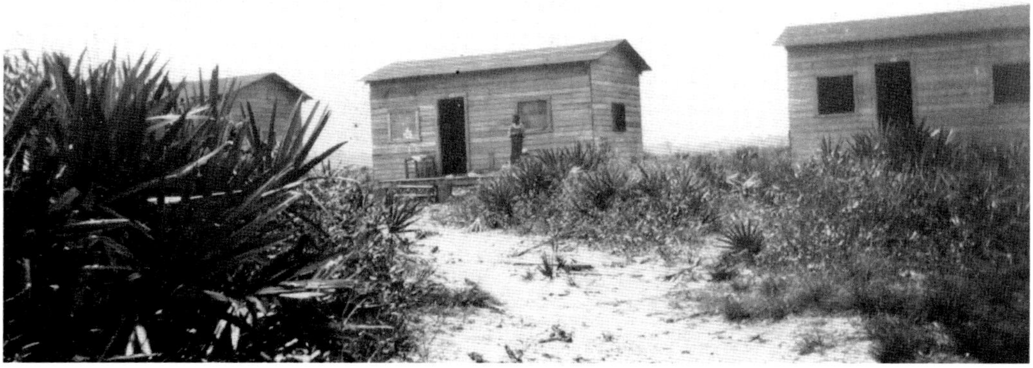

African Americans' shacks at the Buckman and Pritchard Sand Plant. *From the collection of the Beaches Area Historical Society.*

The mine had sent a number of tons of minerals to the alloy company, but now the company wanted more. Expansion of the mining operation would take a lot of money, and Buckman and Pritchard had enough financial worries without adding to them. They had hoped that the company would help them.

Pritchard indicated that a number of company executives came to inspect the plant.

> *We couldn't dare let those executives know that we were almost broke or they would have set back and waited for us to go under. We were out of ammunition, we knew, but we kept on firing.*

Mrs. Pritchard and Mrs. Buckman became quite adept at being able to spot which visitors their husbands wanted to see and which ones they did not, and when the latter came around, the ladies suddenly found it very difficult to find the partners.

Notices finally were served against the mine, and the case was to come up in a Jacksonville Court. However, Buckman pointed out to the judge that the mine was in St. Johns County and not in Duval.

By the time the St. Johns County process server found them, negotiations had been completed for paying for a greatly expanded plant. Pritchard told a *Times-Union* reporter that he and Buckman and their families spent one of their happiest New Year's Eves in 1917, when Mrs. Pritchard sat down and wrote checks to most of their creditors.[106]

MINERAL CITY AND THE MINES

The area of mining became known as Mineral City, and George Prichard became the first U.S. postmaster of Mineral City. The name "Mineral City" was chosen in a contest, and the worker who picked the name was awarded fifty dollars.[107]

Mules were about as important as people in the early mining operations at Mineral City—maybe more so. The mules pulled a device known as a "slip pan" because it looked like a pan and was pulled along the beach. A slip pan was about four feet square, and it could lift about a quarter of a yard of sand in one scoop. Gradually, more and more trucks joined the operation, but they never completely replaced the mules.[108]

The mine operated by Buckman and Pritchard was known as "the Sand Plant" and it was served by an abandoned railroad track that had previously extended from Pablo Beach to the swamps of Palm Valley to accommodate a logging company.[109]

The German Saboteurs in Control

The principal source of titanium, made from ilmenite and rutile, was under German control in Brazil. The only other location of the minerals was in Mineral City, which began to produce large amounts of ores from which titanium was made. Authorities in Washington, D.C., sent for the partners and urgently requested that Buckman and Pritchard supply the badly needed raw materials.

In the interim, the Germans had invented a new metal for armor-plated missiles and airplanes made from zirconium steel. The U.S. Navy again called them to visit Washington, requesting the supply of zircon ore in enormous quantities for a crash experimental program to develop zircon steel.

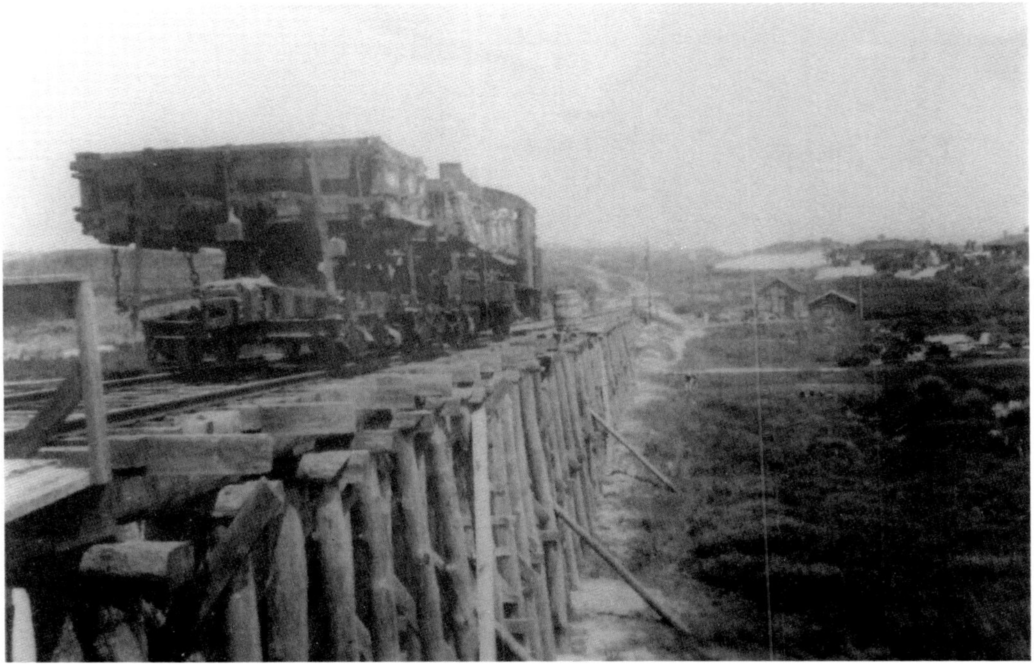

Buckman and Pritchard Sand Plant showing the railroad trestle. Circa 1922. *From the collection of the Beaches Area Historical Society.*

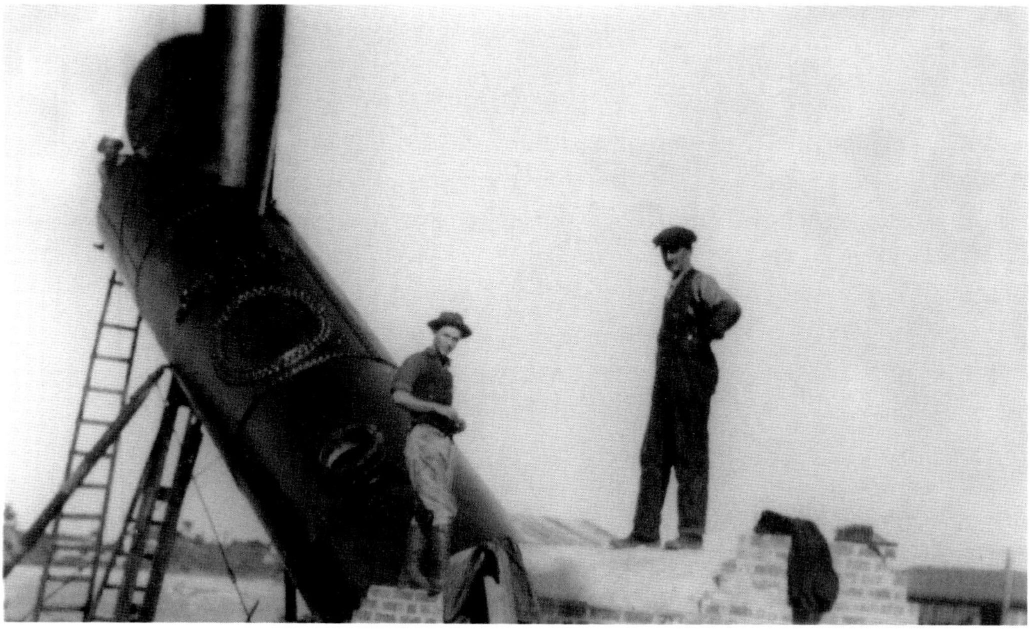

Buckman and Pritchard's Sand Plant showing two unidentified workers during the mining operations. Circa 1922. *From the collection of the Beaches Area Historical Society.*

Paving the way, literally, was Henry Buckman's uncle, Courtland Buckman, who paved the first road to the mine site four miles south of Pablo Beach (now Jacksonville Beach). A spur line was built from the FEC tracks in Pablo Beach to Mineral City.[110]

USES OF THE FOUND ELEMENTS

After the war, these elements were used in making steel, paint, linoleum, auto tires and dyes. Ilmenite became widely used in steel, making the final product more reliable and stronger than ever before. American railroads became major consumers of such steel, using it for improved rails. Zircon, mined at Mineral City, was used in many ways, particularly in porcelain, insulators of high transmission wires, automobile sparkplugs and countless other products in which great heat or high voltage was a factor.

The partnership of Buckman and Pritchard continued for several more years and was no less an achievement than their mining operations. According to members of their families, they never had any formal agreements or written contracts. They simply split everything evenly down the middle. It was said that they remained close friends for the remainder of their lives.

In a 1928 report of beach deposits in Mineral City, it was noted that the following minerals were being mined: ilmenite (black); zircon (white), rutile (brown), monazite (yellow), staurolite (brown), epidote (greenish yellow) and disthene (or kyanite, a bright blue crystal).

The Landrum Family

Buckman and Pritchard hired Roy Landrum Sr. to come with his family to build the railroad from the mining operation north to Ruby Beach (Jacksonville Beach). Roy and Ida Lee Landrum were from Newberry, Florida (west of Gainesville). The family was housed at a nearby farm. The railroad built to haul the ore would replace hauling the minerals to Ruby Beach by mules. Roy Landrum Sr., while working for Buckman and Pritchard, became deputy sheriff for the entire area of northeast St. Johns County.

Roy Landrum Jr. took over as deputy sheriff in 1929. He was assigned to caring for one of the mules hauling the minerals and, in addition, he built an icehouse to furnish the Club House, a store and a filling station. Also in 1937, Roy's wife, Alice, became postmistress, a position she held for thirty-six years.

Mineral City eventually housed about five hundred working miners, and those with children sent them to the elementary school in Pablo Beach (Jacksonville Beach). The center of commerce in Mineral City was the post office, which was designated Mineral City, and the general store. Ida Lee Landrum, wife of Roy Landrum Sr., operated both.[111]

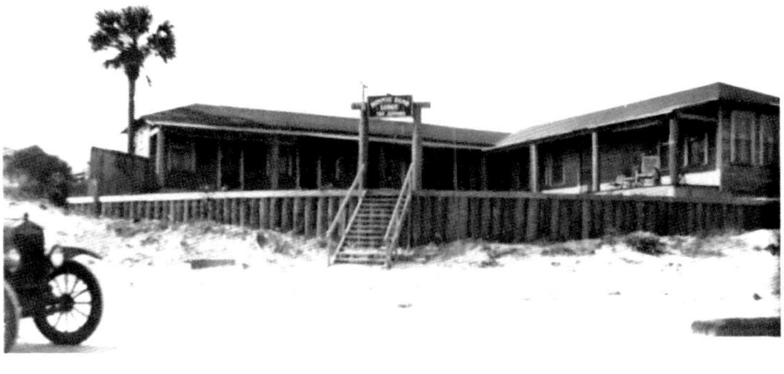

"Bonnie Dune Lodge," Mineral City, Florida. The Jeffers home and sign reads, "Bonnie Dune Lodge: the Jeffers." The home was built by George Pritchard in 1917, and was later turned into a lodge by George Jeffers. Circa 1919. *From the collection of the Beaches Area Historical Society.*

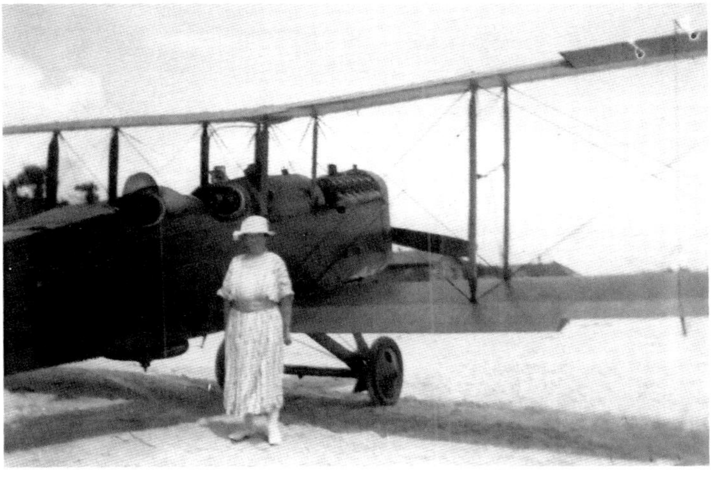

Mrs. George Jeffers standing in front of an airplane that landed on the beach in front of the Bonnie Dune Lodge, Mineral City, Florida. Circa 1922. *From the collection of the Beaches Area Historical Society.*

After 1922, the National Lead Company (NLC) built recreational facilities for its employees, including a rudimentary nine-hole golf course, a log clubhouse and a polo/sports field. The log house and golf course, both of which had been built for the mining employees, were made into a clubhouse and golf course for members. A dog track was added and a polo field was built.

By the end of World War I, the mineral market slowed and production at Mineral City ground to a halt. The NLC needed a new use for its now quiet town.

James R. Stockton Sr., of Telfair Stockton Company, was hired to sell the real estate. Mr. Robert Angus plotted the lots and the original nine-hole golf course, which was named Pablo Beach Golf Course.

The name Mineral City changed in 1928, when the Telfair Stockton Company took over planning for the future use of the property. By 1937, the Ponte Vedra Inn had opened. Gone were the abandoned shacks, the railroad tracks, the miners' cottages and the mining equipment—the surf had wiped out all traces of mining on the beach.

10.
First Church in Palm Valley and Ponte Vedra Beach

Oldest Church in Palm Valley

Palm Valley Baptist Church—originally Diego Baptist Church, which began in 1902—was located at 4890 Palm Valley Road.

Palm Valley Baptist Church celebrated its hundredth anniversary in 2002. In 1902, Diego (Palm Valley) residents William DeGrove, Thomas Patton and Thomas McClamma met with their families and friends to worship at the site where Palm Valley Baptist Church is now located.

> *And, it was the Mary E. and William DeGrove's, father and mother of Mrs. Charles DeGrove and Mrs. Doris Turknett, who donated the land to Messrs. Patton and McClamma, the church's first trustees, for the the Baptist Church of Diego, now Palm Valley Baptist Church.*[112]

Prior to that time, a small congregation held services under the beautiful oak trees, which today still hold the present church in their embrace. Today, in a little cemetery adjoining the church, lie the remains of Mr. and Mrs. William DeGrove and other members of their families.[113]

Palm Valley was known as Diego in the early 1900s because of the first Spanish settlers that arrived in the area. Then, in the late 1930s, charter members of the church and Diego's postmaster, Robert J. Henson Sr. petitioned Washington, D.C., to change the name of the community to Palm Valley. Changing the name of the church to Palm Valley Baptist Church soon followed.

Before the church hired a full-time pastor, the pastor of the First Baptist Church of Jacksonville, Homer Lindsay Sr., came out to Palm Valley to preach. Church members would pay Lindsay with vegetables, not cash, for providing services. Services were held only once a month in the beginning. The first full-time pastor was Reverend Paul D. Carmichael Jr., followed by Reverend M. Andrews.

There were many other "firsts" for the church. The first services were held once monthly and then bimonthly. The first baptisms were held in a water hole dug for that purpose not far from the church, and a few were held in the ocean. After the canal was dug in 1908, baptisms were held there until 1953, at which time they were moved to the First Baptist Church of the Beaches until the church could have its own baptistery. All the children loved to ring the church bell.[114]

On January 17, 1949, Eunice and P.H. Odum deeded the church some property on which to build a parsonage. Reverend McKensie, Reverend W.P. Everson and William West broke ground, even though the parsonage wasn't built until later.

The end of World War II brought the need for weekly services, according to a commemorative history booklet compiled by church members.

A new sanctuary was dedicated in 1957, and classrooms were added. In August 1980, a new Baptist church was built off SR-A1A in Ponte Vedra Beach. The new church took the name Palm Valley Baptist Church, and the old church on Palm Valley Road went back to its original name, Diego Baptist Church.

Later, the early frame church was torn down. Since then, two new additions have been made, and there has been a succession of ministers, including the Reverend Dr. W.P. Everson, who served in 1977.[115]

In 1999, the congregation decided to reclaim the name Palm Valley Baptist Church. The church has grown a lot, but many things remain the same. In the little cemetery, which is located next to the church, lie some of the founders of the church. The church booklet reads:

> *Through all these changes and those yet to come, our roots run deep, just like those of the old oak trees. The trees and the graves under them are continuing reminders of who we are and how we are growing.*[116]

Reverend Jim Witt, named pastor in 2005, was associate and youth minister at the church.

FIRST CHURCH IN PONTE VEDRA BEACH

Christ Episcopal Church at 400 San Juan Drive began in 1949 and now holds services at the following locations: Serenata Beach, DayBreak, Vicar's Landing, Cypress Village and others.

The Episcopal Diocese of Florida came into being January 17, 1838, at Tallahassee with seven parishes. It was not until the 1950s that an Episcopal church began in Ponte Vedra Beach.

Christ Episcopal Church celebrated its fifty-fifth anniversary in 2006. On Christmas Eve 1951, Christ Church held its first worship service to celebrate Christmas and the dedication of the church building.

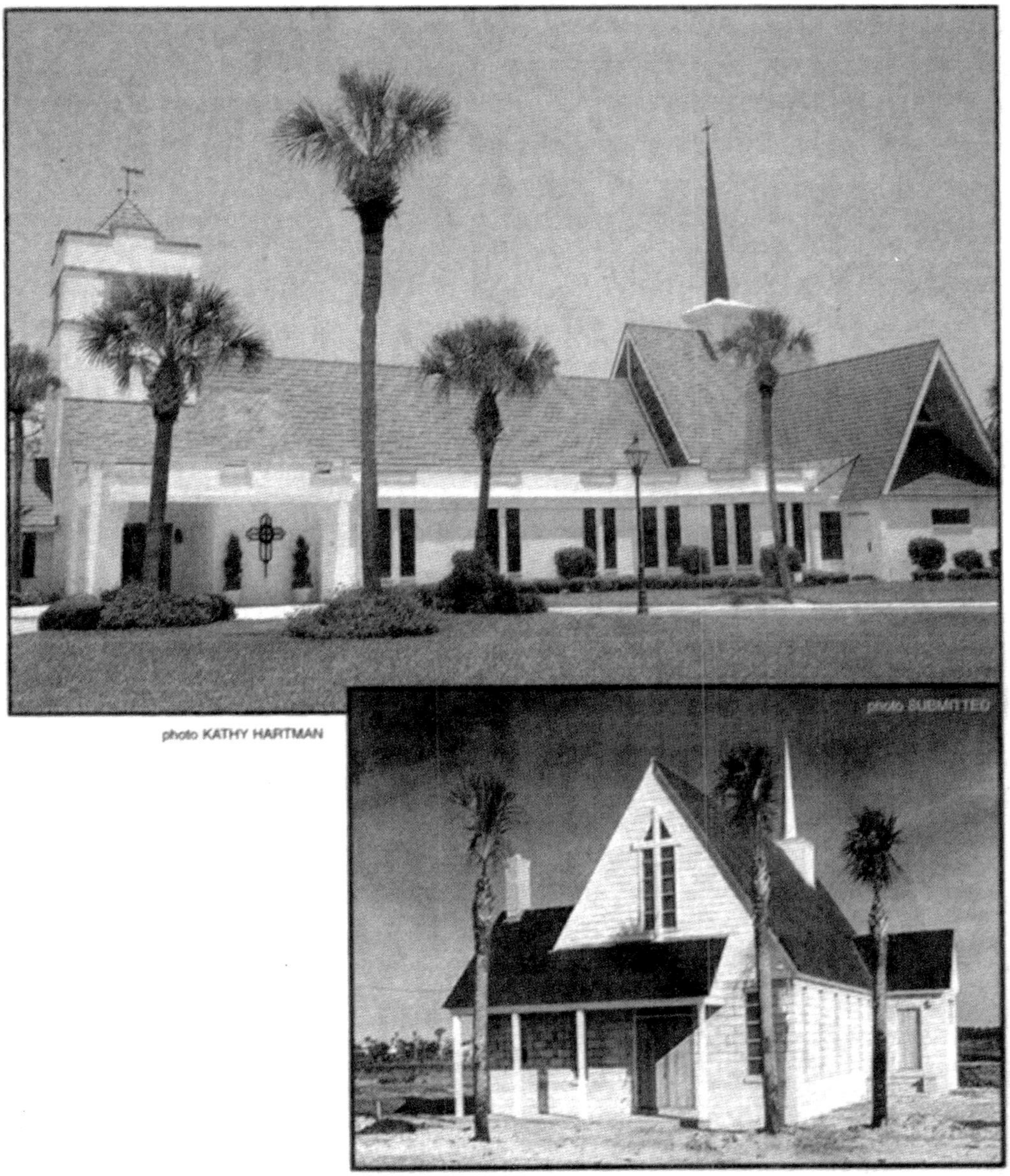

The Christ Episcopal Church building on San Juan Drive during construction in 1951, and as it stood in 2004. The church was designed by architect Wellington Cummer II. Beaches Leader/Ponte Vedra Leader, *March 2005.*

In the beginning, area citizens were interested in establishing a church, and an Episcopal church was the initial congregation's choice. The first meeting of the church's congregation was held in the Surf Club at the Ponte Vedra Inn in the fall of 1950. The Right Reverend Frank A. Juhan (bishop of the diocese) advised some thirty Ponte Vedra residents of the steps necessary to establish a mission within the Parish of St. Paul's By-the-Sea, Jacksonville Beach.[117]

Some of the ladies that began the church were: Henrietta (Hinkey) Gilliard, Myra Brown, Elizabeth Sterling (who helped buy the lot) and others.

At first, on December 15, 1950, Christ Church was a mission that met in many of the members' homes. The first part-time priest was Edward Harrison, from Jacksonville Beach, who conducted services at Christ Episcopal as well as in Jacksonville Beach. Christ Church became a parish on July 24, 1955. The rectory, located at 84 San Juan Drive, was completed on September 15, 1955.

In its fifty-six-year history, the church has had three full-time rectors: the Reverend Alexander "Sandy" Juhan (whose father was an Episcopal bishop), the Reverend Dr. James Cooper and the Reverend Richard S. Westbury Jr. Under Juhan's leadership, Christ Church grew from seventy members to seven hundred. Since that time, the church has expanded its facilities three different times and acquired additional properties.

The architect, Wellington Cummer (parishioner Hettie Rowe's brother-in-law), who just recently died, designed the first church building in 1951 on San Juan Drive.[118]

Christ Church has experienced an explosion of growth. The small but faithful church's congregation came together several years before 1951 as an existing church. Christ Episcopal Church is the oldest church in Ponte Vedra still standing. Today, Christ Church is a worshiping community of over six thousand. More than 50 percent of the present congregation arrived during the last six years. One recent survey listed Christ Church as the third largest Episcopal church in the country.

The church is continuing to expand its facilities and locations to meet the community's needs. The lay ministries play an important role in encouraging the spiritual growth of the diverse congregation.[119]

Harry Johnston (no one ever called him anything but "Harry," despite his old age) said that, in his opinion, two institutions were of major importance in developing a community of spirit (in which he played an important role) in Ponte Vedra: the founding of the Ponte Vedra Volunteer Fire Department and the founding of the Christ Episcopal Church by the prime mover, J.P. LeMaster, on land donated by Stockton, Watley, Davin and Company (SWD).

THE COPPER STEEPLE

A personal observation was obtained from the Jacksonville Historical Society archives regarding the steeple:

> *A piece of copper which adorns the steeple has an interesting background. Ed Smith of Jacksonville Beach told me about this when I spoke to the Beaches Rotary on August 12, 1966. He was program chairman. Mr. Smith has a building supply and insulation materials business.*
>
> *One day a known moon shiner came in with a large piece of copper sheeting and wanted to sell it because* ["the revenuers were getting too close"]. *This man was a moon shiner and that was no secret, but I was curious as to why he wanted me to buy*

> *the copper. Smith knew this man and knew that he could be believed when he affirmed that he was telling the truth. The moon shiner wanted to sell the copper for $20. The price was fair and Smith bought it.*
>
> *The next day a contractor working on the Christ Church came in, saw the copper and asked the price. Mr. Smith told him the story and the price, whereupon the contractor paid the $20 and took it along with him. He incorporated it into the roof of the steeple, signed DS.*[120]

Church Members Reminisce

Fred Woolverton was the first mission board member of Christ Church, along with J.P. LeMaster and other prominent citizens in the community. Fred and Margaret Woolverton became interested in building the church and talked to their contractor friend, Buddy DeChaine, who agreed to serve as contractor without charge, which was a wonderful help.[121]

There are several other members who reminisced about the early beginnings of the church:

Alice Juhan (now living at Vicar's Landing), wife of Reverend Sandy Juhan—who was the first permanent rector of Christ Episcopal Church—recalls coming to Christ Church on January 15, 1953, from Havana, Cuba. The Juhans had lived in Cuba for three years. Before his Havana assignment, Sandy was first assigned as army chaplain in Norfolk, Virginia, and upon his return from Cuba, he was assigned in Richmond, Virginia.

The Christ Church began with retired clergy holding their initial services in homes before the church building was opened in 1951. At the end of the first year, the mission membership totaled eighty-eight. Bill Perry lived across from where the first church was built, and he held Sunday school at his home. Reverend Juhan also gave Father Danaher of Our Lady Catholic Church office space when that church was being formed in 1972. The first church building that was built had open windows and doors (there was no air conditioning at that time) and the chickens and birds would try to enter the building before storm doors were finally installed.[122]

Randy Brown was one of the early residents of Pont Vedra, moving here in 1946. He remembers when most of A1A was called "Possum Trot Trail" and to get anywhere, one had to travel by jeep. "There were only thirteen kids riding the school bus from PV," said Randy, "Alberta West and Mary Hughes were the bus drivers and Mary was still driving his children in 1985."

Randy moved to Jacksonville at age two before coming to Ponte Vedra. He was the first acolyte at Christ Church and has served variously as lay reader, cook, vestryman and chalice bearer since the first service in 1951. His parents were part of the original group petitioning Bishop Juhan for a church in Ponte Vedra.[123]

Randy, still living on Solana Road beside the church, is still a member of the church, and he recalls many memories. Randy's parents were James Randolph and Myra Brown.

The first church meeting was held on Randy's parents' front porch and five couples were involved: Hazel and Bryan Crawford, May and Dutch Williams, the J.T. Woolfords, the LeMasters and the Sterlings, who helped get the church's lot. The first church service was held around 1949. The money for the church construction came from the Beach Bank, Fred Allen's bank in Jacksonville Beach. There were several temporary pastors, but Reverend Newton Middleton, a retired priest, was the main one.

Randy's father, James, remembered that on Christmas Eve 1951, most things were delivered and in place—except the lighting fixtures. Some of us cut one- by three-inch boards, drilled holes in them for candles and wedged them into the window wells since the first service was to be held by candlelight.[124]

The original altar at the first service was a long, cherry table now in the Brown's home. Alice Juhan's father was a physician in Atlanta, and he gave the Browns two menorahs (a candelabrum with seven branches used in ceremonies to symbolize the seven days of creation) to light candles in the church. The candles were used for many years and now reside in the Brown's home. Sandy Juhan's father was the Episcopal bishop of the area at the time the church was established. In 1948, the mission church members held regular services, meeting in homes serving as church circles.[125]

Henrietta "Hinkey" Gilliard—who at this writing was ninety-three years old and living in Cyprus Village—helped start the church in the 1940s, indicating that not everyone was of the Episcopalian religion. Original members tried to start a church that would be acceptable to everyone, and the Episcopalian religion was the choice. Soon, Episcopal services were being held in Ponte Vedra.[126] One day, Hinkey visited Myra Brown with a check for $100 from her mother in Nashville, Tennessee. Hinkey's mother thought starting a church was a good idea, but that it wouldn't get anywhere unless people contributed in cash as well as talk. This began spontaneous giving from those who were interested. They gave the money to Myra, who had a secret hiding place, "so that no one could steal the lord's money."[127]

11. GERMAN SABOTEURS—*OPERATION PASTORIUS*, 1942

GERMAN SABOTEURS LAND IN NEW YORK AND FLORIDA

In 1970, professor of history at Miami-Dade Junior College, North Campus, and retired FBI special agent Leon O. Prior wrote one of the many detailed accounts of this German invasion in his 1970 article for the *Florida Historical Quarterly*. In the article, he described how Americans were taken off guard by this affront.[128]

As part of *Operation Pastorius*, a team of four saboteurs infiltrated the United States via the submarine *U-202* at Amagansett, Long Island, on June 13, 1942, and another four saboteurs landed in Ponte Vedra Beach, Florida, via the submarine *U-584* on or about June 17, 1942. All eight men were armed with explosives and planned to destroy factories, bridges, tunnels, power plants and waterworks. One member of the group that landed on Long Island, New York, eventually turned himself over to the FBI and confessed the entire story. All eight saboteurs were arrested, and six were executed in Washington, D.C., on August 8, 1942.

The first sign of the German High Command's intention to engage in sabotage activities in the United States was disclosed by the apprehension of eight trained German saboteurs by FBI special agents within two weeks after they had landed in the country by German submarines. These eight saboteurs had been thoroughly trained by the High Command of the German army in the most modern methods of destruction, and they were sent to this country for the specific purpose of interfering with the U.S. war effort. The Germans placed particular emphasis on interrupting production at aluminum and magnesium plants.

Sabotage investigations were another FBI responsibility. These men had been trained by Germany in explosives, chemistry, code writing and blending into American surroundings. While still in German clothes, the New York group encountered a Coast Guard sentinel patrolling the beach. A beach sentinel ultimately allowed them to pass. However, afraid of capture, saboteur George Dasch eventually turned himself in and assisted the FBI in locating and arresting the rest of the team, who had been at large for roughly two weeks. All eight saboteurs were in federal custody by June 27, 1942. The swift capture of these Nazi saboteurs helped to allay widespread fear of Axis subversion and bolstered Americans' faith in the FBI.

LANDING ON LONG ISLAND, NEW YORK

The first group of saboteurs landed on the beach at Amagansett, Long Island, on the night of June 13, 1942. Those landing in New York were Ernest Peter Burger, age thirty-six; George John Dasch, age thirty-nine; Richard Quirin, age thirty-four; and Heinrich Harm Heinch, age thirty-five. All of these men had been born in Germany and, at one time or another, had spent a portion of their lives in the United States, during which time they learned the English language and became acquainted with American customs.

All of these men, with the exception of Burger, had returned to Germany after the outbreak of the war. Burger had returned to Germany in 1933, after living in the United States for a period of six years.

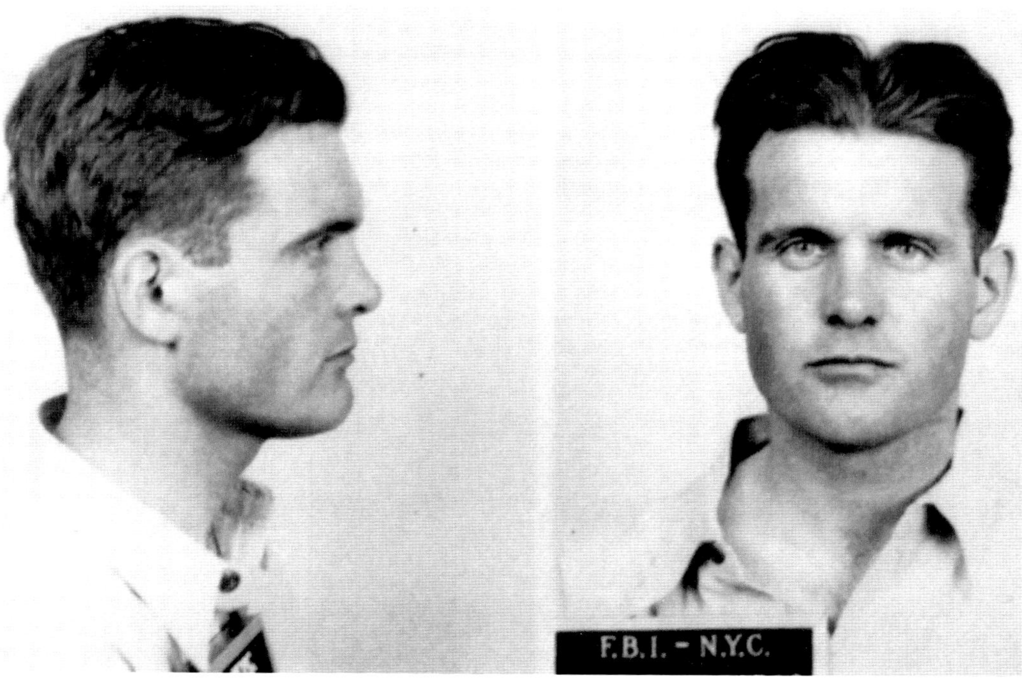

An FBI mug shot of Edward John Kerling, age thirty-four, one of the four Germans with *Operation Pastorius*, who landed in Ponte Vedra and later was sent back to Germany in exchange for releasing information about the operation. *Michael Dobbs,* Saboteurs: The Nazi Raid on America *(2004).*

Landing on Ponte Vedra Beach

On June 17, 1942, four nights after the German landing on Long Island, another German landing took place near the resort in Ponte Vedra Beach, Florida. Arriving onshore after disembarking from *U-584*, four Nazi agents tossed their jackets and caps into the boat and dug four holes.

The saboteurs landing in Ponte Vedra were Herbert Hans Haupt, age twenty-two; Edward John Kerling, age thirty-four; Hermann Otto Neubauer, age thirty-two; and Werner Thiel, age thirty-five.

The landing of the Germans from *U-584* went much more smoothly than that of their counterparts in New York just four days earlier. Even so, there were some anxious moments. As he navigated the shoreline south of Jacksonville (Ponte Vedra), U-boat commander Joachim Deecke had to dodge an American patrol boat and a barrage of zeppelin observation balloons monitoring the coast for enemy submarines. The little zeppelins were particularly tiresome creatures—very difficult to shake off.

Eventually, the submarine came within several hundred feet of a wide, sandy beach near Ponte Vedra. Deecke ordered the bow tanks to be flooded so that his boat nudged against the sand, its decks peeking out of the water. A thin sliver of moon glowed in the sky, making the night a little less impenetrable than the mist-shrouded obscurity that had enveloped *U-202*. But it was dark enough, nonetheless. Unlike their counterparts from *U-202*, the men from *U-584* were dressed only in bathing suits and German marine caps as they came ashore in a rubber dinghy. They assumed that the Nazi swastika insignia on the caps would be sufficient to give them prisoner of war status as German soldiers if they were captured after landing. Their civilian clothes were zipped up in waterproof bags.

After depositing their passengers on the beach, the two crewmen from the submarine scooped up a can of American sand to take back to Germany. They could hear some female bathers chatting and giggling a little to the north of the landing spot. They used flashlights to signal Deecke that the landing had gone according to plan, and the crewmen returned to the U-boat almost immediately.

A slender man with wavy brown hair and a heavy jaw, Kerling made a quick tour of the beach to make sure there were no inhabited houses nearby and that nobody had seen his men land. He then selected a place to hide the four boxes of explosives and other sabotage gear—all practically identical to those brought ashore by Dasch's group. The spot Kerling chose was easy to remember: a grove of palm trees on a little hill next to a wire fence, halfway between the beach and the road. The saboteurs buried the boxes just as a gray dawn was breaking, and they threw the spade into the sea, where it would be taken out by the tide.

Dressed in swimsuits and carrying their clothes in bundles under their arms, they then walked north from Ponte Vedra Beach in the direction of Jacksonville Beach. For the next four hours, they lounged around on the beach, swimming and relaxing like vacationers. While still in their bathing suits, they gave a cheery wave to a passing police patrol car and received a wave in return. At around eleven, they put on their clothes and caught a bus into Jacksonville, some forty-five minutes away.

The next morning, local fisherman found the incriminating evidence—small bombs and incendiary devices.

Like Dasch's group, the four men decided it was safer to split up into pairs. Kerling and Neubauer, the injured soldier with the American wife, checked into the Seminole Hotel in downtown Jacksonville under the names of Edward Kelly and Henry Nichols. Haupt and Thiel found rooms in the Mayflower Hotel, just a block from the bus station. As an American citizen, Haupt registered under his own name: if questioned about where he had been over the last year, he planned to claim that he had just returned from a long trip to Mexico. Thiel signed as William Thomas.

That afternoon, they went on a shopping expedition, just like their comrades from *U-202*. Haupt, who had the most expensive tastes and had felt deprived of consumer goods in Germany, felt particularly at home in American stores. He had his hair cut and got something to eat, and then he proceeded to make a string of purchases: a three-piece tan suit from a fashionable New York tailor, a pink-gold Bulova wristwatch, some neckties and shirts, underclothes, a tan leather suitcase, silk handkerchiefs and several pairs of shoes. The others limited themselves to the basics.

In the evening, they all met for drinks at the Mayflower Hotel and agreed on a plan of action. Kerling and Thiel would travel to Cincinnati and New York and Neubauer would go to Chicago. Haupt was adamant that he also be allowed to return to Chicago, despite warnings from Lieutenant Walter Kappe about contacting his family. Even though Kerling knew of Haupt's fondness for money and doubted his loyalty to the Nazi cause, he decided to entrust him with a canvas zipper bag containing $10,000 in a false bottom, to be left for safekeeping with his uncle in Chicago. His reasoning was that Haupt running around with plenty of spending money posed less of a threat than a financially strapped Haupt, who would be tempted to turn everyone into the FBI for a cash reward.

The plan was for the saboteurs to meet again on July 6, two days after the planned July 4 rendezvous between Kerling and Dasch in Cincinnati. Even though gasoline rationing was being enforced along the East Coast for owners of private automobiles, Kerling and Haupt would somehow find a way to return to Florida and retrieve the explosives.[129]

The objectives of the proposed sabotage were found in the papers buried in both New York and Florida. The Florida team, headed by Kerling, was scheduled to blow up New York's Hell Gate Bridge over the East River; demolish the Horseshoe Curve of the Pennsylvania Railroad at Altoona, Pennsylvania; and destroy New York's water-supply system. They were also to attack the lock and canal installations in St. Louis and Cincinnati. Both teams were to plant bombs in Jewish-owned stores and in locker rooms at major passenger railroad stations to spread fear and panic.

After Dasch revealed the story to the FBI, all saboteurs in New York and Ponte Vedra Beach were immediately arrested. By June 25, 1942, all the would-be Nazi saboteurs had been captured. The two naturalized Americans, Haupt and Ernest Peter Burger, and the other six, who had all called America "home" at one point or another, were found guilty.

Recruitment of Saboteurs

The German saboteurs who were sent to the United States were recruited for this work by Lieutenant Walter Kappe, who was attached to Abwehr 2 (Intelligence 2) of the German High Command and was in charge of German sabotage in the United States. Kappe had lived in the United States from 1925 to 1937, during which time he took part in the creation of the first Nazi organization—known as Teutonia—in this country in Chicago. He later was one of the principal organizers and an officer in the Friends of New Germany, which subsequently became the German-American Bund. In the latter organization, Kappe was press agent, in charge of propaganda, and was editor of the official Bund newspaper in the United States. Fritz Kuhn ousted him from the German-American Bund as a result of some inner-circle rivalries, and Kappe returned to Germany, where he was placed in charge of the American section of the Ausland Institute at Stuttgart, Germany.

It is known that periodic meetings were held in Berlin, and in other cities throughout Germany, for those Germans who had formerly lived in the United States. These groups were known by the name Comradeship USA. Walter Kappe was one of the officials in charge of these meetings that were held for the purpose of keeping up the morale of these Germans because they had grown accustomed to a higher standard of living in the United States than that which was available in Germany at that time. Kappe recruited several of the saboteurs from these groups.

Conclusion

After the Ponte Vedra Beach team reached the shore without problem, questions arose. That same morning, Kerling and Thiel were on a train bound for Cincinnati, and Haupt and Heubauer were en route to Chicago.

It was at that point that the carefully planned operation went wildly awry. George Dasch—who had lived in the United States for years after illegally entering the country in 1922 and had only returned to Germany the previous year after a brief stint in the USAAF—telephoned the FBI and went to Washington. There, he stayed in Room 351 of the Mayflower Hotel and met special agents Duane Traynor and Thomas Donegan on June 18. Within nine days, all members of both teams had been arrested.

Why Dasch surrendered so easily to the FBI still remains something of an enigma. In his interrogation, he revealed not only the identities of his confederates, but also valuable information on the German civilian situation, the Abwehr training school, Walter Kappe and even the depths to which U-boats could be submerged. He later said that one of the turning points in his attitude had been back in Lorient, when he realized that a great deal of the $5,000 he had been given to finance his American adventure was in notes that had been withdrawn from service years before. Recalling this oversight, he remarked:

I kept thinking about the money. If they could be that stupid, how much did they really care about any of us? What chance did we have?

The trial of the eight agents took place in the U.S. Justice Department building. By August 8, 1942, the verdicts had been reached.

Michael Dobbs wrote, in *Saboteurs: The Nazi Raid on America*, that George Dasch was a very bitter man who considered the charges against him "crazy" and the concluding remarks of Cramer "grossly unjust." The tribunal, he would later write, was "not my idea of an honest American trial." But what upset him most was this treatment by the FBI. He thought he would be hailed as a hero for betraying *Operation Pastorius*; instead, he was shunned and ignored.

The sentences were thirty years in prison for Dasch and the electric chair for the other seven. In April 1948, both Dasch and Burger were granted clemency by President Truman and returned to Germany.[130]

This was the first such procedure against civilians since the trial of Lincoln's assassin, and before the case was ended, even the Supreme Court had become involved. The White House issued the following statement on the sentences of the eight Nazi saboteurs who landed by submarine on the Long Island and Florida shores on June 13 and 17, 1942:

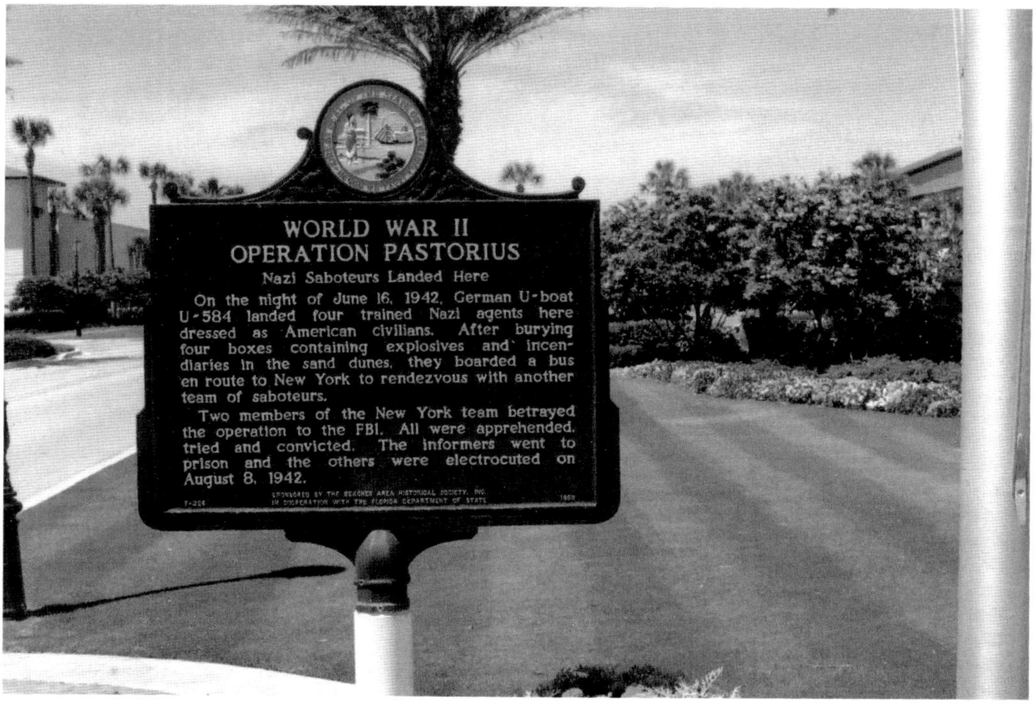

The World War II *Operation Pastorius* landmark located on Ponte Vedra Boulevard at the Ponte Vedra Club, sponsored by the Beaches Area Historical Society. *M. Robinson photograph, 2004.*

> *The President completed his review of the findings and sentences of the Military Commission appointed by him on July 2, 1942, which tried the eight Nazi Saboteurs. The President approved the judgment of the military Commission that all of the prisoners were guilty and that they be given the death sentence by electrocution. However, there was a unanimous recommendation by the Commission, concurred in by the Attorney General and the Judge Advocate General of the Army, that the sentence of two of the prisoners be commuted to life imprisonment because of their assistance to the Government of the United States in the apprehension and conviction of the others. The commutation directed by the President in the case of Burger was to confinement at hard labor for life. In the case of Dasch, the President commuted the sentence for confinement at hard labor for thirty years. The electrocutions began at noon today. Six of the prisoners were electrocuted. The other two were confined to prison. The records in all eight cases will be sealed until the end of the war.*

Sixty-two years later, that the government of the United States released to the public all the documents pertaining to *Operation Pastorius*.

World War II–Operation Pastorius Historical Marker

This Florida historical marker is located on CR-210, in front of the Ponte Vedra Inn and Club and was sponsored by the Beaches Area Historical Society in cooperation with the Florida Department of State.

12. PONTE VEDRA INN AND CLUB HISTORY

EARLY CLUB BEGINNINGS

The inception of the first club began in October 1928 in the offices of the National Lead Company (NLC) on Wall Street in New York City. The NLC had been mining the sands along seventeen miles of Florida beaches, the site of the present Ponte Vedra Club, and the mining operation was petering out. Now it faced the question of what to do with the several thousand acres of ocean-side property.

The Telfair Stockton Company ([TSC], begun in 1884 and later to become Stockton, Whatley, Davin and Co.) was the major land developer in all of Jacksonville. NLC decided, on that fall afternoon in 1928, to ask TSC to take over the planning of the grand design for the future use of its property. TSC, together with NLC, began arrangements with the Ponte Vedra Inn and Country Club.[131]

Shortly after NLC opened the club, it sold all of its holdings to TSC, which began development of the present resort community. The cost, at that time, was about the price of a single oceanfront lot today. Telfair Stockton had grand plans for the oceanfront paradise, and then World War II erupted.

At the club, major changes took place. The Ryder Cup, golf's greatest international tournament, had been scheduled for November 18–19, 1939, on the Inn and Club's Ocean Course, but it was cancelled seven months in advance. Charles Row, secretary of the British Professional Golfers' Association, sent a message via cable to the national office of the PGA of America, stating:

> *When we have settled our differences and peace reigns, we will see that our team comes across to remove the Ryder Cup from your safekeeping.*

In a gesture to soothe the U.S. team—which included legends Byron Nelson and Sam Snead—after having lost the chance to represent their country, Ponte Vedra Inn President Frank Rogers presented the members of the squad with lifetime memberships to the club.

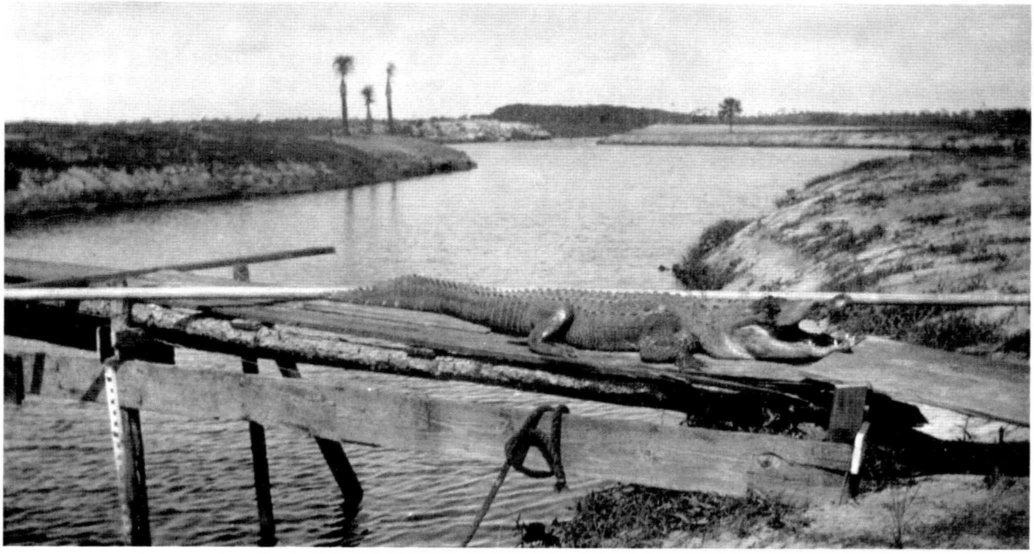

The first golf course under construction, showing the lagoon and an alligator perched on a bridge. Circa 1928. *From the collection of the Beaches Area Historical Society.*

Joe Davin, the land engineer of the firm, was put in charge of land planning and development. Jim Stockton, son of Telfair Stockton, was put in charge of planning, designing and managing the club resort.

THE PRINCETON CONNECTION

Jim Stockton was a true-blue Princeton man of the class of 1916. Off went a letter to every member of the class, all of whom would be in their early forties in the year (1937) of the Ponte Vedra Club's opening. And all of whom, at that age, would presumably be prospering in careers in their hometowns and throughout the country.

The loyal Princetonians must have spread the word immediately, as the early years of Ponte Vedra reflected that the guest register was filled with names from many states.

Joe Davin, vice-chairman of the board, emeritus, of Stockton, Whatley, Davin and Co. (SWD), remembers when his company was approached by the NLC with the idea of developing the area.

> *In the late '20s, they got the idea of making a development out of it and asked us to do it. So we went down, dredged out those lakes, and had the road at Jacksonville Beach extended to St. Augustine.*

The venture started fairly slowly. Due to the sudden economic hardships of the Great Depression, the state lagged behind in building roads into Ponte Vedra.

From the beginning, the emphasis was on the good life.

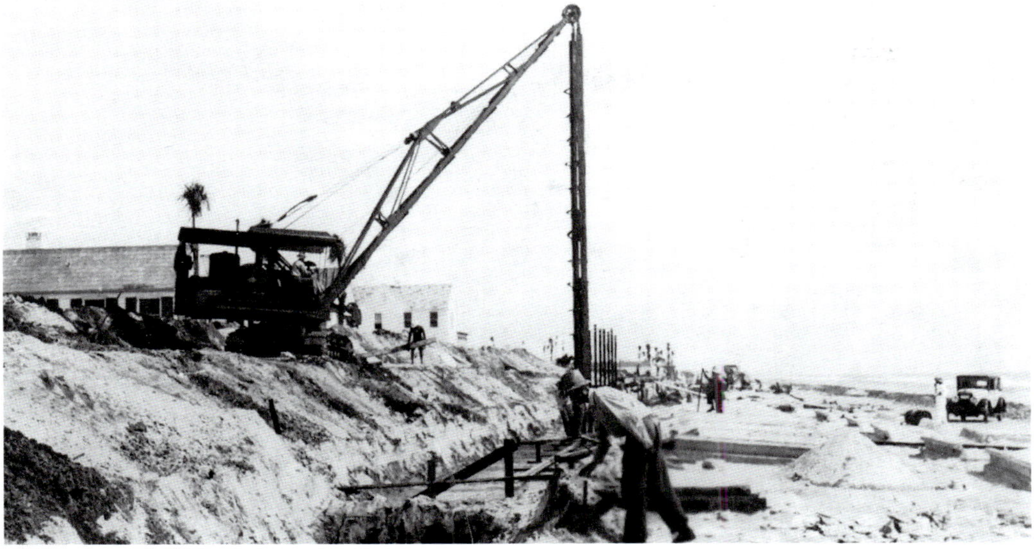

Building the bulkhead, Ponte Vedra Beach, Florida. A crew with a crane is building the seawall. Circa 1914. *From the collection of the Beaches Area Historical Society.*

> *The first thing we built was the Bath Club, then the Surf Club. We built some tennis courts, but the Bath Club was the big thing. It had a dance floor, and that was popular from the beginning. People went on Saturday night and danced.*[132]

A Storied Past

From the boardrooms of Wall Street to the social registers of America, word spread quickly of the charming seaside retreat on Florida's northeast shore. The first guests came from faraway places such as Princeton, New Jersey; Newport, Rhode Island; and Greenwich, Connecticut. Indeed, this quaint, seaside retreat attracted the upper classes from all over the Eastern and Midwestern states. They came for the sun, sand and surf. They came for the sports. They came to socialize. The finest families came to meet the finest families.[133]

The same could not be said, however, of the rest of Ponte Vedra. Joe Davin concedes that there was some doubt as to whether the whole thing would succeed.

> *That was a big doubt. It was slow. We built the first ten houses for National Lead at cost. Then we built another fifteen or so ourselves, all on the ocean. We built a few on the back roads, to get that part inhabited, you might say. But it took a long time for it to get going.*

Vacationers paid rates that were considered high-end, though they seem astoundingly low by today's standards. Accommodations cost as little as $4.00 a day for a single-

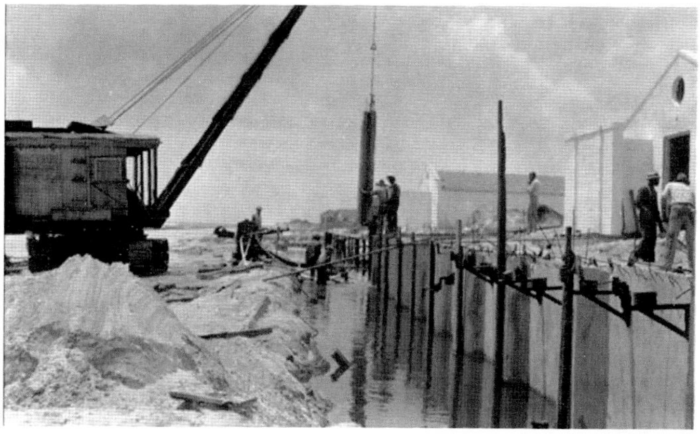

Construction of the bulkhead in front of the Ponte Vedra Bath Club. The construction firm was B.B. McCormick & Sons. Circa 1934. *From the collection of the Beaches Area Historical Society.*

occupancy, no-view room to as much as $14.00 as day for a double-occupancy, oceanfront room, including all meals. Greens fees were $1.50 per day, and annual golf memberships were available at $60.00 for men and $40.00 for women.

From the boardrooms of Wall Street to the social registers throughout the Northeast, word spread quickly of this charming seaside retreat on Florida's northeast shore. The grand plans for "the Inn" and the first cottages began to take shape in 1927. In 1937, the Inn was formally opened.[134]

One of the first settlers, Louis Kurz, indicated that the NLC people had to change the name from Mineral City to something more enticing.

> *One day during a name-discussing conference, one of the developers happened to pick up a newspaper and see a story with a date line "Pontevedra, Spain." Ponte Vedra was Mineral City to Ponte Vedra then unanimously chosen as the name for the new development.*
>
> *The National Lead Company, too busy with military orders to devote much time or interest to resort real estate, sold all of its local holdings to the Ponte Vedra Corporation in 1942.*[135]

In 1937, the Inn opened and Collis Quarterman, chauffeur for the senior Stocktons when Jim Stockton was growing up, was assigned the first "star" of this new cast. Interestingly, he was also a graduate of the Rolls Royce engineering course, which he attended in the North after the Stocktons first purchased a Rolls Royce. Jim Stockton asked Collis to join the staff of the Inn, and it was Collis who checked in the first guest in 1937. When Collis retired in 1979, he had been chief of service for most of his forty years on the staff.[136]

The original Log Cabin, a twelve-room structure built in 1927, was in constant use by guests until the opening of the Inn in 1937. It remained in use as an employee's residence until 1966.

As Jim Stockton had turned to his Princeton classmates for support of his Ponte Vedra venture, he soon turned to his brother-in-law for managerial talent at the Inn.

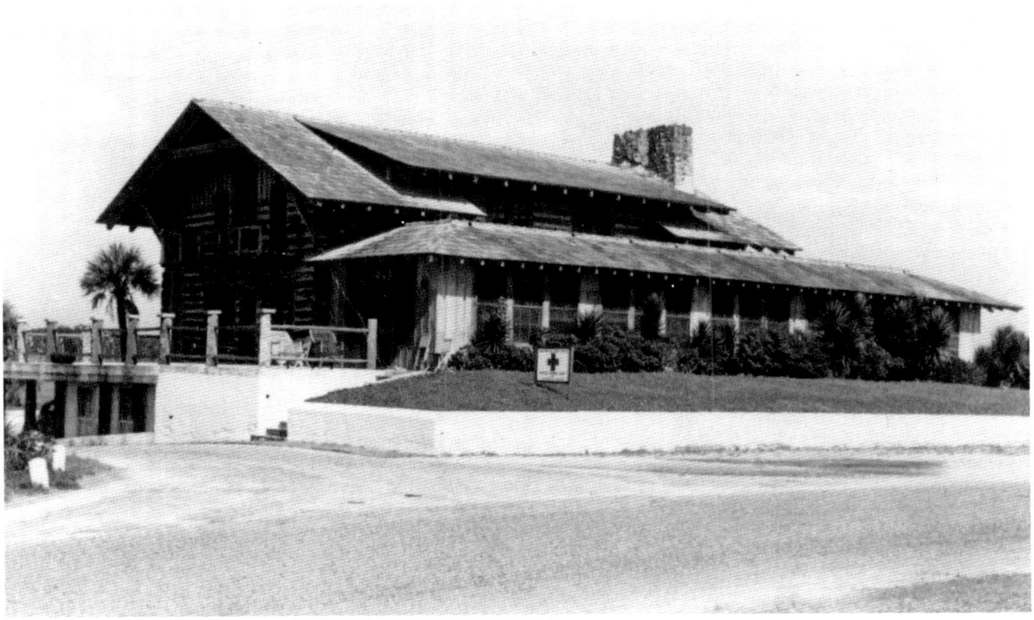

Ponte Vedra Golf Club House showing the Red Cross station during World War II. Circa 1942. *From the collection of the Beaches Area Historical Society.*

Several professional hotel men served as managers in the shakedown days of the Inn, but the Stockton firm felt that one of its own executives, particularly one with a wide acquaintance throughout the South, would be more suitable to forward the interests of the fledgling resort.

Frank Rogers, married to Florence Stockton (Jim's older sister), left his position as vice-president in the life insurance department of the company and came to take over the management of the club in 1938.

Frank and Florence "Stockton" Rogers, leading members of the Jacksonville gentry, were to set the tone of the Ponte Vedra Club for years beyond their tenure as its first leaders.

The Innlet's Ownership

We can't ignore the Innlet, located a mile and a half to the south of the Inn. In 1941, Tommy Sabin, a New York banker and playboy who had been a frequent Ponte Vedra visitor, bought some beachfront land from the Ponte Vedra Corporation south of the Inn and built the thirty-two-room Innlet. In 1944, the Innlet was purchased by Ponte Vedra Corporation and operated as an integral part of the Inn. The Innlet changed ownership many times from the late 1940s to the 1970s, but Ponte Vedra Inn and Club continued to manage the property.[137]

A sad thing happened in 1968 when the Innlet was sold to outsiders and passed out of the Ponte Vedra orbit.[138]

PONTE VEDRA COUNTRY CLUB

SEASON 1937

AMERICAN PLAN RATES

Guest Cottage Rates Including Meals, Storage of Automobiles in Club Garage, and Use of All Bathing Facilities at Bath Club.

GUEST COTTAGES "A" AND "B"
(ON THE OCEAN FRONT)

Single Occupancy	$ 8.00	per day
	50.00	per week
	200.00	per month
Double Occupancy	$ 14.00	per day
	85.00	per week
	350.00	per month

GUEST COTTAGE "C"
(SURROUNDED BY THE GOLF COURSE)

Single Occupancy	$ 7.00	per day
	45.00	per week
	180.00	per month
Double Occupancy	$ 12.00	per day
	75.00	per week
	300.00	per month

EUROPEAN PLAN RATES
(ROOMS ONLY)

GUEST COTTAGES "A" AND "B"

Single Occupancy	$5.00	per day
Double Occupancy	8.00	per day

GUEST COTTAGE "C"

Single Occupancy	$4.00	per day
Double Occupancy	6.00	per day

Ponte Vedra Country Club Golf Course

ROLAND MACKENZIE

of the Congressional Country Club,
Washington, D. C., Winter Professional

GREEN FEES

Per Day	$ 1.50
Per Month—Men	$15.00
—Women	10.00
Per Season—Men	$45.00
(6 Months)—Women	30.00
Per Year—Men	$60.00
—Women	40.00
—Husband and Wife	88.00

The Ponte Vedra Country Club guest rates for cottages and golf in 1937. *Elaine B. Koehl,* Ponte Vedra Club: The First Fifty-Five Years, 1927–1982.

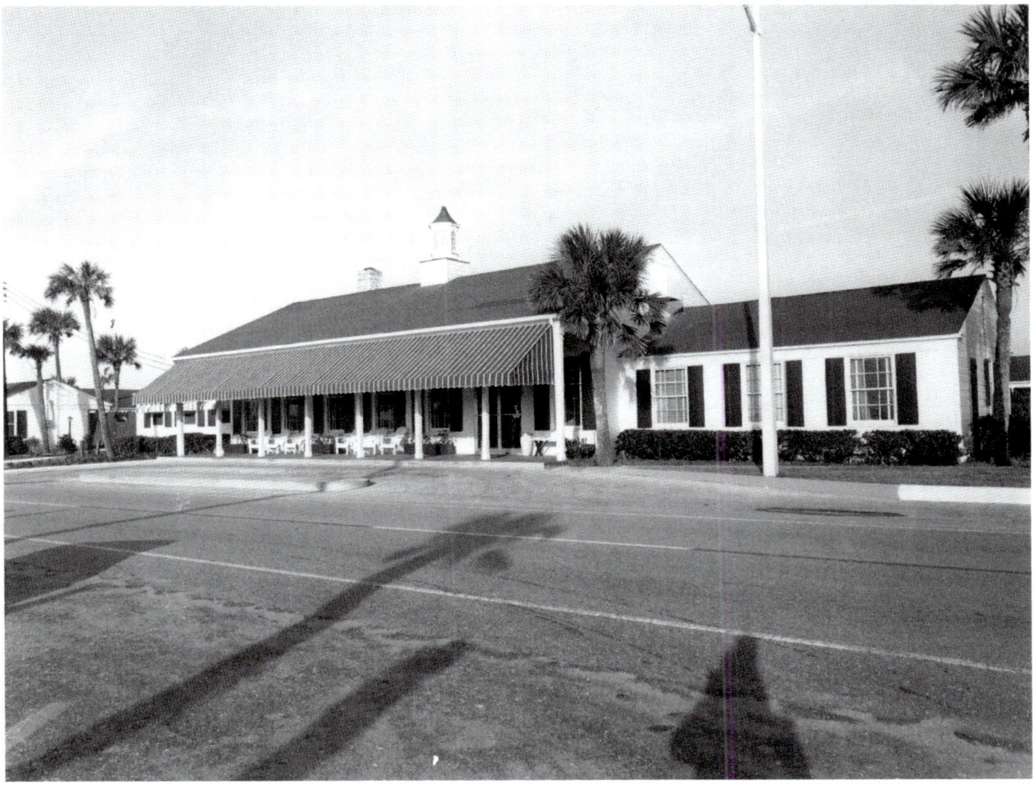

The Innlet on A1A, Ponte Vedra Beach, Florida. Circa 1964. *From the collection of the Beaches Area Historical Society.*

In 1969, the Innlet was sold to the Land Corporation of America, and in 1974, all buildings were removed. It remained vacant until 1987. In 1989, the Fletcher Land Development purchased the ten-acre oceanfront site. Fletcher built the Lodge and Bath Club, a luxury, two-story, sixty-six-room oceanfront resort hotel. In 1997, the Ponte Vedra Corporation purchased the Lodge and Bath Club and changed its name to the Lodge and Club. Again, it was managed by the Ponte Vedra Inn and Club.

NLC arranged for the first eighteen-hole golf course at the club to be designed by British golf course architect Herbert Bertram Strong. Roy Landrum Sr. was the superintendent of the job. The Landrum family, father and sons, was an old local family, and they helped build the course and run the community.[139]

In 1945, when Jim Stockton hired Bob Kroner as general manager of the Inn and the Innlet, he found a great successor to his brother-in-law, Frank Rogers.

It was 1946 when TSC merged with Whatley, Davin and Company to form SWD. For thirty-eight years afterward, the SWD logo was familiar and recognized around the country.

In 1947, the golf course redesign was suggested by Bobby Jones, the greatest golfer at the time, and was completely redone by Trent Jones. It was put on the list of "best courses."

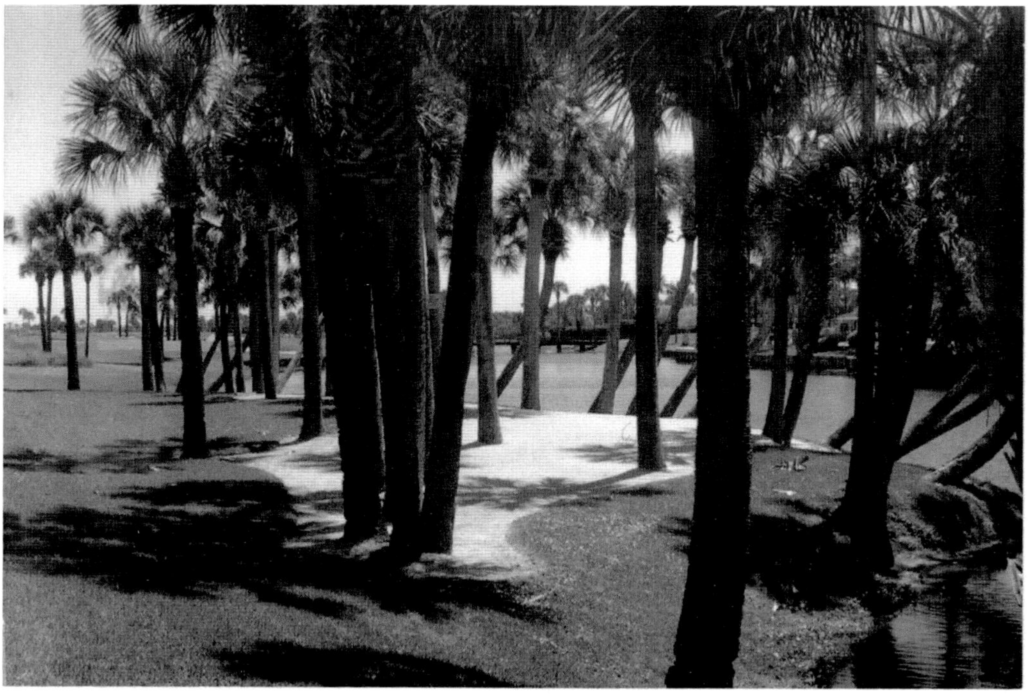

Palm trees and the lagoon off Ponte Vedra Boulevard at the Ponte Vedra Club's golf course. *M. Robinson photograph, 2004.*

In 1948, Jim Stockton decided to retire from complete management of the club and he returned to Jacksonville to the newly formed firm of SWD. He brought into the club another of the company's major partners, J.P. LeMaster, and turned over the management of the resort operation to him.

In 1961, Robert Trent Jones was called back to create another nine "Nine West" holes, enlarging the golf course to twenty-seven holes. In 1977, Joseph Lee, Florida golf architect, redesigned the Nine West and added another nine holes, thus creating the new Lagoon Course, companion to the existing Ocean Course. Today, the resort offers two picturesque, eighteen-hole courses, each with its own distinct seaside links. Meandering lagoons, undulating fairways, elevated Bermuda greens protected by steep-faced bunkers and prevailing sea breezes provide for every kind of shot imaginable.

TENNIS AND RACQUET CLUB

The Ponte Vedra Racquet Club has come a long way from the single court built next to the Inn in 1937. The courts jumped to four in 1958, nine in 1964, eleven in 1969 and fifteen in 1974, plus a new Racquet Club replacing the original white Tennis House. Today, the club offers fifteen Har-Tru Tennis courts. Tennis activities have grown tremendously along with the Sawgrass courts and the Amelia Island courts.

It is difficult to ascertain whether, in the 1930s, as the Ponte Vedra Inn and Club cleared ground for its first lone tennis court on the property, management envisioned one day being the finest tennis resort in the land. If the twenty-five-cents-per-hour court fee was any indication, they were at least intent on encouraging play.

After years of ranking in the top ten and then the top five, in October 2006 the Inn was named number one in *TENNIS* magazine's annual "50 Best U.S. Tennis Resorts," a long-awaited, first-time honor after topping out at number two the previous year.[140]

Frank Rogers reappeared on the scene in 1950, when he and Florence purchased the Innlet. The Innlet, under their leadership, continued to be operated as part of the Ponte Vedra Club, considerably expanding the guest facilities of the Inn.

In the 1950s, as the Rogers took over the Innlet, Jim Crawford was promoted to general manager of the club, succeeding Bob Kroner. However, Kroner was to resurface in 1963 to buy the Innlet from the Rogerses. Jim Crawford resigned in October 1954, and Marjorie Arnold Carpenter continued as resident manager until 1956, when Luther Grimes became manager.[141]

In 1977, architect Joe Lee was brought in to add nine more holes to the Lagoon Course, bringing the total to thirty-six. And just six years later, the Ponte Vedra Inn and Club underwent another major change.

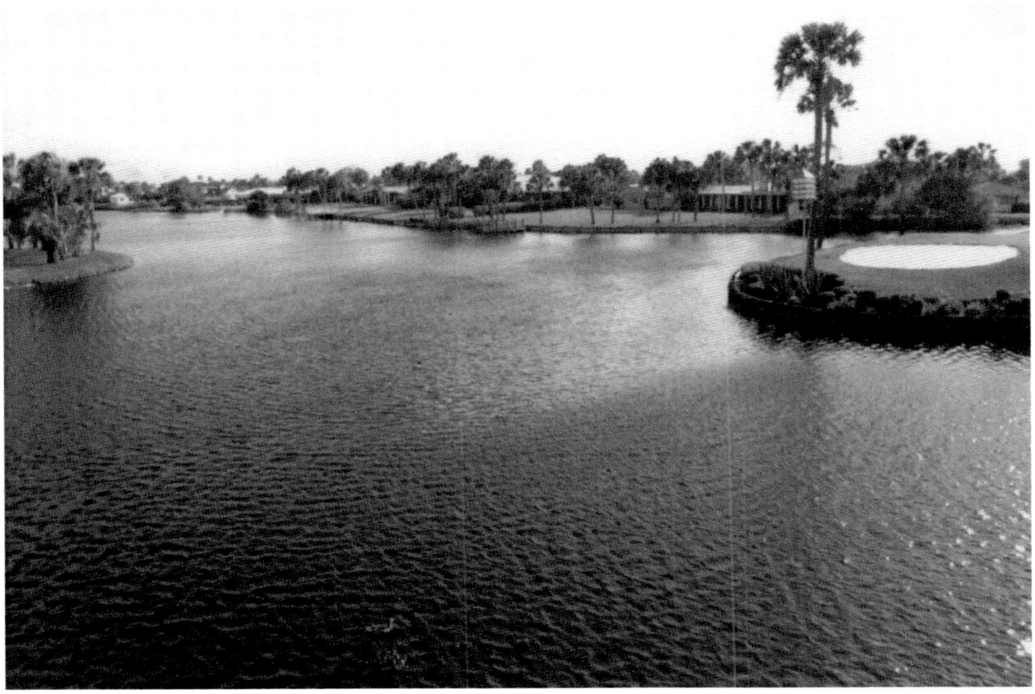

Ponte Vedra Lagoon Golf Course looking south from the eighteenth hole. This postcard was mailed on May 29, 1980. *From the collection of the Beaches Area Historical Society.*

The Oasis Bar

In the 1950s, there wasn't a bypass road (A1A). The Oasis Bar, located on Ponte Vedra Boulevard where the Breakers condominiums are today, was a place where one could get a hamburger, meet girls and drink beer. It was great fun, but it was a terrible mess. The boulevard traffic was horrendous—worse than it is today—with people heading to the bar because Duval County didn't allow alcohol consumption on weekends at that time. One of the pivotal events that affected Ponte Vedra's development in the late sixties was when Jimmy Stockton bought and closed the Oasis Bar.

When the Guana River reached a point adjacent to Barney's, it became known as "the Lagoon." It curved northward between the pretty homes and hotels of Ponte Vedra until it reached the Duval County Line. In earlier days, storm tides occasionally backed ocean water across the road at this location, which became known as "Carter's Run." The road then became inaccessible, reverting travelers to the inland Sand Hill Road, the oldest trail.[142]

The wild cattle problem continued to plague golfers and homeowners alike until, in 1953, a great roundup (western style) took place and three hundred cows were penned up and trucked off to a ranch in Kissimmee, Florida, where presumably they lived happily ever after.[143]

In January 1960, Jim Stockton retired as chairman of the board of SWD. Brown L. Whatley moved up to chairman and J.J. "Jack" Daniel was elected president of SWD. Daniel was to play a very active role in the ongoing fortunes of Ponte Vedra. Along with Jack's other sterling virtues, he was a Princeton man!

J.P. LeMaster returned to the Jacksonville office of SWD to take over the mortgage department, and Jim Stockton again became the president of the Ponte Vedra Corporation, which directed the affairs of the Ponte Vedra Club.

Part of Ponte Vedra lore is the exchange, long ago, between an irate guest and Tubby Courson, later vice-president of the Inn. The guest, complaining bitterly to Tubby and getting no satisfaction, was determined to get to the top. He asked, "Who is your boss?"

Courson replied, "Luther Grimes."

"And who is *his* boss?"

"J.P. LeMaster."

"And who is *his* boss?"

"Jesus Christ," Tubby answered.[144]

Jim Stockton's letter of December 4, 1961, announced the eleven years of presidency served by Edward "Ebbie" (or "E.B.") LeMaster III, J.P.'s son. Ebbie was elected president of Ponte Vedra Club and continued as vice-president of the Ponte Vedra Corporation. Ebbie and Harriet LeMaster set a standard of style and elegance that the members recognized as a quality resort atmosphere.

This well-known and popular bar and grill (the Oasis Bar, better known as "Barney's") was the hangout for the Jacksonville Beach crowd. Barney Compton owned the Oasis Bar, which opened in 1965. The Ponte Vedra Lodge bought the Oasis and its property in 1968 for $250,000 and tore the facility down. Now there exists an Oasis Bar and Grill

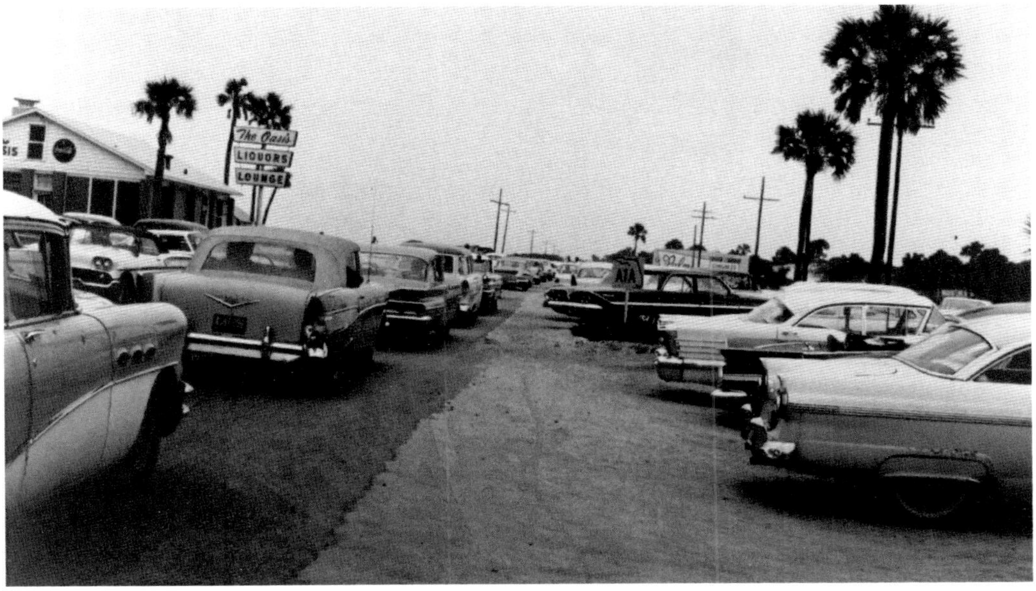

A1A traffic at the Oasis Liquors and Lounge on the left (owned by Barney Compton). Circa 1962. *From the collection of the Beaches Area Historical Society.*

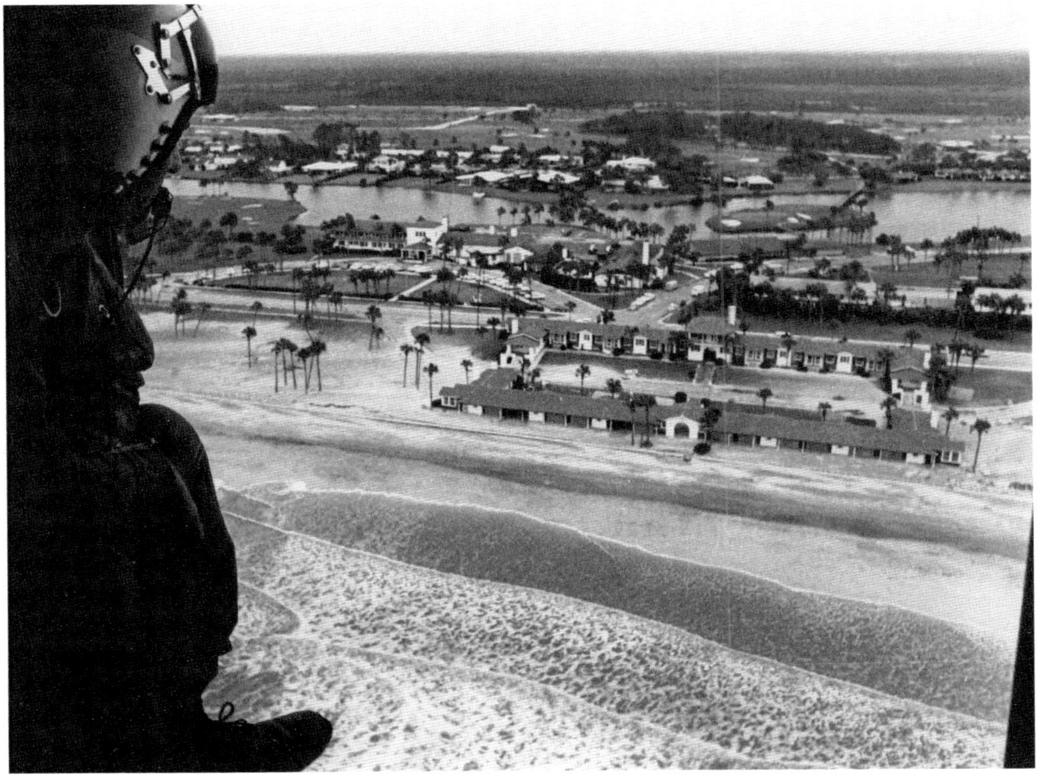

An aerial view of the Ponte Vedra Club taken after Hurricane Dora hit Ponte Vedra Beach, Florida, in September 1964. *State Library and Archives of Florida in Tallahassee.*

within the lodge that takes its name from the old Oasis Bar, which was located just south of today's site.

In 1964, two of the felicitous events were the purchase of SWD (and all of its properties at Ponte Vedra) by the General American Oil Company of Dallas, and Hurricane Dora. Dora tore down the Surf Club, the pool and the seawall and damaged the Inn itself.

When Ebbie left in 1972, Jack Daniel provided continuity and leadership as temporary president until appointing Bob Reed as the new president in 1973.[145]

PEYTON PURCHASES THE INN

It was in 1983 that Jacksonville businessman Herbert Peyton and his privately held company, Gate Petroleum, would acquire and purchase the SWD Real Estate Division. The acquisition came about when General American Oil Company of Dallas tried to prevent a hostile takeover. Phillips Petroleum Company agreed to the purchase and offered $1.3 billion for General American. Phillips was short of money and decided to sell SWD—after all, they were in the petroleum business, not real estate.

After Peyton considered purchasing this division, his only hope was if Phillips Petroleum would guarantee a bank loan because Gate Petroleum already received credit from its gasoline purchases. Some of the officers from Phillips and Gate advised Peyton not to make an offer to purchase the SWD property. After much discussion, Phillips Petroleum agreed to loan Gate the money.

The property to be purchased consisted of Deerwood and Deerwood Center, property at J. Turner Butler and Southside Boulevard, Ponte Vedra, Regency property, Guana Lake and all beach frontages around Ponte Vedra. Peyton valued the property at $100 million and initially talked about offering $66 million for this trademark of Phillips 66. Peyton and the Gate board decided to bid $60 million.

The other bidders made a serious mistake in bidding for the entire SWD, instead of separating the bid for the Ponte Vedra Inn and Club from the real estate. After much discussion with Phillips, Gate proved solvency for the $60 million and was declared the high bidder. After further discussion with the several bankers, Peyton finally convinced them to accept the total $60 million debt at 12 percent interest.[146]

Although some members were concerned that a large corporation such as Gate might change the club's atmosphere and allure, Peyton—who as a young man had dreamed of being a member of the club—had every intention of making the resort even better than before.

Also in 1983, the Ponte Vedra Club Realty, Inc. (PVCR) became an offspring of the first real spurt of development in the 1960s led by SWD. This means that the PVCR has been specializing in Ponte Vedra Beach properties since the first oceanfront home was constructed in 1936. It became a unique office that takes great pride in area history and knowledge of the beaches. It has been recognized as a top residential producer in the northeastern Florida area.

After the purchase of the Ponte Vedra Inn and Club, a long-range comprehensive plan was set into motion to improve the atmosphere and excellence of the facility. Beginning in 1986, when an oceanfront Surf Club was erected, the resort also saw the addition of a new golf club, pro shop and restaurant in 1997; a conference center and expanded fitness facilities in 1998; and restoration of the Ocean Course.

In 1997, the Ponte Vedra Lodge and Bath, which had once been the Innlet, was purchased again and became part of the Ponte Vedra Inn and Club family. The boutique hotel was built on the same site where Tommy Sabin, a New York banker and frequent Ponte Vedra Inn and Club guest, had opened a hotel a half century earlier.

The Ponte Vedra Inn and Club and the Ponte Vedra Lodge and Club were joined together in 1997 under the umbrella of Ponte Vedra Beach Resorts. That year, the Ponte Vedra Inn and Club also opened Atlantic House, a spectacular addition to its accommodations, bringing the total to 221 elegantly appointed rooms and suites. And just months later, the Ocean Course saw the completion of its most recent facelift, courtesy of golf course architect Bobby Weed.

In 1987, the Ponte Vedra Inn and Club opened North Florida's original spa, where guests were first introduced to the world of pampering. Twenty years later, Ponte Vedra's spa continued to lead the way. The Ponte Vedra Inn and Club unveiled a new and

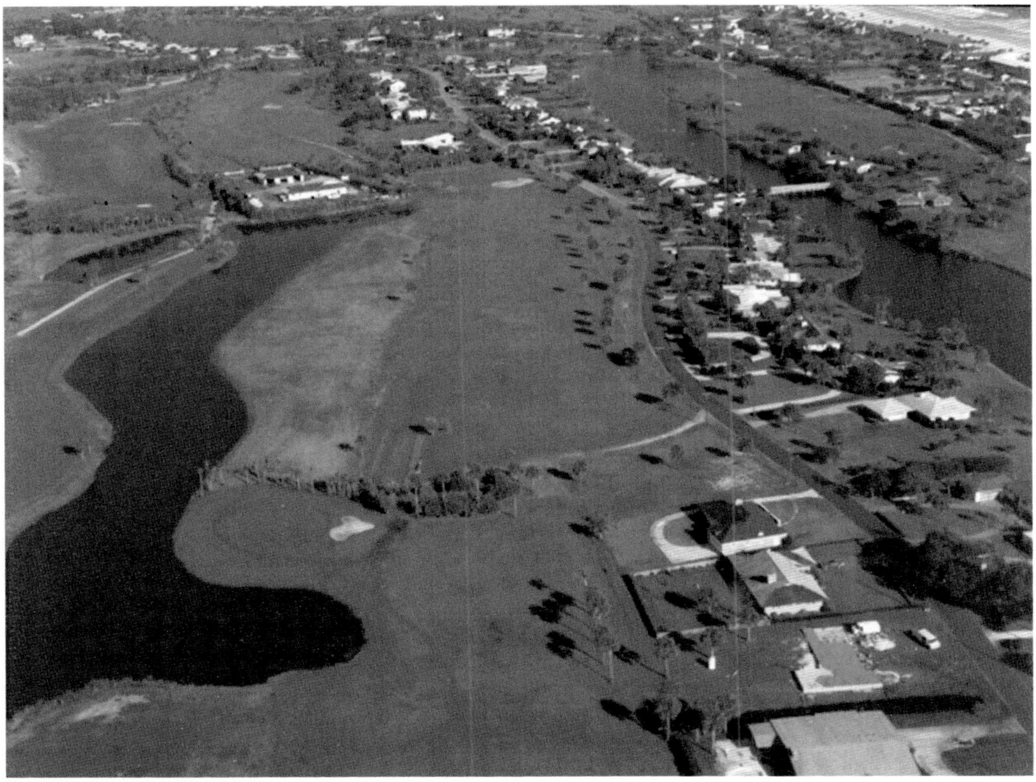

Ponte Vedra Club Golf Course, south nine holes. Circa 1980. *From the collection of the Beaches Area Historical Society.*

ultrasophisticated spa in November 2006—the region's largest, with thirty thousand square feet, including the latest in technologies and therapies. This is the club's new sophisticated "Oasis," designed to appeal to both men and women, young and old.

In April 2005, Herb Peyton and the Ponte Vedra Club Realty bought out Jimmy Stockton's real estate company (Stockton Realty) and its real estate office building on A1A.

HEROICS OF THE PHIL AND JULIANNA HOWE FAMILY[147]

The Howes moved to the beach in the 1960s from Avondale after many years of vacationing at the beach. It was interesting that the Howes and only a few neighbors who lived on Duval Drive were considered a part of Ponte Vedra, even though they were in Jacksonville Beach but picked up their mail in Ponte Vedra.

The Howes played a part in Ponte Vedra's history by lending a hand during World War II. According to Phil Howe:

> *My father had a yacht, an old Mathews. The navy decided it was the perfect vessel for the war effort and borrowed it. Outfitting it with antisubmarine guns, they used it to patrol off Ponte Vedra for German submarines. As it turns out, the yacht helped sink one of them.*

A picture of that yacht hangs in the Howes' living room, showing it docked at the old Florida Yacht Club and looking a lot better than it did when the navy finally returned it to Phil's father.

Julianna relays very vividly the event at the Ponte Vedra Club, when her fifteen-year-old son, Gardner (now, a Navy Seal), saved a lady's life at the club when she fell down and stopped breathing. Gardner had just come in off his sailboat when the club members were looking for someone to assist and to try to get the fallen woman breathing again. Gardner's application of CPR kept her breathing until a doctor arrived, but he was told to continue. Soon, the rescue squad came, but they asked if he would stay with her. Upon arrival at the hospital, Gardner was still asked to assist her to breathe. Needless to say, the community publicly awarded him for his heroics that day.

A SUPER, SUPER PERSON (PUBLICITY DIRECTOR)

In 1977, Elaine Koehl, director of publicity and public relations for the Ponte Vedra Club, was recognized as one of the top women executives in the Greater Jacksonville area.

Elaine Koehl came to the Ponte Vedra Club in 1970 at the request of Ebbie LeMaster, who was club president at the time. LeMaster recognized talent when he saw it. When

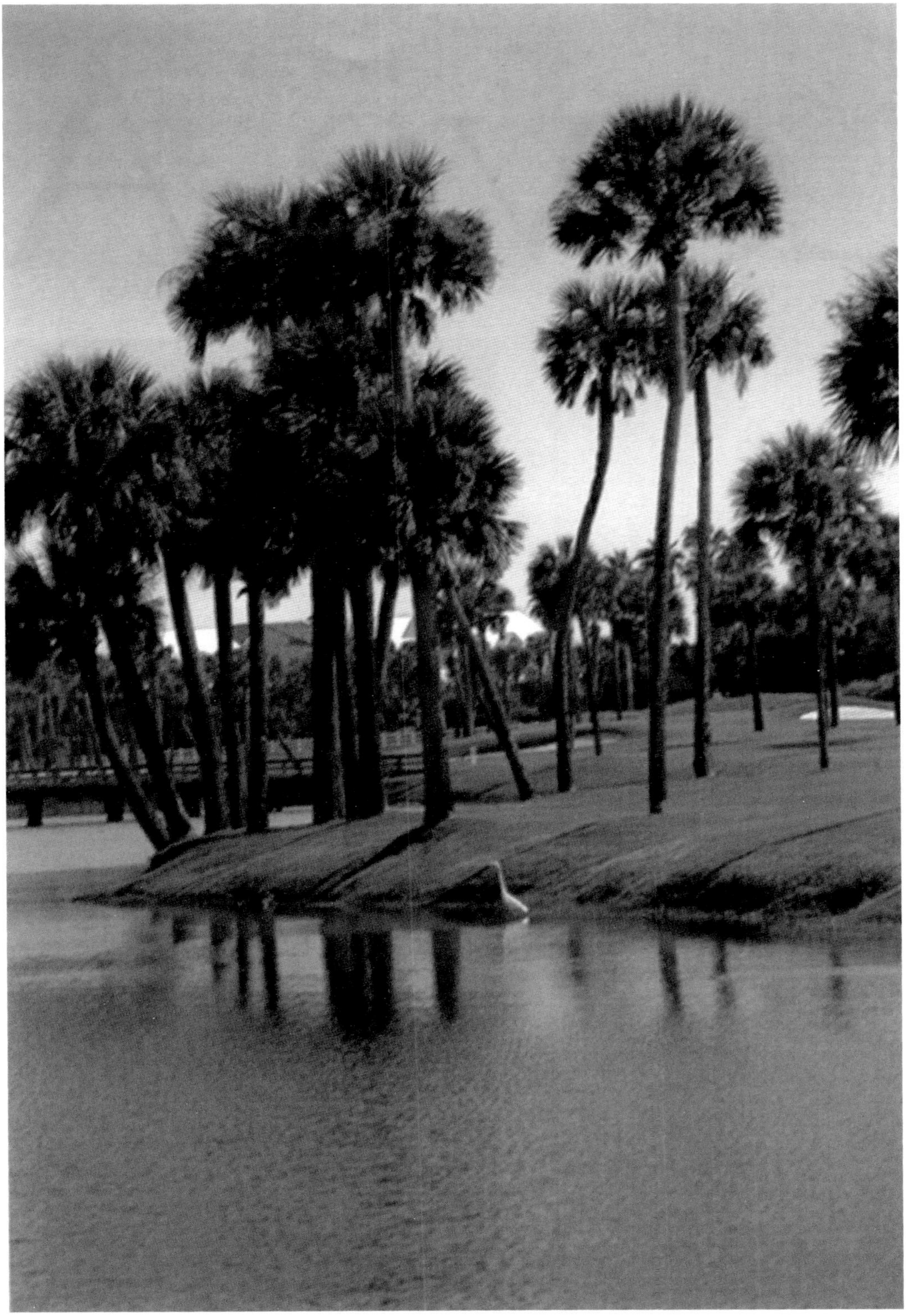

An egret on one of the holes at the Ponte Vedra Golf Course. Legacy: The Magazine of Ponte Vedra Inn & Club, *2003*.

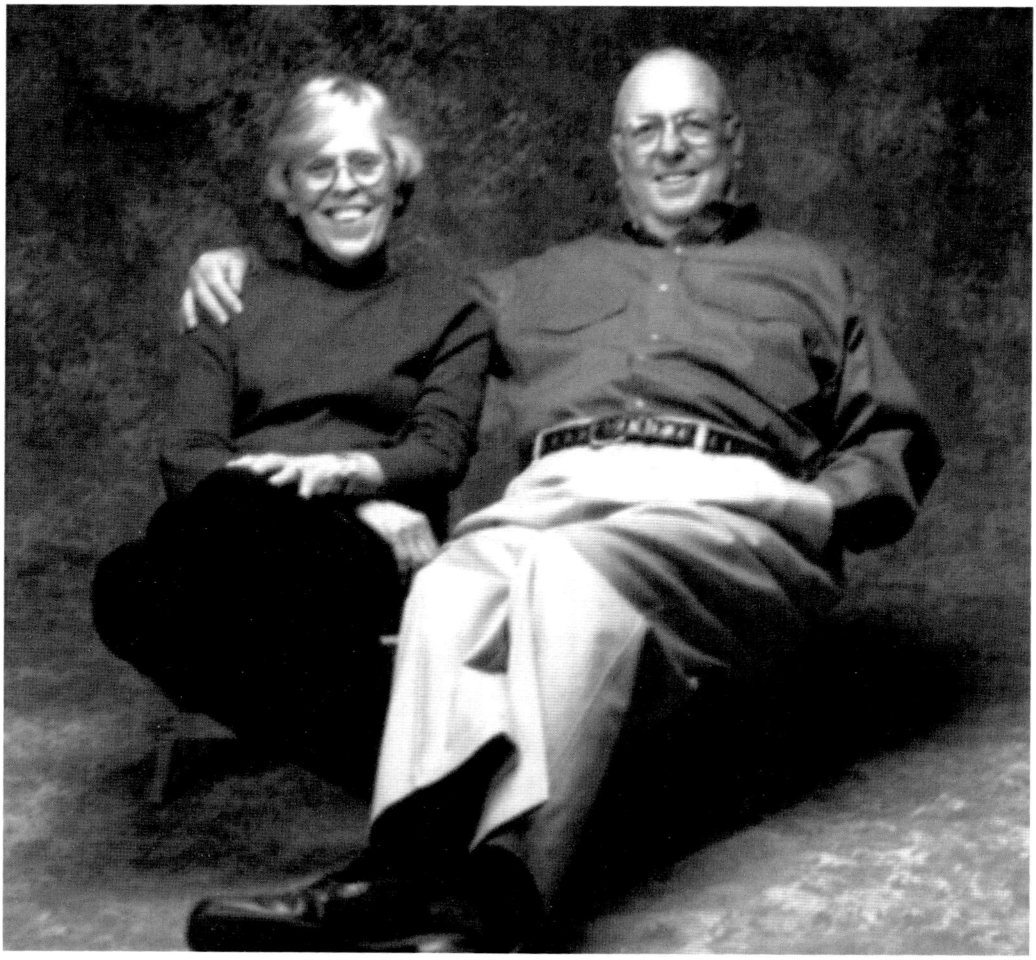

Phil and Julianna Howe, longtime Ponte Vedra Club members and current residents on Duval Drive. Julianna was one of the originators of the Jacksonville Beaches Historical Society, and Phil's father loaned their yacht to be used by the navy in World War II. Ponte Vedra Lifestyles, *June 2001.*

Elaine accepted the position at the Ponte Vedra Club, following her husband's untimely death, she moved into the Lagoon Apartments and worked for the club eight months of the year. She spent the rest of her time with her two sons, or at Ardsley-on-the-Hudson. After residing and working at the club for several years, she made a big decision and purchased a delightful home in 1976, thus becoming a "full-fledged" Ponte Vedran.[148]

Among Elaine's accomplishments were her abilities and boundless energies at her job. She composed the Ponte Vedra Club newsletters, designed all the graphics, set up numerous club golf and tennis house parties, youth and adult activities, organized art exhibits and cultural events—you name the event, she was behind it.

Elaine's most interesting accomplishment was her book, *Ponte Vedra Club: The First Fifty-Five Years, 1927–1982.* Elaine writes about the history of the club since its beginning, telling us about how the club began, grew and, more importantly, the interesting club

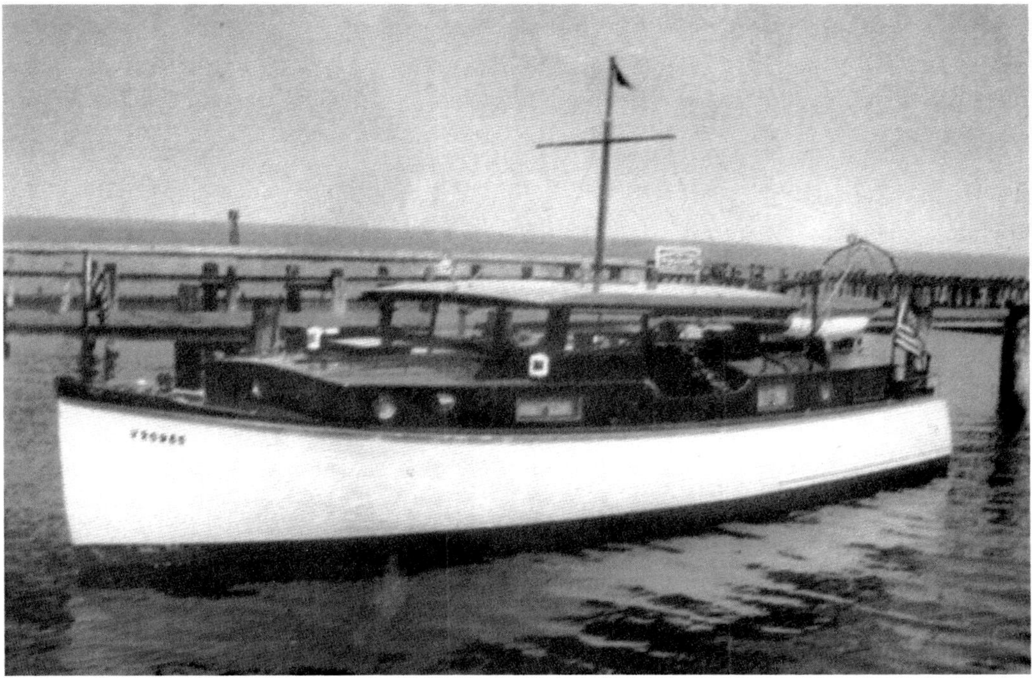

Phil Howe's father's yacht, which the navy "borrowed" to help in the war effort in the 1940s. Ponte Vedra Lifestyles, *March 2001.*

members and the many dedicated staff employees who made personal contributions to the club's successful history.

A Membership Portrait

Since its inception, the Ponte Vedra Inn and Club has served as both resort destination and private membership club. Its unique atmosphere emphasizes personalized attention; creative, ever-changing cuisine; and upscale amenities—all to the advantage of both the member and guest. This blending of two cultures contributes significantly to the overall attraction of Ponte Vedra.[149]

13. Ponte Vedra Beach Volunteer Fire Department—Station Number 10

The Ponte Vedra Volunteer Fire Department (PVFD) was established in 1951. The first building was a garage at the Ponte Vedra Inn on Miranda Road used for both equipment and volunteers. The current building was completed in 1992 on Library Boulevard, where it is housed today.

Fire Apparatus

The first fire apparatus was a 1951 secondhand Chevrolet truck. In 1952, the first new fire engine was purchased for $3,288, secured by the first fire chief, Howard Bissell. Another secondhand truck was purchased in 1958 from the surplus store at Camp Blanding. A Seagrave fire truck was purchased in 1963 with a center-mounted pump.

Staffing

The PVFD maintained a roster of twenty-four adult and four student volunteer firemen in 1959. In 1972, the roster consisted of nineteen volunteers, with Fred Woolverton as chief, along with seven junior volunteers, including both Kurt Kanauth and Steve Sciotto, who became chiefs at St. Augustine and Jacksonville Beach.

In 1972, the Ponte Vedra community enjoyed a Fire Underwriters rating of eight, which is the best available for a volunteer fire department.

Funding

In the 1960s and 1970s, the Ponte Vedra citizens paid a twenty-five-dollar association fee to the fire department to help support the cost, along with the small amount that the county gave the department each year.

We will always remember the volunteers' "Boot Collection" for funds raised each year on the highway that help run the fire department. This event was so successful that it became an annual event.[150]

CHIEFS AND MEMORIES

Harry Johnston, after several visits to the Inn, bought a home on the first fairway at 1 Miranda Road and gave up a successful banking career for the role of community leader. Harry was instrumental in founding the Ponte Vedra Volunteer Fire Department in 1951.

Murle Harrison, the Ponte Vedra Club manager during 1978–83 and also, later, volunteer fire chief for five years, relayed an interesting story about Harry Johnston:

> *The event occurred back on July 4, 1973, when Fred Woolverton was chief and Harry Johnston lived on the first hole of the golf course. Smoke was coming from Johnston's house on the Fourth of July holiday in 1973. Harry could not determine exactly where the smoke was originating from within his house. All he could see and smell was the smoke, so he knew there must be a fire somewhere. When the fire department arrived, they had a problem also determining where the fire had started. They searched everywhere but they could only smell the smoke. It was finally decided that the lightning storm had caused a fire on one of the wires that was in the wall of the house. The problem wire was finally found and the fire was contained before any further damage occurred.*

Harry was so grateful to the fire department for saving his house that he wanted to give a ball, including dinner, for the firemen for their heroic deeds. This dinner at the Ponte Vedra Club for the firemen and their wives began a tradition for an annual appreciation dinner sponsored by Harry every year. The first firemen's ball was held at the Ponte Vedra Club on February 20, 1974.[151]

Fred T. Woolverton Jr. joined the department in 1953 and was named chief in 1957. He held that position until 1974. Fred lived in Ponte Vedra with his family when he was a child, and he remembered the following events that occurred during his volunteering days.

Fred related to me the story of the Christmas morning fire at the Ponte Vedra Boulevard home of Maxine Preas in the early 1960s. "Everybody [the volunteers] came, but no one brought the fire truck."

In a 1985 *Ponte Vedra Recorder* interview, Fred and Murle Harrison both reminisced about their days at the Ponte Vedra Volunteer Department. "The most memorable fire we had was the night of the firemen's ball," Woolverton said.

> *The Ponte Vedra Volunteers used to annually hold a very festive and social benefit ball and approximately fifteen years ago* [in 1970] *just after most firemen had arrived home from the ball, the fire alarm was sounded. The Surf Club, scene of the firemen's ball, was on fire.*

Fire was coming through the roof of the Surf Club. You could see it 1½ miles away. It was the darndest conglomeration of drunks trying to put out a fire you ever saw.

Harrison did not attend the firemen's ball that evening but was at home, sober, when he heard the fire alarm. "Fred was the only non-drinking fireman we had," Harrison said. He added that fighting the Surf Club fire was "just a great big comedy of errors," but it was a learning experience when the volunteers critiqued their performance afterwards.[152]

The fireman boot money collection on A1A at Solana Road began an annual event for the volunteers that continues until the present day. It is an opportunity for all of the area's citizens to contribute to the fire department.

14. The Ponte Vedra Beach Branch Library

Ponte Vedra Beach Library and Friends of the Library Mission

Our mission is to make the Ponte Vedra Beach Branch of the St. Johns County Public Library System an outstanding educational, cultural, civic and recreational center for the community. This will be achieved by providing supplemental books, materials, volunteers and programs and fundraising and advocating on behalf of the Ponte Vedra Beach Branch Library. By enlisting support of all those dedicated to disseminating knowledge, we believe the community will be enhanced and enriched.[153]

The Early Days

In the early 1980s, the only public library in St. Johns County was located on the second floor of an old home in St. Augustine (now occupied by the St. Augustine Historical Society). Long recognized as inadequate, the library finally attracted the energies of the American Association of University Women, which launched a campaign for a county library building fund. A referendum approved in 1983 established that fund.

At that point, library consultants, HBW Associates (now Himmel and Wilson), recommended that the first two libraries to be constructed should be the main library in St. Augustine and a temporary branch library in Ponte Vedra Beach, with a permanent one to follow by 1990.

The Palm Valley Volunteer Library[154]

Earlier in 1984, local citizens organized a volunteer library for northeast St. Johns County, housed in the Palm Valley Community Center. The Northeast St. Johns County Volunteer Library, a public library open to all residents of Northeast St. Johns County, opened

February 18, 1984, in the Palm Valley Community Association building on Canal Street (now Canal Boulevard).

Monies donated by the Ponte Vedra Community Association, Palm Valley Community Association, Sawgrass Master Association, DeLeon Shores Community Association, L'Atrium Homeowners Association and the Players Club Association provided materials for the first bookshelves and some supplies.

TEMPORARY COUNTY BRANCH LIBRARY

In 1987, the temporary county branch library for Ponte Vedra Beach opened in a small room in the county annex building on CR-210, where for the next several years Doug Cisney became the community's much-appreciated librarian. The urgent need for a county library here had finally been recognized. Membership in the Friends of the Library, which was formed in 1985, grew by leaps and bounds.

Plans for a permanent building in Ponte Vedra Beach were delayed for several reasons. The Friends focused on the ten-acre parcel, still zoned residential, just south of Sandia (now Library) Boulevard. Construction began, but money was needed for books.

The Friends were determined that the library would have enough books when it opened, and they organized a "caravan" of many Ponte Vedrans to fill the auditorium of the county commissioners. The commissioners approved a $350,000 book fund for the new building.

The Friends even worked on changing the library's name to fit the area it serves. The Friends convinced the county first to change the branch's designation from Northeast St. Johns County to Ponte Vedra–Palm Valley, and later to Ponte Vedra Beach, so *all* patrons could feel it was *their* community's library.

The Friends organized large celebrations for the grand opening in May 1993. But the Friends still had work to do, since the building was too small the day it opened.

...AND LATER

In March 1999, a revised plan for the expansion was submitted. The Friends offered a $250,000 donation to increase the expansion square footage. A temporary library was established in the same Palm Valley Community Center building that housed the first volunteer library in the early 1980s.

The official grand reopening and the official ribbon-cutting of the library took place on August 11, 2002. The St. Johns County Library administrator singled out Jack Morgan as "the patriarch of the PVB Library," citing that he led the cause to build the first library and continued to promote the library throughout its history. She also credited the contributions of the Friends, the PGA Tour, the county commissioners for approving the building and staff who worked on the project.

The library has become a center for cultural, educational and community activities in "our town." The auditorium and conference rooms are in constant demand for the meetings of many organizations, large and small. Educational opportunities and programs abound. The Friends utilize the community room for much-appreciated lectures by authors, other regular programs on travel and world affairs and special programs for children.

No history of the library and its importance to the community would be complete without mentioning the great contributions of the librarians themselves. The directors, local managers and the local staff have individually and collectively given the library a friendly and accessible personality.

The Friends' board of directors are also volunteers who put in many hours to keep the Friends' machinery running smoothly, plan programs, decide policy, interact with county library authorities and direct outreach to the community.

As library patrons are aware, the library is supported not only financially by members of the Friends, but by the work of volunteers who log hundreds of hours, demonstrating again the great appreciation the community has for its library. The Friends' mission is to enrich our quality of life.

For seven months before the grand reopening, the library was closed because of the renovations that were being made to the expansion of the structure. During the library construction period, a temporary library was held back in the Palm Valley Community Center, with help from the Neptune Beach branch of the Jacksonville Library.[155]

In 1999, Ponte Vedra Beach–based PGA Tour charities pledged a ten-year, $10,000-a-year donation to build and outfit the multimedia room, which provides northeastern Florida's only public access video conferencing capability.

Later, the PGA Tour also donated $258,000 to build the community room, plus $70,000 to equip the multimedia room, and the partnership between the Friends and the PGA Tour is certainly held up as a national model.[156]

Today, we have a beautiful, functional and expanded library building for all of our citizens, thanks to St. Johns County, the Friends and the PGA Tour.

15. Beginning of the First Elementary and High School

Ponte Vedra–Palm Valley Elementary School[157]

At one time, there were acres and acres of untouched land where the Ponte Vedra–Palm Valley Elementary School stands today.

That lush land belonged to Eunice Pitt Odum Semmes. Mrs. Semmes donated forty acres for the school back in 1957. According to Ebbie LeMaster:

> *The Odum family members were early pioneers. They owned all the land developed around Innlet Beach. We wouldn't have had enough money to build a really viable school if Mrs. Semmes hadn't given such a generous gift.*

Mrs. Semmes stated, matter-of-factly:

> *They didn't have any money for a school…it was very expensive. I had plenty of land, so I just gave them some. I said, "Pick your land."*

LeMaster remembered the land north of the school, which was a pine forest back before the school was built. The deputy sheriff, Roy Landrum, had the trees planted. "It was his gift to the school," LeMaster recalled.

"One of the less serious moments happened when the land was being cleared by bulldozers," LeMaster said, with a chuckle. He got a call from one of the construction crewmembers telling him they had found a "moonshine still" hidden in the underbrush. The crew had to clear around it until the owner was located. "The moonshine operator moved his business overnight," he said.

Ponte Vedra–Palm Valley Elementary School has been a part of Ponte Vedra's growth, thanks to the gift of land from Mrs. Odum Semmes in memory of John and William Pitt.

FIRST PONTE VEDRA–PALM VALLEY ELEMENTARY SCHOOL PRINCIPAL

In 1984, Mrs. Merkin Purcell, the first principal of the Ponte Vedra–Palm Valley Elementary School, was interviewed for the preparation of the twenty-fifth anniversary. The school began in September 1958, when the students were taught in makeshift classrooms at Ocean Park Baptist Church in Jacksonville Beach.

When they finally transferred to the new school, Mrs. Purcell was ready to plunge into new territory. Mrs. Purcell was an innovator. She was the first educator in the area to try a no-grade system. Students were placed in classes that were later tuned to their individual learning pace.

Mrs. Purcell put in her application for principal for the new Ponte Vedra–Palm Valley School (grades K–9). It was approved, and she stayed in her job as principal for seventeen years through the 1975–76 school year.

ALLEN D. NEASE HIGH SCHOOL

Nease High School was opened and began enrollment of students in August 1980. At the school's beginning, the students covered the entire northern portion of St. Johns County for grades seven through ten. Later, after sophomores became seniors, grades seven and eight were moved to the new middle school. With the new high school built in the northwest portion of the county, Nease included only the students in the northern portion of the county.

Nease High School has been an excellent academic high school in St. Johns County and the entire area since it began enrollment in 1980. Nease has been an International Baccalaureate (IB) World School since January 1996. Academics have been the top priority at Nease for each of the principals. Sports have played an important role in the school's development—whether football, soccer, golf or any other, Nease has produced many athletes and championships.

The first principal, Halver Stedman, retired in 1987. Stedman was very familiar with the county officers and he convinced the state to donate the property for the school before 1980. Recent principals have been Bill Mignon, Robert (Bob) Schiavone and, currently, Linda Thomson.[158]

In 2005, Margie Nease, at a Nease school function, indicated that the land for the high school, which was cattle land, had been in her husband's family for years. The "D." is an important part of the name and that's why it is included in the name of the school. It stands for Dowling, Allen's original birth name. Allen took the last name of Nease when his stepfather adopted him at age ten.[159]

Allen Dowling Nease Sr. named for the High School[160]

Who was Allen Nease, whose name was used for the high school serving the northern St. Johns County area? Nease was born on February 1, 1913, in Duval County, Florida. In 1936, he got his degree in forestry from North Carolina State University and went to work with the U.S. Forest Service in the Apalachicola National Forest. He planted trees, cruised timber, supervised timber sales and fought "redneck" poachers, who were determined to undermine his efforts to make the forests of "Apalach" a viable, sustainable resource.

Nease ran a prisoner of war camp in Georgia for two years during World War II before coming to St. Johns County as general manager of Robinson Improvement Company, which owned fifteen thousand acres of timberland.

Nease began his career of "greening up the state" in Washington County as a kind of referee between irate turpentiners and desperate cattlemen who were blackening the forests, setting fire to pinelands to get enough fresh grass to keep their starving herds alive. Nease was hired as the first "county forester" in the state, but as he combed the woods from the Apalachicola River to the Alabama state line at Pensacola with some giveaway proposals (eighteen million pine trees) to restore the forests and "law and order," local citizens called him everything *but* county forester.

In 1940, Nease was hired by the Florida Forest Service as the first county forester in the state selling the need for forest and soil conservation all the way from Suwannee County to Washington County. Nease carried on forestry programs in Suwannee, Hamilton, Columbia and Escambia Counties. He supervised the planting of two hundred thousand acres in the Black Water Forest after the government bought the land and resettled families to spots where the soil was better for raising food.

Prior to 1940, Nease was shot at more than once by "firebugs," and once four men pulled four knives on him at one time when he went to a house to try and make an arrest. "I literally talked them out of killing me. I'm pretty good at talking," Nease once told a reporter.

A more notable story was when he just missed being the third victim of a two-man murder.

> *A farmer had stolen my plough and I went to the house to try and get it back. Knocked on the door but didn't get an answer so I walked around to the barn and saw the plough behind the building, put it in the truck and drove away. Minutes later, two federal men came to arrest the farmer for moonshining. When, they made the mistake of opening the barn door where he stored the whiskey, the farmer came down off the roof where he was hiding and shot and killed them. If I'd opened that door I'd have got it too.*

Nease recalled that a smart lawyer got the man off the murder charge. The next day, Nease reported that the farmer appeared at the attorney's office with a hound dog under each arm and said, "This is all I have left to pay the fee."

From 1971 until his death in 1984, Nease continued his timber growing and conservation efforts on his landholdings, in addition to raising a herd of two hundred cattle and developing pasture to support them. He was also a successful timber/pulpwood dealer and consulting forester.

The other significant related accomplishments by Nease include:

He was a charter member of the Florida Forestry Association.

In 1955, he organized the St. Johns County Timber growers Association and was its only president until his death.

He battled for the construction of the St. Augustine Technical Center.

He helped to locate and acquire land for the construction of St. Johns River College and served four years on the board of trustees.

He was one of the founders of the St. Johns County Fairgrounds Association.

In 1980, the Florida Association of County Agricultural Agents honored him as the "Outstanding Agriculturist."

In 1984, he posthumously received the "Mr. T-Terrific" Award from the Florida Forestry Association.

After much growth in the area, a new high school, Ponte Vedra High, will be opening in 2008, just west of the Intracoastal Waterway.

16.
Post Office History

Diego ("Deigo")/Palm Valley Post Office

Toward the end of the nineteenth century, Diego Plains residents had begun to be served by the U.S. Post Office Department. By the close of the twentieth century, residents were served by the U.S. Postal Service.

The U.S. postage rate was two cents per half ounce when the Diego Plains post office began on May 20, 1898, but it increased to forty-one cents per ounce in 2008. The Diego Post Office, which was started in St. Johns County, was misspelled "Deigo" in 1898. This mistake was quickly changed to "Diego" on March 10, 1899. After petitioning Washington, D.C., the local post office name was officially changed to Palm Valley on March 28, 1908, and was eventually discontinued on April 30, 1932, when mail was being handled at the Jacksonville Beach Post Office in Duval County.

Apparently, the first postal carrier and post office was established in the Diego area, now called Palm Valley, beginning on November 11, 1904, and was in operation until May 30, 1908. In November 1904, the U.S. postmaster general was Robert J. Wynne under President Theodore Roosevelt.

The first "Deigo" postmaster, in the late nineteenth century, was Eli H. Brodnax when the post office was established in Diego. In 1899, William M. DeGrove began as the second "Deigo" mail carrier and postmaster in Diego Plains when the post office's name was corrected to "Diego." DeGrove lived at the corner of Canal and Palm Valley Road.

The mail in those early days was carried in a locked pouch from Diego to Dewey (known as Pitts Still, a turpentine still operated by the Pitts). The pouch was unlocked, the mail from Dewey was added to it and then it was taken up to Pablo (now Jacksonville Beach) and put on a train for Jacksonville (originally Cowford).

Of course, we are speaking of the mail route in the days before the canal was built. The path taken by the mailman was about where the present Roscoe Boulevard (named for Joseph Roscoe, formally Oleander Drive) is located (called Cabbage Swamp). The mailman then crossed through the swamp to Piney Woods, and then on to Pitts Still. The mail came through three times a week.[161]

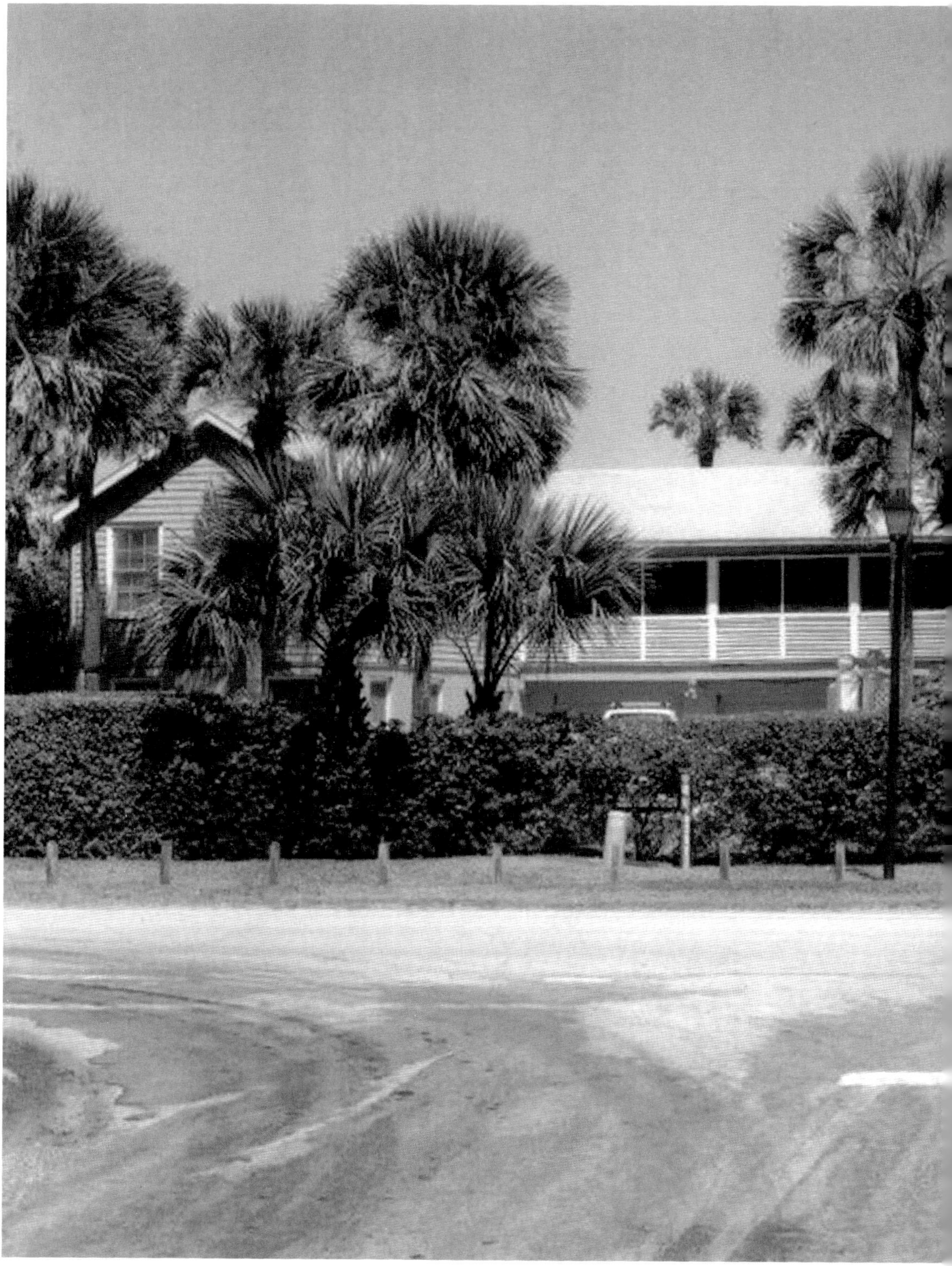

One of the oldest houses on the beach on Ponte Vedra Boulevard at Solana Road, originally used by the Ponte Vedra Club for one of their managers. It was torn down in 2007. *M. Robinson photograph, 2004.*

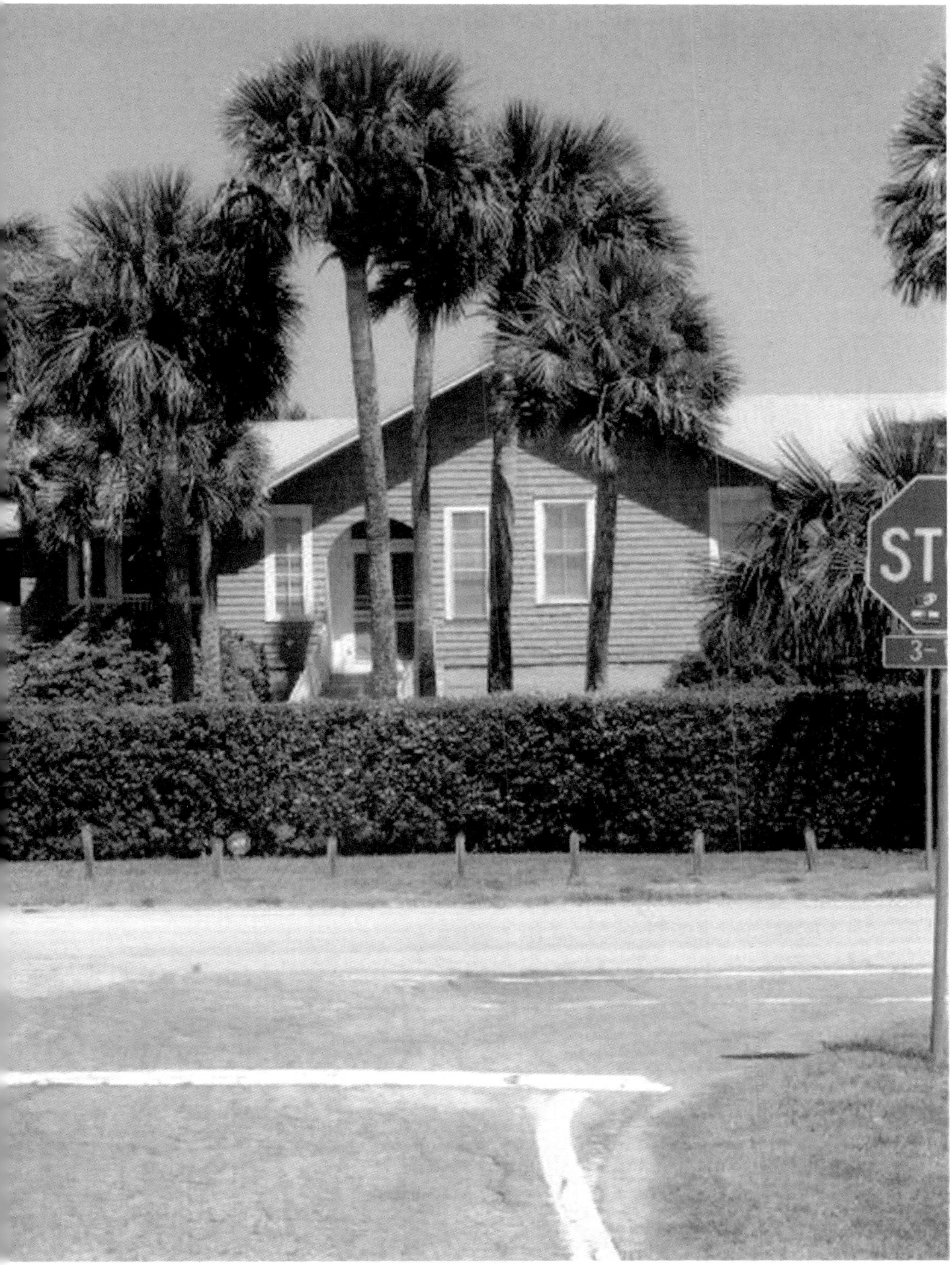

In 1910, there were 50,580 post offices in the United States, of which Palm Valley was one, but the number of post offices was reduced to 27,792 by 2002.

By 1912, new customers were required to provide mail slots or receptacles, and postmasters were urged to encourage existing customers to provide them as well. As late as 1914, a letter carrier spent thirty minutes to an hour each day waiting at doors where there was person-to-person delivery. By the 1930s, as a convenience to customers living on the margins of a city, (like Palm Valley), letter carriers began delivering to customers with "suitable boxes at the curb line." The second residential delivery was discontinued in 1950.

Daily mail delivery in the community (Palm Valley) did not begin until the year 1918.[162]

MINERAL CITY/PONTE VEDRA BEACH POST OFFICE

The first post office was actually in Mineral City, founded on May 28, 1919, and it was housed in a white cottage building across from the Surf Club. Adjacent to the post office was the local grocery store.[163] George A. Pritchard was the first U.S. postmaster. This office was discontinued on June 30, 1928, with mail handled at the Jacksonville Beach Post Office. On October 26, 1937, the first Ponte Vedra postmistress was Alice Landrum, whose husband was the Ponte Vedra sheriff and for whom the Landrum Middle School is named.

A new post office building was completed in March 1955 adjacent to the Store and the Bath Club. The post office personnel, besides Alice Landrum, included Mrs. Sadie Gates, Mrs. Charles DeGrove and Flavian Mickler, clerks; and Charles DeGrove, who continued to be the mail carrier for South Ponte Vedra and Palm Valley.[164]

In 1969, the original fifty-year-old post office building at the Ponte Vedra Club was then converted to house the Gate Store, a youth center and additional conference rooms; however, the building later burned to the ground. Today, that area is the site of a new landscaped parking lot that serves the Ponte Vedra Club.

In 1980, the old post office, a fifty-year-old landmark located at the Inn at the Ponte Vedra Club, was moved to a site 2.1 miles south on A1A, where the library and fire department are located today. The old post office was remodeled as a youth center headquarters, which served as the central meeting place for the entire neighborhood youth, as well as the children visiting the Inn.

In 1989, the Ponte Vedra Post Office was again moved to a site five miles south on A1A in the Ponte Vedra Pointe Shopping Center. Later, a new, modern building was built off A1A and Palm Valley Road (SR-210) at 130 Corridor Road.

History of the Beaches' Newspapers (1888 to Date)[165]

The beaches' weekly newspapers have been the staples of coastal living from 1888 to the present. It was apparently back in the late 1800s that Jacksonville Beach began the first new, weekly newspaper, the *Pablo Beach Breeze*, until the *Beaches Leader* began a weekly newspaper in 1963. A Ponte Vedra Beach weekly paper the *Ponte Vedra Recorder* was founded in 1969 and continues today.

Pablo Beach Breeze (1888) John Frank and W.R. Freeman, publishers
Pablo Beach News (1918) Colonel A.E. Koehler, publisher
Atlantic Beach Herald (April 1921) Colonel A.E. Koehler, publisher
Mayport Times (April 1921) Colonel A.E. Koehler, publisher
Jacksonville Beach News (1925) Colonel A.E. Koehler, publisher
Boardwalk Gazette (1931) Frank Brennan and Leslie Reese, publishers
Gazette (1931, Summer)
Post Dispatch (April 3, 1932) Ben Treadwell, publisher
Ocean Beach Reporter (1935–1959) Most-read beaches' paper for twenty-five years; Ed Compton (1935), George Tobi (1944) and John Perry (1946), publishers
Beach News & Advertiser (1950–65) Frances McCondichie, first owner; Joel and Sherry Burnstein, last publishers
*Beach Citi*zen (1955) Short-lived; Jack Miller, editor
Pablo Observer (1955) Short-lived; Henry and Grace Isaacs, publishers
Jacksonville Journal (1959) A daily by John Perry, owner
Beaches Leader (1963) Frances McCondichie, associate editor
Ponte Vedra Recorder (1969) Gretchen Carpenter and Peg Bradford, launched as a monthly newsletter
Sun Times (1979) Purchased by the *Beaches Leader* in 1985
Ponte Vedra Leader (1996) Special edition for Ponte Vedra began
Beaches Leader–Ponte Vedra Leader (Fortieth-anniversary paper was issued June 27, 2003)

17. BEACHES AREA HISTORICAL SOCIETY

MISSION STATEMENT

To nurture civic pride for the distinct history of the beaches, while providing education, information and entertainment for those who live, work and vacation in our communities.[166]

There was an organization meeting on March 30, 1978, for the newly formed Beaches Area Historical Society (BAHS). The meeting, called by Jean McCormick, was held at Fletcher Senior High School.

McCormick had expressed a desire to see the history of the beaches area preserved for future generations, and was seeking support and approval of a Historical Society that would include all the Beaches from Mayport south through South Ponte Vedra and Palm Valley.

At the meeting, J.B. Dobbins, a former resident of Neptune Beach, stated:

> *There is a void here that needs filling in the preservation of history of the area, and you are the people who must shoulder the responsibility and move forward to a time of accomplishment of your goals. The direction you choose to take will determine what part of the local heritage will survive to instruct and enlighten tomorrow's children about yesterday and today.*[167]

BAHS had established temporary headquarters at 233 North Fourteenth Avenue in Jacksonville Beach. BAHS was cooperating with the Florida State Historical Society to collect and preserve materials of statewide significance so that the material could be made available to students and scholars. It was Julianne Howe, on Duval Drive, who assisted as the history organizer, along with Jean, during these beginning stages.

Mr. William Brown had donated a house to BAHS that was constructed in 1900 by the Florida East Coast Railway (FEC) as the section foreman's residence. The house was moved to the new historical park provided by the City of Jacksonville Beach. The new site is very near its original location at 1206 South First Street, just one block east of the original site.[168]

February 6, 1998 — THE PONTE VEDRA RECORDER — Section A-7

That's Palm Valley, Fl., USA

There will never again be a Palm Valley postmark, but the U.S. Postal Service may be willing to deliver mail addressed to "Palm Valley, Fl."

"We have made that accommodation in various places," particularly for historic communities hoping to preserve an identity, said postal service spokesman Joseph Breckenridge.

Palm Valley, originally all the land west of State Road A1A in what is now Ponte Vedra, has been transformed in recent decades as upscale developments have sprouted.

Some valley residents resent being included in a proposed Town of Ponte Vedra Beach and have won the right to opt out, if Palm Valley votes no in the fall.

"We were here first," said Mary Kohnke of Palm Valley. So was the Palm Valley post office

Flavian Mickler, a member of a Palm Valley pioneering family, said the "Palm Valley" postmark originated about 1906 to 1908, and about three post offices operated in the valley until the late 1930s or early '40s.

After that, the post office moved to what is now Ponte Vedra Boulevard, next to a store and gas station, he said. Since then it has been the Ponte Vedra post office.

Breckenridge said the postal service may allow the "Palm Valley" address if it wouldn't slow delivery. But, he said, most items mailed in Ponte Vedra would continue to be postmarked "Jacksonville," and there could be no separate Palm Valley zip code.

"If we gave out zip codes for every community within a city, we would need nine-digit, or ten-digit, zip codes," he said.

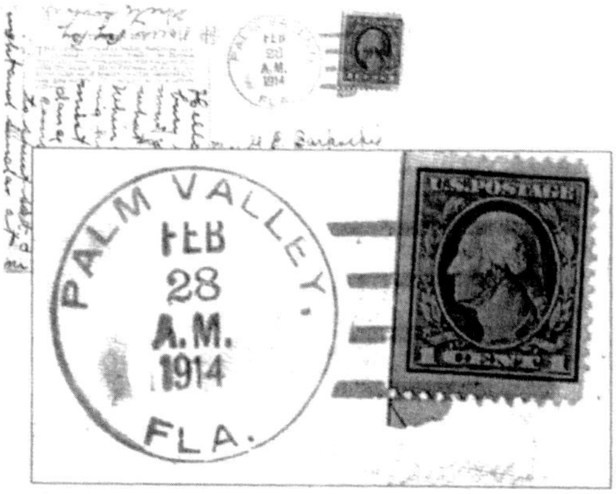

This card has a postmark of 1914, several years after the post office name was changed from "Diego." The card was written to an uncle of Flavian Mickler of Palm Valley from an aunt of Flavian's wife, Jacqueline

The Palm Valley postmark in 1914 after the post office name was changed from "Diego." *From the collection of the Beaches Area Historical Society.*

The largest acquisition in 1983 was a standard gauge H.K. Porter locomotive and cab, built in 1911 and donated by the City of St. Augustine, which may be viewed at the Pablo Historical Park today. The restoration of the depot and the completion of the railroad museum was an important addition to the historical park, since there are no remaining railroads stations at any beaches location.[169]

A research library was started and was housed with the archives at the Southern Bell Building at 415 Pablo Avenue. The Florida East Coast Railway Mayport Depot was moved adjacent to the locomotive and was restored to house railroad memorabilia and displays.

Former BAHS archivist, Dwight Wilson, remembers when the society's archives were stored in an office that was not much larger than a broom closet.

> *The archivist before me, Juanita Dixon, took me to a room in the old Southern Bell Building on Pablo Avenue, handed me the keys and said, "You're now the archivist."*[170]

The donated office space served as the society's library and collection center until 1997, when J.T. McCormick purchased the former archives site at 380 Pablo Ave. When J.T. showed the property to his wife, Jean, she knew that the historical society did not have that kind of money. So J.T. bought the building for them.

The society wasn't in its new, sixteen-hundred-square-foot digs long before its members realized the space was too small.

The land adjacent to the small office, at that time, was located next to the two-story section foreman's house, the old train terminal from Mayport, the twenty-eight-ton steam locomotive encased in a glass exhibit hall and a 1903 post office.[171]

The new building plan in 2004 began with many fundraisers. Construction on the two-story Cracker-style building was slated to begin on the new museum in Jacksonville Beach on November 15, 2004.

The 12,097-square-foot museum at Pablo Historical Park, a three-block campus on Beach Boulevard, was built where the Jean J. McCormick Archives stood. It features a central lobby, museum store, archives research room, collections, archival storage space, office space for up to six staff people, a gallery designed for traveling exhibitions and a permanent exhibitions hall.

The Cracker-style structure, while modern in its construction and technology, has a rustic, "Old Florida" appeal, to blend with the existing historic structures situated in the park.[172]

Area residents, through a capital campaign initiated in 2001, as well as donations from Neptune Beach, Atlantic Beach and Jacksonville Beach and grants from the Cultural Council of Greater Jacksonville and the Florida Division of Cultural Affairs, raised funds for the $2 million museum.

"It's a twenty-five-year-long dream come true," said Jean McCormick of Ponte Vedra Beach, "and it's an inspiration to see the community's participation."[173]

The museum features a permanent exhibit called "Shore Stories: Down the Boardwalk." The exhibit is set within the gallery along a traditional boardwalk surface. It is so realistic that it appears in some areas as though sand and water lap at the pilings underneath the visitor's feet. An introductory video presentation sets the stage for the upcoming walk through time using visual techniques, light and sound.

The façade of the presentation theatre reflects typical beachfront architecture from the early twentieth century. Inside, large photomurals that depict a much earlier time in the beaches' history line the walls and provide a glimpse of the upcoming presentation.

The visitor steps onto the boardwalk where the journey begins at the village of Mayport and continues south through Atlantic Beach, Neptune and Jacksonville Beach, through Palm Valley and ends in Ponte Vedra.[174]

An interpretive overlay of classic artifacts and objects of everyday life, intermingled with photomurals, banners and high-quality laminated test panels, work together to draw the visitor down the coast, highlighting each community and showcasing important historical characters, businesses and locations specific to each. The second floor includes a reading room that allows professional and amateur researchers to view our past through historic photographs, maps, newspapers, postcards, books and genealogical materials.

According to Sam Van Leer, president of the BAHS:

> *It is so satisfying to see the dream of our BAHS founders come to fruition and to know that the hard work and education of our members and volunteers will ensure that the heritage of our beaches will be forever honored and enjoyed by local residents, schoolchildren and visitors to our area.*[175]

18.
Preserving the Guana Tract

The Guana Tract has seen five thousand years of human occupation on its 12,415 acres, and the Guana Tolomato Matanzas National Estuarine Research Reserve Environmental Education Center was opened to the public in 2005.

The Guana Tract includes two areas and both are located on a barrier island in Ponte Vedra Beach, Florida, midway between St. Augustine and Jacksonville Beach on SR-A1A. Guana River State Park on the south end is a 2,600-acre coastal park located on the barrier island. The Florida Game and Fresh Water Fish Commission Wildlife Management Area on the north end comprises some 9,815 acres of public conservation and recreational land. The ten-mile-long Guana Lake is a managed preserve that is popular among waterfowl hunters and includes an observation tower and dam from which to observe wildlife.

History of the "Guana" Name

The name "Guana" means, in the Spanish Florida designation, "Spanish moss and palm straw" used to make the clothing worn by natives. The word is probably Cuban in origin, as it was used there as a generic name for various species of palms.

Originally spelled "Guano," the park's name was changed by Governor Bob Graham in 1984 so as not to confuse it with "guano," which translates to "bird droppings" to scientists today, although two hundred or more years worth of maps use the name "Guano."

Guana's Prehistoric History

The Guana area began human habitation in about the year 3000 BC, or approximately five thousand years ago. The earliest occupational evidence takes the form of projectile points, which have been found scattered along the eroded shoreline of the Tolomato

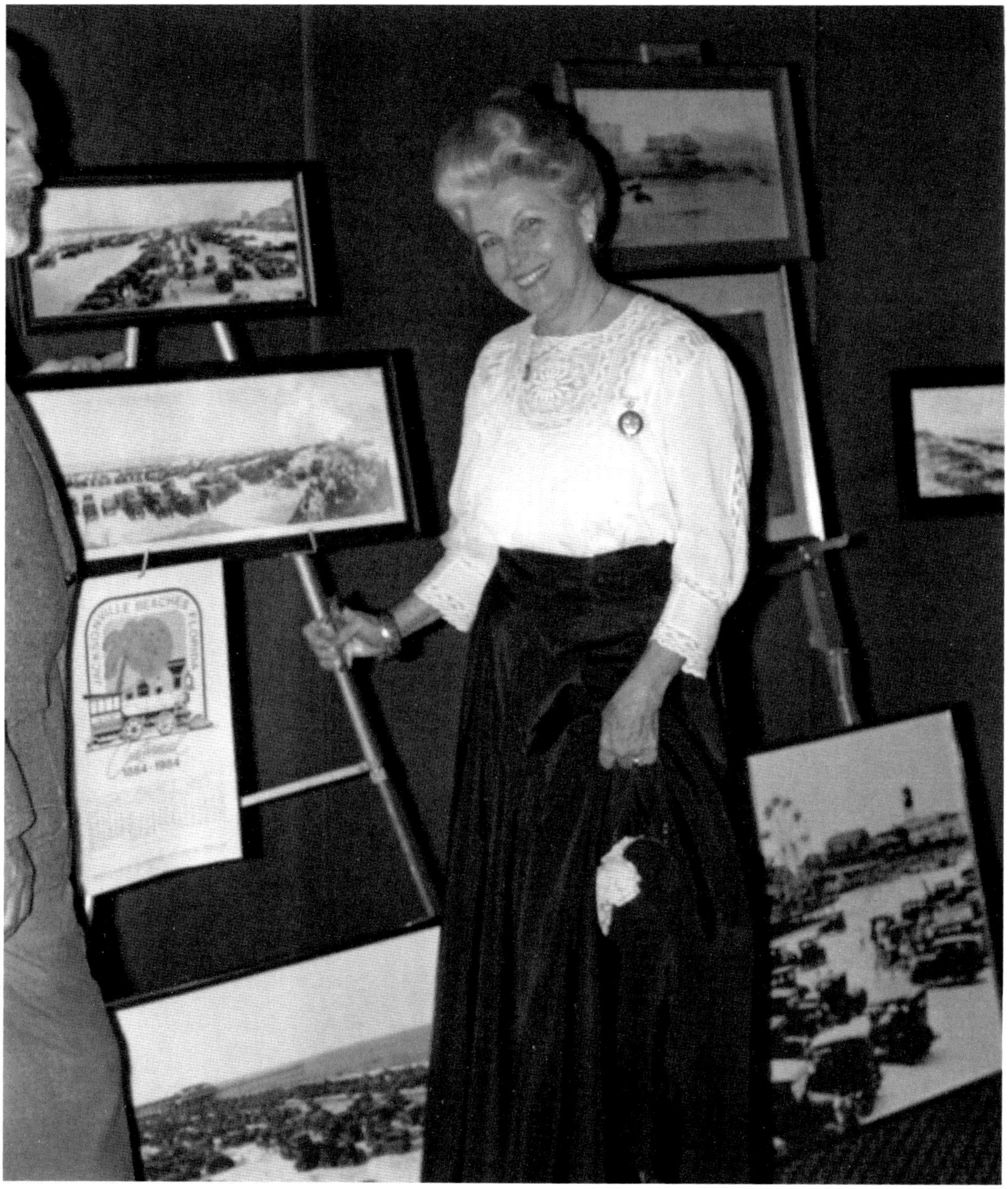

Jean H. McCormick (Mrs. J.T.) at the Beaches Centennial Commission press party held at Sawgrass Golf Club. Circa 1984. *From the collection of the Beaches Area Historical Society.*

River. It is believed that the points have washed out of early deposits either underlying, or at the base of, some of the shell middens found on the peninsula. The middens, most of which are representative of the St. Johns period, are full of oyster and clamshell, pottery shards and bits of faunal material. It was also during this period that the Sanchez burial mound, excavated during the 1880s by A.E. Douglass, was probably constructed.

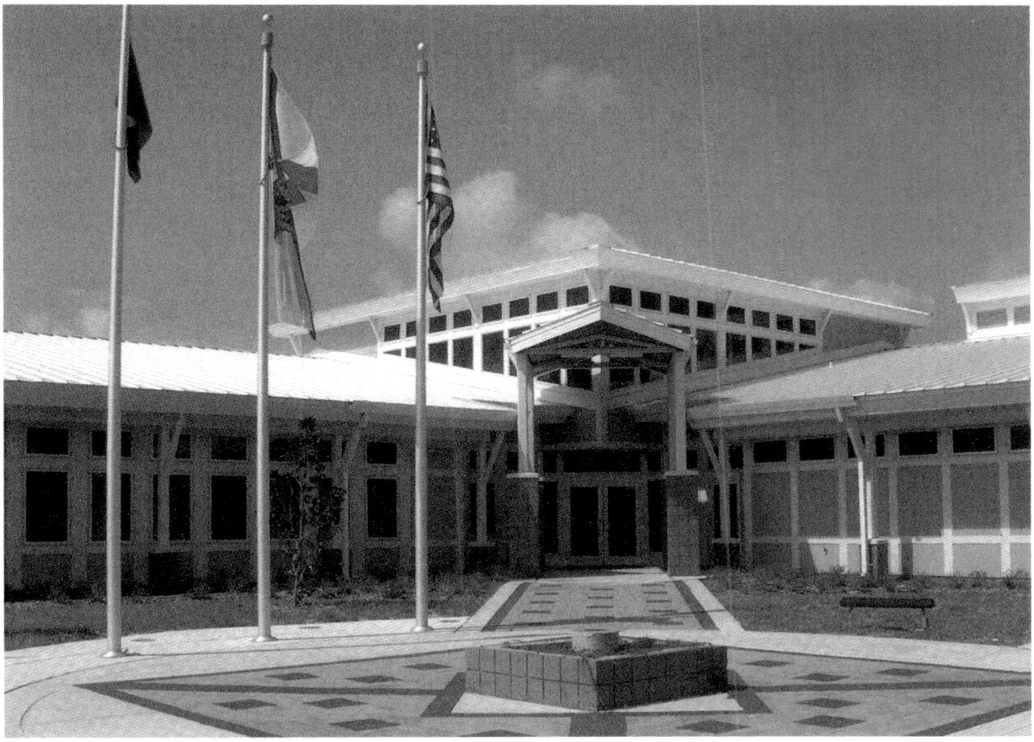

The Environmental Education Center at the Guana Tolomato Matanzas National Estuarine Research Reserve on Guana River Road in South Ponte Vedra Beach. *National Oceanic and Atmospheric Administraction, September 2005.*

Reportedly twenty bundle burials were found in the center of the mound, along with twenty-five stone celts.[176]

One of the more unusual prehistoric sites found on the Guana Tract is the shell ring. Shell rings are more common to coastal South Carolina and Georgia. The Guana ring may be the southernmost example of this site type. Louis Tesar and Henry Baker of the Bureau of Archaeological Research first recorded the ring in 1985. They estimated the ring to be approximately a hundred meters in diameter and one meter high. Previously excavated shell ring sites in South Carolina and Georgia date to the Late Archaic Period, and some of the earliest pottery in the southeast has been found there.

Gate Petroleum Sells the Guana Property

Gate Petroleum Company (Herbert Peyton) had bought the Guana property from the SWD Real Estate Division, but it had to start selling assets quickly because it was paying about $25,000 a day interest and its days were numbered.

The board of Gate Petroleum was of the opinion that it should keep the Guana property and sell the Ponte Vedra Inn property. Peyton was determined that he would sell the Guana property, and after much discussion, the majority of the board agreed.

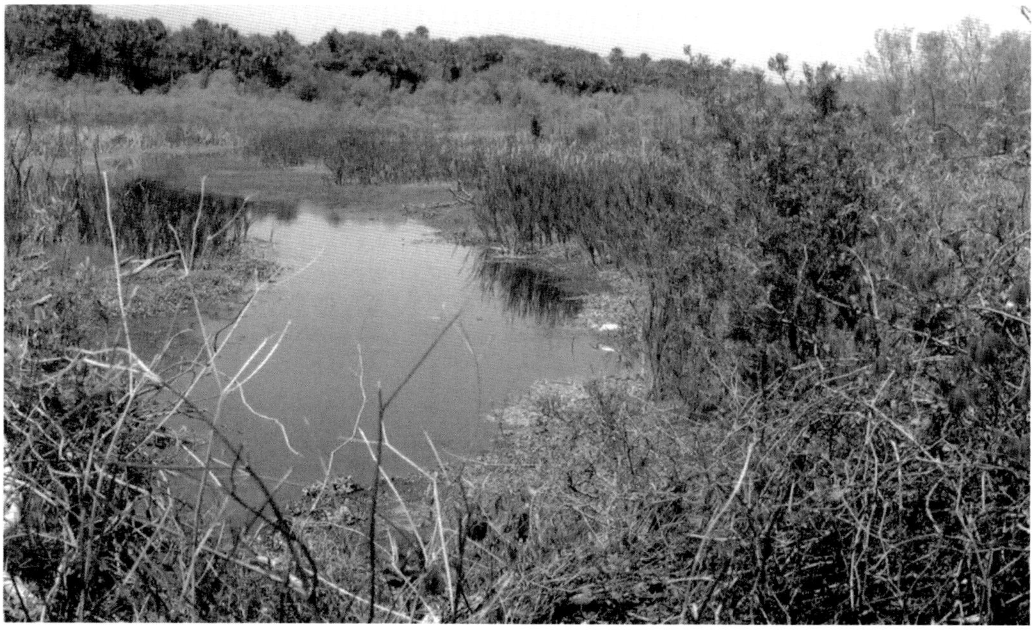

Guana River Watershed, east of SR-210 on Ponte Vedra Boulevard, where the fresh water runs down under A1A to the Guana River. *M. Robinson photograph, 2004.*

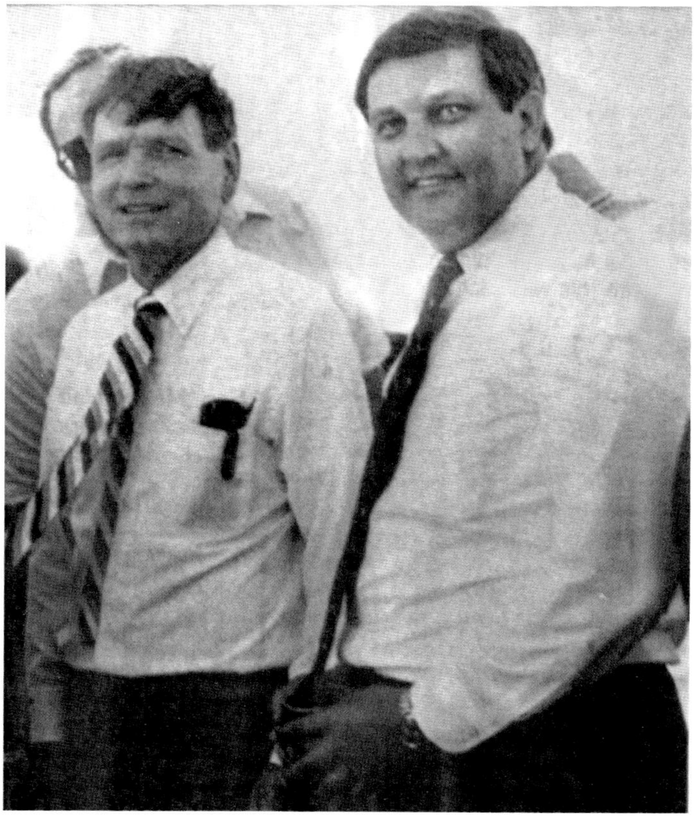

Herb Peyton and Representative Bill Bankhead at Guana Track in 1984, when Peyton sold the twelve thousand acres to CARL (Conservation and Recreation Lands) for $48 million. Ponte Vedra Recorder *picture by Ted Gaggett, July 27, 1984.*

It was obvious to Peyton that the only way Ponte Vedra Inn could be saved was to sell Guana Lake to the State of Florida rather than trying to rezone the area for a residential development. There had been previous discussions between SWD about putting the land on the CARL (Conservation and Recreational Lands) list. The state was interested in buying it, but it took two months to show serious interest.

The state sent a young man to meet with Peyton and negotiate the sale of Guana. The representative knew Peyton had paid $60 million for all the SWD properties. Peyton set the price at about the appraisal value of $53 million. Just after Peyton mentioned that a developer wanted to buy the island, the conversation stopped. Finally, the state representative said, "Okay, but let me ask you one thing. I want to keep it under $50 million because it sounds so much better than fifty. I want to make it forty-nine something." They shook hands, and the deal was made.[177]

Park's Education Exhibits

Construction started in August 2003 on the $4 million educational center at the Guana River State Park in Ponte Vedra Beach. Construction was finally completed at the southeast corner of the Guana River Dam, west of A1A and just north of the Gate Service station on South Ponte Vedra Beach Boulevard.

Florida's historical marker is located at Guana Park Entrance (A1A), sponsored by St. Johns County and the Florida Department of State.

19.
The Fletcher Legacy

John Z. Fletcher, a Havana/Florida native, rose from humble beginnings to become one of Jacksonville's most respected businessmen. John lost his business in the 1930s' stock market crash, but he went to the Telfair Stockton Company (TSC) as vice-president and head of their insurance department. John left TSC in 1936 and formed the John Z. Fletcher & Associates, which became one of the largest general insurance agencies in the area.[178]

Jerome Fletcher acquired control of the local insurance business after his father's death and expanded it to twenty-two offices nationwide. It was sold by Jerome in 1979 and is now part of AON, an international brokerage. John Z. Fletcher was also an amateur golf champion, entrepreneur and father of John (deceased), Jerome, Paul and Tucker. He had a summer home at 507 Ponte Vedra Boulevard, the fifth house built on Ponte Vedra's beachfront in 1939.[179]

Jerome was born in Orlando. When his parents divorced, Jerome, along with his mother and brother, lived with his grandparents in Miami. He then moved with his mother (who was a radio and stage actress) to New York City, but he often visited his father. When his father remarried, he had other sons, and it is Jerome's half brother Paul who has been his partner in their real estate development company since 1960.[180]

Since early childhood, Jerome has spent a part of each year in Ponte Vedra and he has been a full-time resident of Sawgrass/Marsh Landing since 1980. Jerome attended Staunton Military Academy in Virginia and graduated from Yale University (Class of 1951). Jerome's ivy league education also instilled in him a love of history, both American and European, and an appreciation for timeless architecture.

Paul attended Bolles School, and, like his brother, went on to Yale in 1955, where he majored in liberal arts.[181]

In 1942, Paul, who was only a small child at the time, remembers his father pointing out the glow from a burning vessel offshore (the *Gulfamerica*). The United States entered World War II on December 7, 1941, and the Fletchers remember the German boats that heavily preyed on the shores off Ponte Vedra.

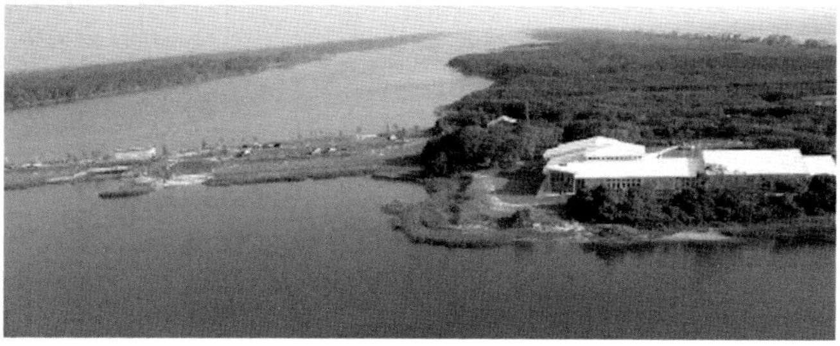

An aerial view of Guana Lake and dam on the left, the Atlantic Ocean on the top right and, below, the major Environmental Education Center at Guana River State Park for hands-on environmental education. *Guana Tolomato Matanzas National Estuarine Research Reserve photo, 2005.*

THE *GULFAMERICA*, 1942[182]

The night skies of April 10, 1942, suddenly exploded in a fiery flash off Jacksonville Beach as a German submarine torpedoed the oil tanker *Gulfamerica* and began moving in to finish her off with deck guns.

Gulf Oil Corporation's SS *Gulfamerica* had begun her maiden voyage in early April 1942 by loading ninety thousand barrels of fuel oil at Port Arthur, Texas. Little did the *Gulfamerica* crew know that the German *U-123*, commanded by Lieutenant Commander Reinhard Hardegen, sighted the *Gulfamerica.*

The U-boat chased the large ship for over an hour, just past Ponte Vedra, until it was four miles off Jacksonville Beach. At 10:24 p.m., the torpedo scored a direct hit and the tanker exploded. *Gulfamerica*'s captain ordered the engines stopped, lifeboats lowered and everyone to abandon ship.

The day after the *Gulfamerica* explosion, local governmental bodies issued rules to try to dim coastal lights so as to hinder the sighting of shops (and houses) by offshore submarines. Nighttime driving on the beach was forbidden, and cars east of the Intracoastal Waterway were to use only parking lights. Neon lights were banned, and oceanfront houses and buildings were to be blacked out or heavily curtained.

Ironically, in 1991, Reinhard Hardegen returned to Ponte Vedra as a retired German executive, speaking perfect English and promoting a book chronicling his exploits, *Operation Drumbeat*, written by Michael Gannon, a University of Florida historian.

LAND DEVELOPMENT IN PONTE VEDRA BEACH

After Paul's graduation from Yale University, he and Jerome founded the predecessor of the Fletcher Land Corporation in 1962. Fletcher Land Corporation, the major operating entity of Fletcher Industries, Inc., has been active in land development continuously since 1962.

In 1968, Frank and Mary Kelly, visitors to Ponte Vedra from Chicago, purchased approximately fifty-eight hundred acres of undeveloped land in Ponte Vedra for approximately $1.2 million.

In 1971, Frank Kelly, after selling off five hundred acres to James (Jimmy) Stockton Jr. for the development of the thousand-acre Sawgrass Country Club, joined forces in a joint venture with a Yale classmate of Jerome's, Frank Gardner. They proceeded with a plan to develop the remaining fifty-three hundred acres into a massive twenty-five-thousand–modular unit retirement community.

The first phase, at this time, was known as "Cabellas Del Mar" (Horses of the Sea), later called "Thousand Oaks" and now "Oakbridge." Approximately one hundred modular (mobile-like home) units were for sale. These were subsequently changed to rental units. Later, the modulars were removed and apartments were built on the site for the Arbor Club, now Ocean Grove of Ponte Vedra.

In October 1973, Paul and Jerome purchased the fifty-three hundred acres and improvements, the Innlet Hotel and Apartments and the adjacent Barney's "Oasis" property for a total of $10 million. The Innlet Hotel, built in 1941 and called "the Lodge," was purchased in 1942 by the owners of the Ponte Vedra Hotel and Club.

The Innlet Hotel, a nostalgic Ponte Vedra landmark, was owned by Paul and Jerome Fletcher. The name "Innlet" confused many visitors. They thought that there was an "ocean inlet" nearby. The hotel, closed and unoccupied since 1970, burned and was gutted by fire in September 1974. Plans had been in the works for some time to build an exclusive modern ocean beach club and dining facility on the Innlet property, in conjunction with the development of Thousand Oaks by Fletcher Properties.[183] The Innlet on Ponte Vedra Boulevard was razed in July 1975.

In 1974, the Fletchers sold off the southern fifteen hundred acres to Leland Burpee and the "Towers Group," who, in 1986, developed the "Plantation."

Innlet Beach Development

The Fletchers' first Ponte Vedra development was Innlet Beach. Jerome and Paul Fletcher hosted several hundred persons at the "invitation only" review of their newly planned recreational community, Innlet Beach, in November 1976. Innlet Beach is now a part of Sawgrass TPC, previously a five-hundred-acre, single-family community surrounding the eighteen-hole golf course. By 1980, the Fletchers had completed over four hundred homes.

Sawgrass and the PGA

In 1979, the Fletchers sold 415 acres of their remaining 3,000 acres to Beman and the PGA Tour for one dollar to serve as the site of their national headquarters.

In 1980, the Fletchers sold to Arvida Corporation the Innlet Beach community and golf club (now Oak Bridge), an additional fourteen hundred acres of land adjacent to the PGA Tour and their 1,230 feet of oceanfront land for approximate $11 million.

In 1982, Arvida Realty came to the Fletchers to buy the land surrounding the new TPC Golf course. It wanted to be near the tournament action and built the Sawgrass Players Club and oceanfront Spinnakers Reach holdings. Within the entire Sawgrass complex, Arvida developed more than fifteen hundred lots and homes.

The investments, by everyone involved, were paying off handsomely. Jerome Fletcher indicated:

> *By about 1980 we had sold off much of the original 5,000 acres. But we kept everything north of Solana Road. Paul felt that land had the most potential because it stretched clear to the Intracoastal.*

MARSH LANDING DEVELOPMENT

The Fletchers began to develop their exclusive Marsh Landing Country Club west to the Intracoastal Waterway. The Fletchers also built a golf course, an Ed Seay signature design. The original name for their development was Marsh Landing at Sawgrass, but in a couple of years, the name was shortened to Marsh Landing.

"We literally sold 120 lots in one day," Paul Fletcher said, "even before we began construction."

Jerome concurred.

> *We platted and numbered 160 lots, and laid out the lakes and fairways, and superimposed that onto an aerial photo. It looked very realistic. That's what we used to sell those Founders Lots.*

From the original fifty-three hundred acres, the Fletchers retained the north twelve hundred acres along the Intracoastal Waterway for the development of Marsh Landing, starting the first phase in 1982 with the country club opening in 1986. To date, there have been over a thousand lots and homes sold and only a few lots remain to be developed.

In 1987, Paul and Jerome assembled a group of prominent investors and reacquired the remaining 630 feet of oceanfront (the old Innlet Hotel and Apartments site) and approximately six acres west of Ponte Vedra Boulevard from Treco. There they developed the Lodge and Bath Club. "The Lodge" opened in 1989 on the eight-acre tract at Corona Road and Ponte Vedra Boulevard. It wasn't until 1996 that Herb Peyton bought out the other investors and entered into a partnership with the Fletchers.

In 1989, Paul and Jerome were very involved with the conceptual design and arranged for the Association of Tennis Professionals (ATP) world headquarters on the "free site" near the PGA Tour. The ATP represents all professional male tennis players in the world and controls most of the sanctioned tournaments. Ponte Vedra is now world headquarters for men's golf and tennis.

SOUTH PONTE VEDRA BEACH

In 1999, Paul Fletcher was involved in various components of the Serenata Beach development in South Ponte Vedra Beach. When plans for Serenata Beach started coming together in 1999, the $160 million condominiums and clubhouse project had the backing of some impressive corporate headliners, including not only Paul Fletcher, but also Jaguar owner Tom Petway and Pittsburgh multibillionaire Henry Hillman.[184]

Fletcher indicated that

> *putting upscale condominium homes and a clubhouse on the last beachfront stretch of South Ponte Vedra Beach—a sacred fifty-acre parcel long held by the Davis family's DDI Inc.—was an investment hard to pass up. The reason we became so enamored with the site is that from every direction, the views are truly spectacular.*[185]

Found Forest in Marsh Landing[186]

Before the Fletchers created Marsh Landing in the early 1980s, they began accumulating the twenty-two hundred tiny undeveloped lots in two planned sections called Pinecrest and Surfside in Jacksonville Beach in the 1920s.

People who paid for these parcels some eighty years ago in what is now Ponte Vedra were buying into developments that existed in name only. The land was never developed, and no one seems to know exactly who put the plan together. But in 2004, as a result of a twenty-five-year effort by Fletcher Land Corporation to buy and consolidate enough of the twenty-two hundred pieces into one big marketable chunk of real estate, very different lines were drawn, laying a grand design over a piece of tangled history. In 2004, the twenty massive new lots became a part of the Marsh Landing development called Found Forest.

The Found Forest development is "the first and the last of its kind based on the location and unique lot sizes, which is rarer for northeast Florida, especially in the Beaches area," said Ray Rodriguez, owner of the Real Estate Strategy Center with North Florida, Inc.

The Ponte Vedra area, with a population of fifty-six hundred in 1980, has grown to over thirty-five thousand by 2008. The new home developments in the area have become very few in number because there were very few areas left to develop. This phenomenal growth in the last thirty years can be attributed to three basic catalysts occurring in the late 1970s:

1) The involvement of Arvida in purchasing and expanding the Sawgrass Club in 1976 and later developing the Players Club Community.
2) The location of the PGA Tour headquarters and annual TPC Tournament (1979).
3) The extension of J. Turner Butler Boulevard (1979) connecting I-95 directly to A1A.[187]

20.
PGA Headquarters' Beginning and the TPC

Golf's Beginning in the United States[188]

Many years ago in Scotland, a new game was invented. It was ruled by "Gentlemen Only, Ladies Forbidden" and thus the word "golf" entered the English language.[189] What would be the significance of golf in the United States without a brief explanation of its beginning in this country. Historians of the PGA Tour, headquartered in Ponte Vedra, can supply us with many clues. "We do know," they write, "that [golf] professionals competed, against each other from the earliest days of the game in this country." That date would have to be sometime in the 1880s, perhaps even earlier, since the first golf club to be organized in the United States was in Yonkers, New York, in 1888.

Two concurrent phenomena contributed to the explosion of golf's popularity in the 1950s: television and another institution named Arnold Palmer. It was not until 1968 that touring professionals finally took over their own destinies. That year, they chose Joseph C. Dey as the first commissioner of what was then was called the Tournament Players Division of the PGA, succeeded in 1974 by Deane Beman and headed up today by Timothy W. Finchem (since June 1, 1994).

Today, in the twenty-first century, it is Tiger Woods whose name continues on the leader board, followed by two Ponte Vedrians, Vijay Singh and Jim Furyk.

The "One-Dollar" Deal[190] —The Fletchers' Contribution

About thirty years ago, developers were preparing to set up some twenty-five thousand mobile homes in Ponte Vedra Beach. They planned a sprawling low-rent retirement community on five thousand acres west of A1A. The community never came to fruition, as we all well know—the Ponte Vedra Beach of today is not a huge trailer park.

For that, the community owes three individuals: PGA Tour commissioner Deane Beman and real estate developers Jerome and Paul Fletcher. Together, they have been largely responsible for something very big that happened and is still happening in this once sleepy beach community.

The Fletchers and Beman had a vision for Ponte Vedra. The tools were golf and residential real estate and the results have been phenomenal.

There is no sea of house trailers here. Instead, due to the Fletchers, Ponte Vedra today is an eclectic mix of upscale housing, liberally sprinkled with exclusive golf course developments. The area thrives in large measure because of what the PGA Tour has brought to the party, thanks to Beman.

But Ponte Vedra Beach west of A1A and Ponte Vedra Beach East were still vastly different entities. Another infusion was needed.

Enter Deane Beman, who had been appointed commissioner of the PGA Tour in 1974. He first visited northern Florida in 1976.

"It was in 1976 that the PGA Tour made a multiyear commitment to come to Jacksonville," Beman said. That commitment was for the Tournament Players Championship. "So we already had made a commitment to the community before we purchased any land here." At that time, in the mid-1970s, Beman began to look for a permanent home for a unique tournament.

"I felt the object was to make a tournament special to the players and make it an extra-special event." Beman indicated.

> *The best way to do that, we felt, was to anchor ourselves in one place, at one golf course. Then we decided that it didn't make business sense to invest that kind of money in someone else's course. So we decided to look for our own property.*

Beman liked the Jacksonville area. He especially liked its people, and the depth of their devotion to professional golf.

> *The whole thing started with the volunteers at the Greater Jacksonville Open. That's the real root of this, the community support we found here for golf. The volunteers attracted us here. They were willing to transfer their enthusiasm from their own tournament, the Greater Jacksonville Open, to ours, The Players Championship. Those volunteers could see not only how things were, but how they could be.*

They had vision. It is a trait Beman respects and shares.

But while he was sure of northeast Florida, Beman wasn't sold, at first, on Ponte Vedra Beach. The Sawgrass Country Club was in receivership at the time, and sales of homesites were nil. The PGA Tour attempted to purchase only the golf course, not the attached real estate. There was no deal.

But Beman kept at it. "We looked at land everywhere, from as far north as St. Marys, Georgia, to south of St. Augustine, and as far inland as Green Cove Springs."

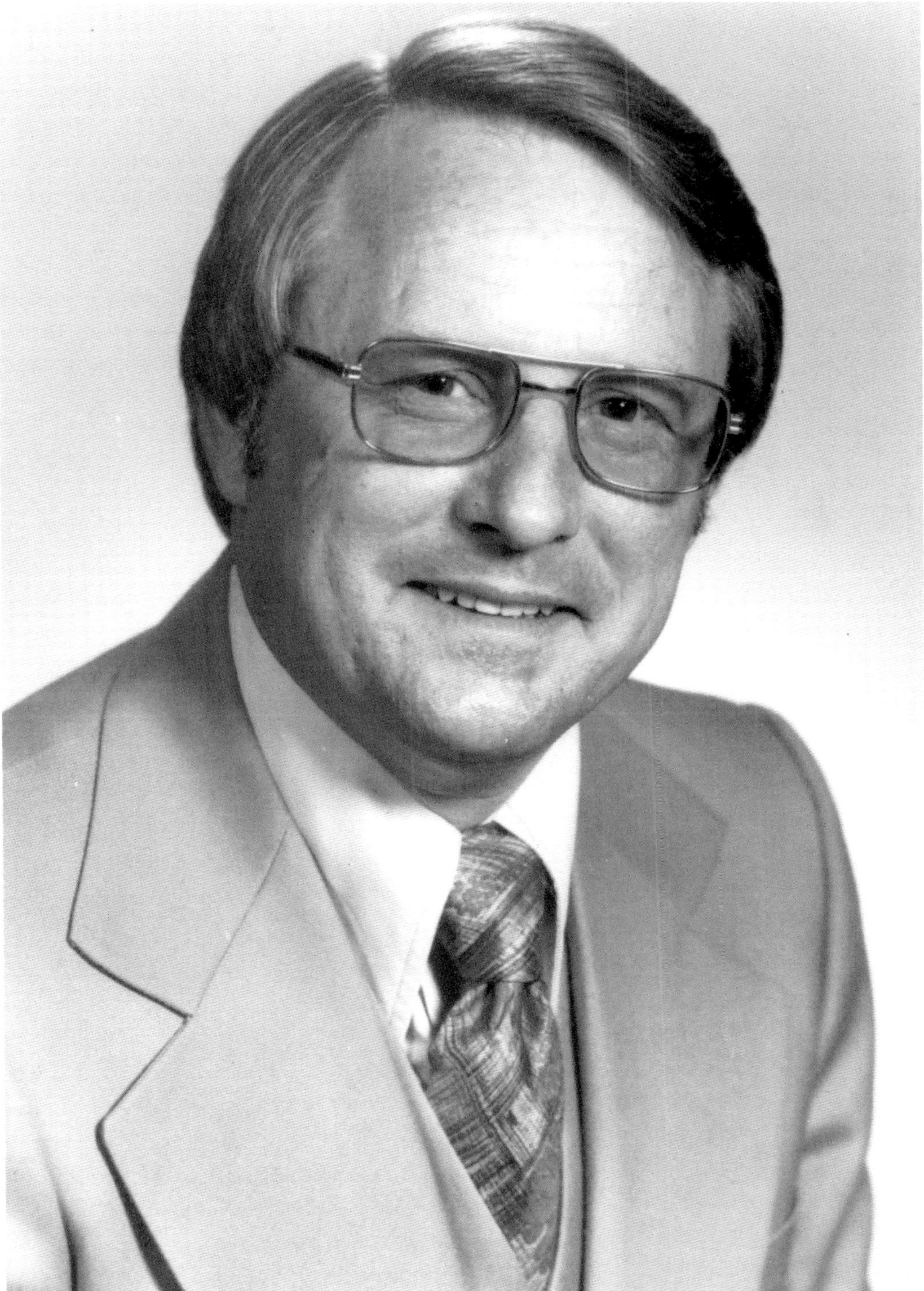

Deane R. Beman, PGA TOUR commissioner for two decades (1974–94), in his TPC portrait. He relocated the key professional golf organization from Washington, D.C., to northeast Florida. *From the collection of the Beaches Area Historical Society, Jacksonville Beach, Florida.*

At this point, the Fletchers made the now-famous "One Dollar Deal." They offered to give Beman enough land on which to build a golf course, for one slim, silver dollar. Part of their original five-thousand-acre purchase, the property was adjacent to the lagging Innlet Beach development.

"Even when you're giving Deane so much land for so little money, nothing is simple," said Jerome Fletcher. "Deane is single-minded. I think Paul and I have some vision, but Deane is a true visionary."

Paul Fletcher concurred. "We didn't sell Deane, we accommodated him."

In fact, the Fletchers reported, six weeks passed before Beman called back to accept their offer. The One Dollar Deal also included land for a possible national headquarters building for the PGA Tour. In return, Beman promised to use the property for no other commercial purposes, and made a fifteen-year commitment to hold the tournament on that course.

THE COURSE TAKES SHAPE

The Tournament Players Club (TPC) at Sawgrass was under construction, and so was a new highway to the beach—J. Turner Butler Boulevard (JTB toll road). As Beman said,

> *We waited to close the deal until we had some pretty strong assurances that the road would be built, and that people would be able to get to the tournament.*

As the new golf course took shape, Beman began to move the PGA Tour's national headquarters from the Washington, D.C. area to Ponte Vedra Beach.

"Two or three things happened in the right sequence at the right time to make that possible," Beman said.

> *We were renting clearly inadequate facilities in D.C., and nearing the end of a five-year lease. We couldn't get proper zoning clearances on land we wanted there. And we were involved with a major project here. So we decided the best thing to do was to be here.*

PGA Tour Headquarters opened its doors in Ponte Vedra Beach in the fall of 1980, just a few months before the Stadium golf course was completed.

The course that sprung up from the swamp—the Stadium course at the Tournament Players Club at Sawgrass—would become one of the most famous in the world, but, more importantly, it served as the model for an ever-expanding network of facilities, each unique in character, yet consistent in quality

The groundbreaking ceremony was nice, but breaking new ground was the true occasion. Certainly, no one had ever seen anything like the TPC at the Sawgrass Stadium course when it opened in 1980.

The rest is history. From the moment the Fletchers began their work, the PGA Tour was enhanced with international recognition.

Little Billy Goats Grazed[191]

With the beginning of the TPC came the little billy goats grazing the golf course. It is said that Vernon Kelly, former president of PGA Tour Golf Properties, wanted to keep an old Scottish tradition alive and therefore wanted goats on his greens.

At first, the animals were kept in a pen between the first and second holes, but "people thought they were so cute that we started letting them out as soon they were all over," Kelly is reported to have said.

Though they consistently manicured the greens, the curious animals soon found their way into golf carts and even onto the roof of the TPC clubhouse. When one goat crept too close to one of the lagoons, an alligator thought it would be a tasty treat and dragged the goat under. To the surprise of nearby golfers, the goat escaped and scrambled back to shore, with a round of applause from the onlookers.

The First TPC Tournament

In 1982, the new TPC at Sawgrass hosted its first PGA tournament. Jerry Pate won and then threw Beman and course designer Pete Dye in the lake at the eighteenth green. The event christened the course and the moment.

The PGA tournament was here to stay. With it, much more than golf came to Ponte Vedra Beach.

Beman and the Fletchers Continue Progress

The PGA Tour still grew, adding a second headquarters building across the road from the first, to house the tour's rapidly expanding staff.

Beman stated:

> *The Tour, the TPC at Sawgrass, The Players Championship, and golf in general have made a strong impact on all of Northeast Florida, not just Ponte Vedra. I think we've been influential in attracting business to the area—the Marriott at Sawgrass, the Mayo Clinic and the Lodge.*

What's ahead for the PGA Tour? According to Beman:

> *Our objective for the years ahead is to continue to do what we do better. We've had tremendous expansion in both activities and staff. We've got a lot on our plates. Now we have to be down in there in the pits running them, making sure that these opportunities meet their original promise.*
>
> *The future may not be nearly so glamorous, but it's just as necessary.*

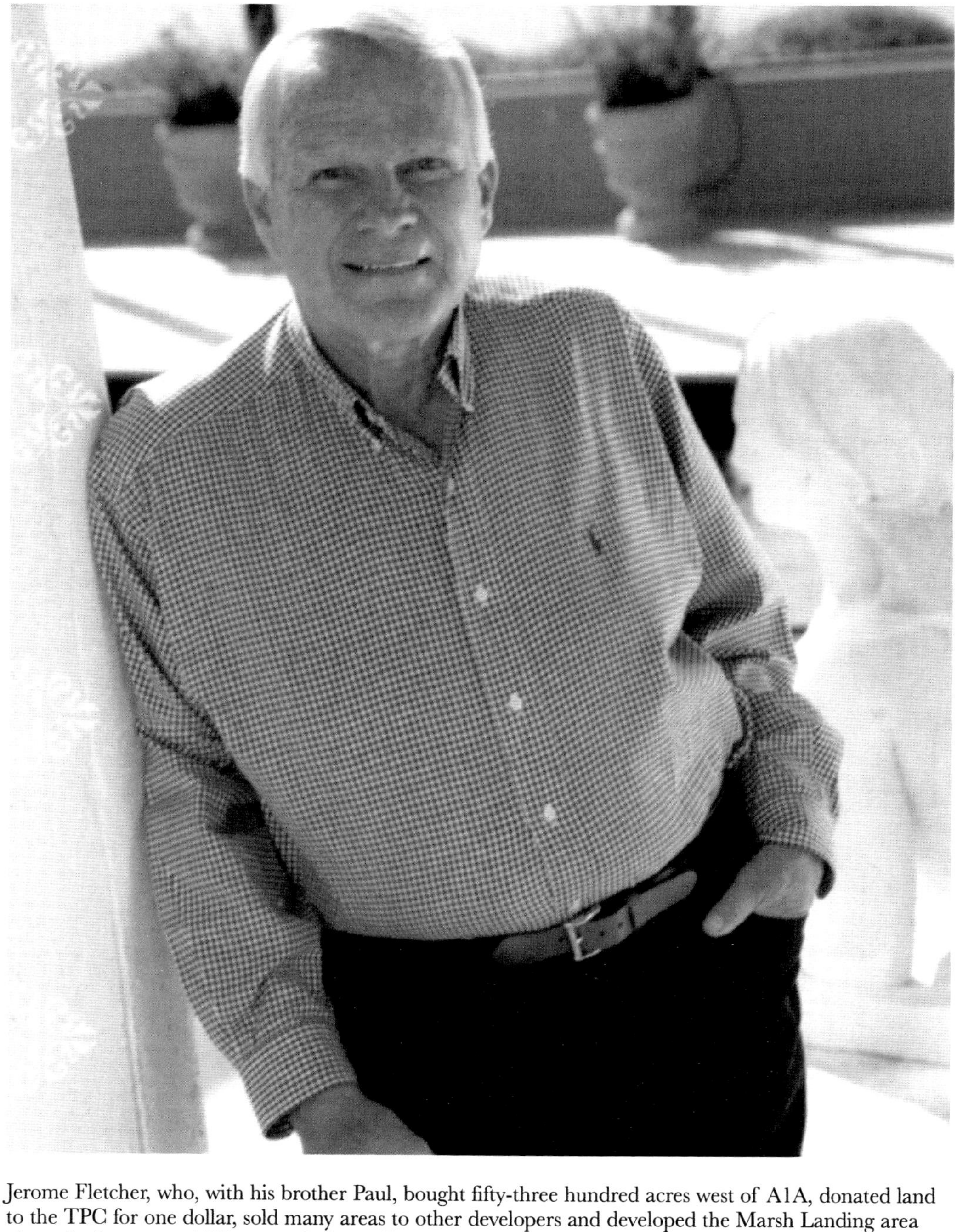

Jerome Fletcher, who, with his brother Paul, bought fifty-three hundred acres west of A1A, donated land to the TPC for one dollar, sold many areas to other developers and developed the Marsh Landing area along the Intracoastal Waterway. Jacksonville Home & Hospitality *publication, photo by Scott Smith, March 2007.*

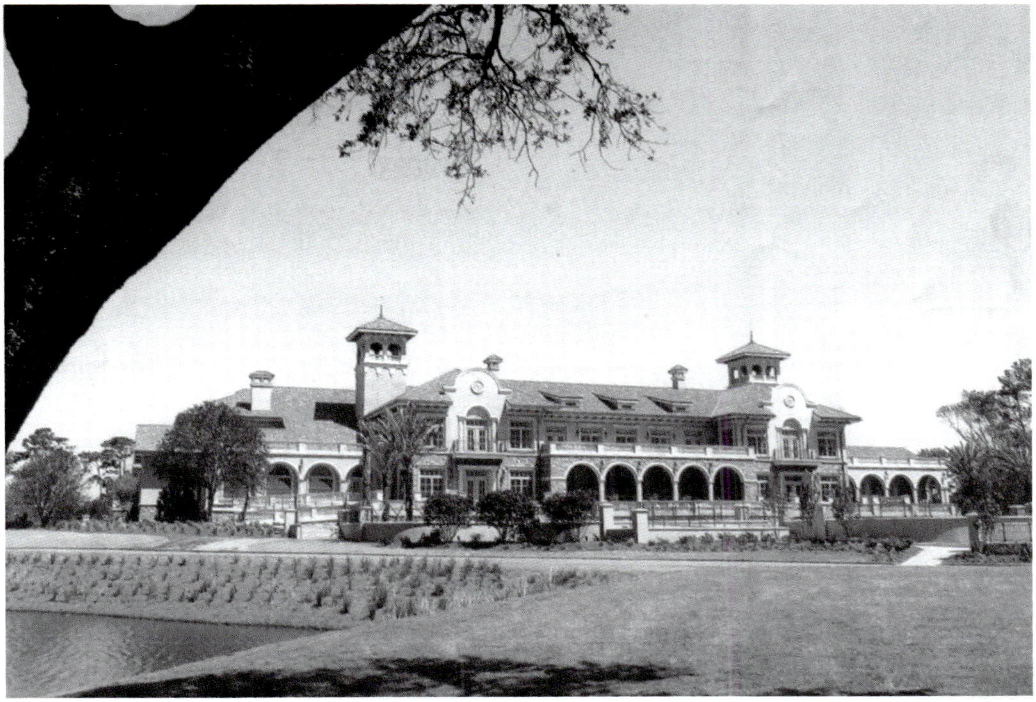

A golf course view of the new seventy-seven-thousand-square-foot clubhouse at TPC Sawgrass, completed in 2007 and home of the Players on the PGA Tour. The Dawning of a New Era, *a feature of the* Florida Times-Union, *Jacksonville, Florida.*

Jerome and Paul Fletcher are pleased that things have worked out the way they have for the community at large. So is Deane Beman.

> *After all, we at the Tour live here in Ponte Vedra. We all benefit from this community. Yes, we've made a contribution, but we get something back every day. It's been very much a two-way street.*

In 2006, The tour shortened the name from the Players Championship (known to locals as the TPC) to simply the Players.

2007 Changes

It was in 2006 that the Players and the PGA Commissioner Tim Finchem decided to build a new seventy-seven-thousand-square-foot clubhouse, revise the golf course and move the tournament to May.

Prior to the 2007 Players tournament, Finchem stressed three things that Beman brought to the PGA Tour during his presentation of a Lifetime Achievement Award to Beman at the new clubhouse.

First, he believed firmly that in any situation, look at the facts and then do the right thing, second, he had great tenacity. And he was an innovator. He did not care what was in the past. He had a vision for the future. If he had built the new clubhouse, it probably would have been completed in four months. And third, he is credited with these achievements: development of TV rights; creating the sports charity arm of the PGA Tour; the player retirement program; the Champions Tour; and the Nationwide Tour.[192]

THE NEW TPC CLUBHOUSE[193]

The new TPC clubhouse was totally rebuilt, and the Stadium Course was renovated before the Players tournament was played in May 2007.

A powerhouse of regal beauty, the clubhouse at the home of the PGA Tour and the Players Stadium Course is as much for the players, past champions and corporate sponsors as it is for the people of northeast Florida. In fact, that was the original intention of former PGA Tour commissioner and golf visionary Deane Beman in the 1970s—to build a spectator-friendly golf course for all to enjoy.

The clubhouse is a shining example of the hallmarks of style from the Mediterranean revival period of the 1920s.

In helping to preserve the history and to honor the rich tradition of the Players Championship, a volunteer docent program of qualified speakers was formed. These storytellers offer visitors a tour into the game of golf and bring back to life unbelievable moments of the Players Championship—it is truly a museum-like experience for visitors.

21. ATP (Association of Tennis Professionals) International Headquarters

The "Parking Lot News Conference"

This is the name by which it will be remembered in tennis lore. In 1988, the Association of Tennis Professionals (ATP), the men's professional tennis players' association, used a parking lot at the U.S. Open to announce that it would assume control of the game. It was a gesture as symbolic as it was strategic. Since the players were barred from using an on-site setting at the U.S. Open, ATP chief Hamilton Jordan seized the opportunity to demonstrate how the players were on the outside looking in.

The players found themselves poised to make another stab at controlling their own destiny when a group of them gathered behind their leader, Hamilton Jordan, for a press conference outside the main gate at Flushing Meadow in 1988.

It was a handful of players who set up shop in the car park in order to let their views be known. It was the first, but not the last, tactical mistake made on the part of the establishment in an argument they were always destined to lose simply because generals cannot fight without troops and the ATP had the troops—all of them.[194]

It was the defining moment in the evolution from the ATP, formed in 1972 under the leadership of superstar Jack Kramer, to become the ATP Tour, the governing body of the worldwide men's professional tennis circuit. "Tennis at the Crossroads," a plan presented at the U.S. Open by Jordan and top players such as Mats Wilander and Tim Mayotte, detailed the problems and conflicts confronting men's professional tennis, as well as the tremendous opportunities available for promoting and marketing the game.

Jordan, former chief of staff for U.S. President Jimmy Carter, had been campaigning during the year for a greater voice for the players in how the men's game was run. The Men's Tennis Council, the governing body of the circuit, however, rejected Jordan's suggestions.

So Jordan got his lectern in the car parking lot and a sound system that actually worked and announced that, after proposals submitted to MTC (Men's Tennis Council) had been summarily rejected, the ATP had decided that it could no longer tolerate such a small voice in the running of the professional game and that it would run its own showcase tour.

It was Philippe Chatrier of the ITF (International Tennis Federation) and his colleagues who expressed shock and dismay at the players' wanting to run their own tour. They could not understand why the professional players would want to ruin something that was so successful, but they, themselves, were fed up with being branded as amateurs because they were not.

During the weeks following the ATP's dramatic announcement, skepticism directed toward the players' motives and ability to organize a tour on their own was rife.

What they wanted most was a tour they could believe in and enjoy; a tour where every event was a certain size and of a certain importance, with the crowds, stadium and atmosphere to match.

Sensing the criticism that would follow, John McEnroe spelled it out at one of his press conferences.

> *It is not about money, that's what needs to be said straight off. In fact, we will probably end up making less money out of the events on our tour. What we are trying to do is to present a better image of tennis to the public, so they will see more big matches between the top players. My primary aim now is to enjoy my tennis and that means playing against the other top guys.*[195]

One of the options also outlined in "Tennis at the Crossroads" was for the players to form a new tour in which they would play a major role and bear greater responsibility for the future of the sport. The idea was quickly embraced by the membership. Eighty-five of the top one hundred ranked players signed a letter of support for a new tour within weeks after the news conference. By the fall of 1988, twenty-four top players had signed contracts to play on the ATP Tour, which began operation in January 1990.

> *Looking back* [at the beginning of the ATP], *it has been a long journey; longer, more exciting and more rewarding than many of us had dared imagine when we gathered for the first Open Wimbledon all of forty years ago.*
>
> *The focus of attention centered on* [the] *sport today is so much more intense, with every played shot and every uttered word analyzed and fussed over by those qualified to do so and by some who are not.*[196]

ATP Headquarters Comes to Ponte Vedra Beach

It was Jerome and Paul Fletcher of the Fletcher Land Corporation who recognized that the ATP should be located in Ponte Vedra Beach adjacent to the PGA Tour headquarters. The Fletchers donated the "eleven-acre free site" to the ATP.[197]

Former player Brian Gottfried, president of the ATP players' union at the time, was instrumental in moving the headquarters from Arlington, Texas. The international headquarters for the ATP stands on ATP Boulevard, adjacent to Florida's A1A and just south of the entrance to the TPC at Sawgrass and the PGA Tour headquarters.

The ATP headquarters is nestled among huge live oaks and maple trees. The three-story ATP headquarters was completed in 1993 and today houses many of the company's employees. The original tennis facilities built for the ATP across the street from the current headquarters building was sold to the Bolles School in 1999.

In October 2000, the ATP announced a couple of changes, which came into effect on January 1, 2001. These changes included a new logo to better reflect the professional and progressive nature of the ATP Tour in the twenty-first century and a shortening of the organization's name to ATP.

ATP Tennis, Europe division, of the ATP International is located in Monte Carlo, Monaco.

The ATP is the worldwide governing body of the men's professional tennis circuit, comprising sixty-four tournaments in thirty countries on six continents.

Ponte Vedra Tennis Before the Arrival of ATP

The *TENNIS* (publication) recognized Ponte Vedra Inn and Club as the number three tennis resort of the nation's top fifty in 2002. Andy Radovic, vice-president of sales and marketing, indicated that the "Ponte Vedra Inn and Club is honored that its Racquet Club is held in such high regard by one of the top tennis publications in the country."[198]

Ponte Vedra Beach is, now, not only the headquarters for the ATP, but also the home of the renowned Racquet Club at the Ponte Vedra Inn and Club, which has evolved from a single clay court in the early 1930s to one of the top tennis centers in the nation today.

Appendix
Chronological History of Ponte Vedra Beach

Brief Early Pre-Columbian History

Prehistoric Period to Fifteenth Century BC

15000 BC and prior	Florida's coastline was changing.
15000 BC–AD 1500	Florida's people and cultures prior to the recorded discovery by Ponce de León.
3000 BC to Present	Guana history—prehistorical cultural sites—five thousand years of human occupation.

Post-Columbian History: Fifteenth–Nineteenth Centuries

1500s

1497	Depicting a peninsula like Florida, white men may have seen the area but there is no record of landing.
1498	England's John Cabot supposedly viewed Miami's Biscayne Bay.
1513	Don Juan Ponce de León landed at Guana, looking for the Fountain of Youth. First recorded arrival of the Spanish in North America's Florida.
1520	Juan Bono Quexo discovered the St. Johns River.
1562	Jean Ribault, explorer for France, and his Huguenots landed in St. Johns River.
1565–1763	The first Spanish period and Spanish control of Florida.

1565	Don Pedro Menéndez de Avilés arrived in St. Augustine at the Timucuan town of Seloy and began the first permanent European/Spanish settlement.
1572	Jesuits were gone from Spanish Florida.
1573	Franciscan missionaries began their work with the Native Americans in Florida.
1586	Sir Francis Drake, British seafarer, burned the city of St. Augustine.
1598	The first hospital in the United States was Nuestra Señora de la Soledad, or Our Lady of Solitude, in St. Augustine.

1600S

Early 1600s	Palm Valley's early development as Diego Plains.
1605	The Franciscan friars established a mission among the Timucuan Indians in northeast Florida as the first U.S. school and schoolteachers.
1607	Founding of Jamestown, Virginia (ninety-four years after Ponce de León's discovery).
1620–1702	Mission la Natividad de Nuestra Señora de Guadalupe de Tolomato was established at Guana (two leagues north of St. Augustine/Guale area).
1670	Founding of Charleston, South Carolina.
1687	Eight men, two women and a child fled from slavery in South Carolina to freedom in Florida.
1690	A mission town three leagues north of St. Augustine at Guana was Santa Cruz (Cruce or Holy Cross).
1693	King Charles II declared that slaves fleeing English possession would be set free upon arrival in Spanish territory.
1696	Jonathan Dickenson's journey through Santa Cruz (Cruce) Indian Town.

1700S

1702	Governor James Moore of South Carolina and Colonel Robert Daniel destroyed the Tolomato mission at Guana.
	Don Diego Espinosa built a home in Diego Plains, named "Dago."
July 1704	Governor James Moore burned all the Florida missions.
1708	Colonel Barnwell of South Carolina invaded Florida.
1710–1717	Timucuan Indian civilization vanished from disease and wars.

1715	The Yamassees of Carolina and Georgia came to Fort Mose. Ten Spanish treasure ships were driven onto the reefs on the east coast of Florida.
1717	A third Tolomato mission reemerged on the 1717 census at Wright's Landing.
1724	Ten more runaway South Carolina slaves reached St. Augustine.
1727	Colonel John Palmer of South Carolina invaded Florida.
February 12, 1733	James Edward Oglethorpe arrived at Beaufort, South Carolina, from England.
ca. 1736	Fort San Diego in Diego Plains was built by the Espinosa, Sanchez and Zavalia families.
1736 and 1740	General James Oglethorpe of Georgia attacked on Fort San Diego.
1738	Fort Mose, the first freed slaves' fort, was built north of St. Augustine in St. Johns.
1740	Fort San Diego was captured by the Englishman Oglethorpe.
1750s	Fort Diego was passed to the Sanchez and Villareal families.
1752	Fort Mose was rebuilt in its second location.
1763–1784	Arrival and influence of the British for a twenty-year period.
1763	The Spanish Crown, backing the defeated French in the Seven Years' War, surrendered Florida to England. Spain evacuated its Florida colonists to Cuba after 250 years. Florida was divided into East and West Florida, with the East Florida capital in St. Augustine. Don Francisco Xavier Sanchez's plantation, San Diego, was built in Diego Plains.
March 14, 1764	The last of 3,104 priests had left Florida, most heading to Havana.
1764	British Governor James Grant arrived in East Florida.
1765	Governor Grant established three-hundred-acre plantation, Grant's Villa, with fifty to sixty planted acres.
1768	Grant's Villa established indigo fields in the area (now Guana Park).
1776	The northern section of the King's Road from St. Augustine to the St. Mary's River near Coleraine, Georgia, was built by British Governor Grant.
1780–1784	David Yeats assumed Grant's Villa, naming it Mount Pleasant Plantation.
1780	Dragoons, a Spanish military outpost, was established at Twenty Mile Station.
1781	Battle of Pensacola in West Florida. The Spanish defeated the British on May 17, 1783.

	The *East Florida Gazette*, Florida's first newspaper, was printed in St. Augustine.
1783	The Spanish regained control after losing it for twenty-one years.
1784–1821	Jorge Clarke, Domingo Sanco, Tory Travers and Vicente Lacrous were Diego landowners.
1784	The Spanish Crown awarded large East Florida land grants.
	Twenty Mile Station, "La Posada Media," was established in Diego Plains on Twenty Mile Road.
1787	Twenty Mile House (Outpost) was rebuilt at the southernmost tip of the Dee-Dot Ranch.
1790	Spain established head right land grants.
1790s	Daniel McGirtt, Scottish outlaw, ended his terror in Diego Plains.
1795	Guana, South Ponte Vedra Beach, was a Spanish fort attacked and destroyed by the Georgia state militia.

1800S

1800–1803	Native American wars damaged the recovering area plantations.
1817–1818	The First Seminole War took place in Florida.
1818	Major Andrew Jackson invaded Florida.
	Nicholas Sanchez owned the 300-acre Quigui on Diego Plains.
	Philip Solano owned the 245-acre Two Sisters on Diego Plains.
	Adams-Onis Treaty—Spain agreed to sell Florida to the United States under the "Florida Purchase Treaty."
1821–1845	Florida's territorial period lasted for twenty-five years.
February 22, 1821	Spain sold Florida to the United States through Andrew Jackson.
	Most Spanish landowners evacuated Florida to the islands and South America.
	Florida became a territory of the United States.
	Territory of Florida divided East and West Florida into two counties, St. Johns and Escambia.
	First Florida sheriff (James R. Hanham) was in St. Johns County.
	Andrew Jackson became the first (absentee) Florida governor in St. Johns County.
	The first Mickler family in Diego were the Jacob Micklers.
1822	City of Jacksonville (Cowford) and Duval County were founded.
1824	The U.S. Post Office Department began using the King's Road.
	Pedro Mestre was the owner of 645 acres in Diego Plains.
	Andres Papy owned the Fort Diego land.

1835–1842	The Second Seminole War was fought in Florida.
March 3, 1845	United States declared Florida the twenty-seventh state.
	David Levy Yulee became Florida and the United State's first Jewish senator in St. Augustine
1845–1861	Florida's American statehood period.
1855–1858	The Third Seminole War occurred in Florida.
January 10, 1861	Florida withdrew from the United States.
1861–1865	Florida participated in the Civil War.
1865–1877	Reconstruction period in Florida.
1868	Florida was readmitted to the Union.
1873	The Oesterreicher homestead in Palm Valley on Twenty Mile Road was built.
1874	Pioneer Yulee Mickler arrived in Palm Valley.
1880–1927	Intracoastal Waterway/East Coast Canal, was initially dug and operated through Diego/Palm Valley by the FCLC & TC.[199]
1882	School No. 26 was built in Diego, west of the Intracoastal Waterway.
1883–1904	School No. 27 was established at Twenty Mile Ridge in Durbin.
1884	Telfair Stockton Co. began its real estate company in Jacksonville.
1888	The First Beach's newspaper was established and published.
1880s	The JSTAHRR[200] ran between St. Augustine and Jacksonville.
1898	Spanish-American War occurred in Florida.
	Eli H. Broadnax, first Deigo postmaster, worked out of his home.
1899	Deigo Post Office's spelling was changed to Diego.
	William M. DeGrove was the second Diego postmaster.

Current History: Twenty–Twenty-first Centuries

1900–1925

1902	Diego Baptist Church (now Palm Valley Baptist) became the first church in Diego.
1906	Robert J. Henson, third Diego postmaster, lived in his 1875 home.
	Intracoastal Canal was more deeply dug through Palm Valley.
	Diego Plains name changed to Palm Valley.
	Post office name officially changed from Diego to Palm Valley.
1910	First U.S. Post Office building was located in Palm Valley.

	First family, before the beach area was named Mineral City, was the Pritchard family.
	Mining operations occurred along the beach by Buckman and Pritchard.
	Turnstile sort of bridge on the canal was built with bridge toll for boats only.
	Dixie Highway, along Old King's Road, was constructed.
	Palm Valley residents built a twenty-five-pupil school near Cracker Landing.
ca. 1916	Shore Sawmill, at Cracker Landing (or Craddock Landing),was built in Palm Valley.
1916–1917	Beach pavilion was built for dances on Mickler's Beach.
1917	William M. DeGrove and Telfair Stockton were members of the Florida House of Representatives.
	Buckman sold the beaches' mineral rights to the National Lead Company.
1918	World War I ended, demand for minerals declined and miners left.
	"Mineral City" was the name chosen by the miners.
1918	First Post Office in Mineral City was established by George Anson Pritchard, postmaster.
1922	National Lead Company bought out Buckman and Pritchard.
	First nine-hole golf course was built in Mineral City.

1926–1950

1927	Intracoastal Waterway, through Palm Valley, finally connected Jacksonville to Fort Pierce.
1928	The mineral market collapsed mining in Mineral City.
	Ponte Vedra Beach (PVB) was named after Pontevedra, Spain.
	Original log cabin, a twelve-room structure, was built for the Ponte Vedra Inn venture.
1929	Telfair Stockton and Co. was hired by National Lead Co. (NLC) to manage Ponte Vedra Club.
1930s	Herbert Strong, a British immigrant, was the architect of Ponte Vedra Golf Course.
	The Outpost, a hundred-acre preserve on Lake Guana, was opened by the Ponte Vedra Inn.
1932	State Road No. 1 (A1A) was completed from Ponte Vedra Beach to Vilano.
1933	A barge bridge was erected north of the current Palm Valley Bridge.
	Moonshine industry thrived in the Palm Valley area before and after the repeal of the Volstead Act.

1934	The Meredith brothers took over the two-story Ponte Vedra Inn.
	Intracoastal wooden bridge erected by the FCLC & TC[201] was dismantled at Palm Valley.
	U.S. Army Corps of Engineers erected a temporary intracoastal pontoon structure at Palm Valley.
	Ponte Vedra Club manager's cottage was completed at 423 Ponte Vedra Boulevard (torn down in 2006).
1935–1947	Mickler's Atlantic Ocean Fishing Pier was built and survived.
1935	Palm Valley Road was established as State Road No. 306.
	Intracoastal Waterway was redredged, a hundred feet wide by eight feet deep, from Jacksonville to Miami.
1937	Palm Valley Drawbridge across the Intracoastal Waterway was built.
	Joseph W. Davin formed the real estate company Whatley, Davin and Co., which merged with Telfair Stockton and Co. in 1946.
1937	Ponte Vedra Inn, facing on the shore road (now Ponte Vedra Boulevard), opened.
October 5, 1937	First postmistress in Ponte Vedra was Alice Landrum.
1940s	The Fletcher family lived in Ponte Vedra Beach.
1941	Tommy Sabin, a New York banker built the Innlet.
	James Stockton bought an eight-hundred-acre stake and eight miles of oceanfront from the National Lead Co.
1942	National Lead Co. sold its remaining buildings to the Ponte Vedra Company.
	The Stocktons built Fort Davis, the log cabin at Dee-Dot Ranch.
April 10, 1942	U.S. tanker *Gulfamerica* was torpedoed off the coast by the Germans.
June 17, 1942	A German submarine landed with four saboteurs.
1944	The Innlet was sold to the Ponte Vedra Inn and Club.
1945	State Road No. 306 was changed to State Road No. 210.
	Christ Episcopal Church's first congregation met in Ponte Vedra.
1946	Highway No. 1's name was changed to A1A.
	Ponte Vedra Community Association was founded by F. Lee, president.
	Telfair Stockton and Co. merged with Whatley, Davin and Co. to become Stockton, Whatley, Davin and Co. (SWD).
	Vilano Bridge was built connecting A1A (South Ponte Vedra) with St. Augustine
	The Stocktons acquire the ten-thousand-acre Guana from the Hale and Upchurch families.
1947	The new community, South Ponte Vedra Beach, was named.
	Robert Trent Jones, designer, expanded Ponte Vedra Golf Course to twenty-seven holes.

1948	George Hunter's grocery and service station opened on Palm Valley Road, now Ponte Vedra Valley Cemetery.
	Palm Valley residents obtained electricity.
1949	A legislative act closed traffic on the beach from Duval line to the Innlet.
	Beach Boulevard opened over the inland waterway, the second major artery to the beaches and Ponte Vedra.

1951–1975

1951	Harry Johnston began the Ponte Vedra Volunteer Fire Department.
	Church building was completed for Christ Episcopal Church.
1957	Guana River Dam was built by private owners to create Guana Lake.
	Canal Road was renamed after a local resident as Roscoe Boulevard.
1958	Eunice Odum Semmes donated forty acres for Ponte Vedra/Palm Valley School.
	New Jacksonville Beach Hospital opened to serve the beaches.
1961	Legislative act closed traffic on the beach from the Innlet to Mickler Pier Road.
1963	The *Beaches Leader*, local newspaper, began publication.
October 1963	First Ponte Vedra incorporation request failed.
September 9, 1964	Hurricane Dora directly hit the beaches.
1964	General American Oil purchased Stockton, Whatley, Davin and Co.
	Sawgrass began development with James "Jimmy" R. Stockton Jr.
	Mosquito Control Station of Anastasia opened off A1A.
1966	A1A Highway bypass was built west of Ponte Vedra Boulevard.
	James Stockton Jr. formed his own real estate company in Ponte Vedra Beach.
1967	Ponte Vedra Beach incorporation vote was again defeated.
	All vehicle access was closed off to Ponte Vedra beaches.
	Land Corp of America (LCA) was formed by Frank Kelly.
	Miami attorney Frank Gardner bought fifty-three hundred acres west of Ponte Vedra Boulevard and the Innlet Hotel.
	Ponte Vedra Recorder newspaper was launched.
February 1968	Ponte Vedra Beach was declared a bird sanctuary.
1970s	Stockton Properties assembled eleven hundred acres and continued Sawgrass development.
	The Sawgrass Lagoon golf course was redesigned.

1972	Sawgrass Community West broke ground for an eleven-hundred-acre development.
	South Ponte Vedra Association of area neighbors was founded.
1973	The citizens again turned down the incorporation of the Ponte Vedra Beach area.
	The Fletcher brothers purchased five thousand acres west of A1A for $10 million.
	First volunteer firemen's ball began an annual firemen's event.
1974	Deane Beman, commissioner of PGA, explored sites for golf tournaments.
	James Stockton Jr.'s Sawgrass was sold to a banking consortium.

1976–1999

1976	PGA Tour came to Ponte Vedra Beach.
1977	The Arvida Corporation purchased Sawgrass from Industrial-America.
	The Tournament Players Championship (TPC) golf tournament was held at Sawgrass.
1978	Beaches Area Historical Society was founded by Jean McCormick.
1979	J. Turner Butler Boulevard and bridge was completed to A1A.
	PGA Tour relocated headquarters from Washington, D.C. to Ponte Vedra Beach.
1980	Oak Bridge (once Innlet Beach),purchased by Arvida Corp, joined Sawgrass.
	Ponte Vedra Community Association was again rejected for incorporation.
	Annual firemen's ball was changed to the "Summer Party."
	Ponte Vedra Beach Post Office relocated two miles south on A1A.
	Shipwrecked *Rocket* was beached near the shore in South Ponte Vedra Beach.
1982	Land for Tournament Players Championship was bought from the Fletchers for one dollar.
	The Ponte Vedra Municipal Service District (MSD) was organized.
	Marsh Landing's twelve hundred acres was opened by the Fletcher Brothers.
January 1982	Phillip's Petroleum purchased General American Oil Company.
1983	Nease High School began, named after Allen D. Nease Sr.
	Sawgrass's Arvida was sold to Bass Brothers and Arvida Management.

July 1983	First commercial shopping center, Sawgrass Village, was built.
	Walt Disney Productions acquired Arvida (Sawgrass).
	Gate Land Co. sold twelve thousand acres at Guana to the State of Florida.
	Sawgrass Oceanside golf course, South Nine, opened.
1984	Gates Petroleum Company purchased the Stockton, Whatley, Davin and Co. real estate holdings, including the Ponte Vedra Inn and Club.
1985	First Ponte Vedra library was founded on Canal Blvd, then moved to SR-210 in 1993 and finally settled, in 2001, on Library Boulevard.
1987	Sawgrass Marriott Resort opened after plans were announced in September 1985.
1988	The Association of Tennis Professionals (ATP) tour moved to Ponte Vedra from Texas.
	The ATP was renamed the Players Championship.
	Vicar's Landing Retirement Community at Sawgrass opened.
1989	The post office moved again two miles south to Ponte Vedra Pointe on A1A.
	The Lodge and Bath Club opened.
1991	Alice B. Landrum Middle School opened.
1992	Marjorie K. Rawlings Elementary School opened.
1993	Ponte Vedra Public Library moved to A1A.
1995	Ponte Vedra–Ponte Vedra Connection was organized.
1996	Ocean Palms Elementary School opened.
	The Ponte Vedra Beach Chamber of Commerce was formed.
	The Cultural Center of Ponte Vedra was founded.
1997	Palm trees were planted in median of A1A in November.
	Whatley Interchange (Butler and A1A) was completed.
1998	Voters again rejected a charter form of government.
1999	The Winston Family YMCA opened on Landrum Lane.
	New U.S. Postal Service facility was built on Corridor Road.
	Local newspaper, the *Recorder*, was sold to Add, Inc.
	Bolles Lower School at Ponte Vedra Beach opened.
1999–2001	Ponte Vedra Inn and Club redesigned and expanded its golf course.

2000 TO DATE

2000	Beaches Cultural Collaborative Council began.
2001	Serenata[202] Beach opened in South Ponte Vedra.
	Ponte Vedra Library moved to current location on Library Boulevard.

	Ocean Grande at Serenata opened on the Intracoastal Waterway in South Ponte Vedra.
	New overhead Palm Valley Bridge replaced the drawbridge over the Intracoastal Waterway.
2003	Oak Bridge Club and Golf Course in Sawgrass Players Club was sold.
2005	New traffic circle was built at the intersection of Mickler and SR-210.
	Guana Tolomato Matanzas National Estuarine Research Reserve Environmental Education Center opened.
2006	Construction began on Nocatee in the area now named Ponte Vedra.
	The new Beaches Museum and History Center opened in Jacksonville Beach.
2008	New Ponte Vedra High School to open in September.

NOTES

ST. JOHNS TIMUCUAN INDIANS —SATURIWA TRIBE

1. Suzanne Lussagnet, *The French in Florida* (Paris: Presses Universitaires de France, 1958), 212–13.
2. Translated from R. Pareja, *Cathecismo, y Examen para los que Comulgen, en Lengue Castellana, y Timuquan* (Mexico City: Imprenta de Juan Ruyz, 1627).
3. John H. Hann, *A History of the Timucua Indians and Missions* (Gainesville: University Press of Florida, 1996), 325.
4. Jerald T. Milanich, *The Timucua: The Peoples of America* (Oxford: Blackwell Publishing Inc., 1996), 195–95.
5. Jerald T. Milanich, "The Timucua Indians: After the Europeans Came (1562–1767)," May 2000.

AMERICA'S EARLY EXPLORERS, 1492–1526

6. George R. Fairbanks, *The History and Antiquities of the City of St. Augustine, Florida* (New York: Charles B. Norton, 1958), ch. 11 "First Discovery, 1512 to 1565," 13.
7. Michael Gannon, *The New History of Florida* (Gainesville: University Press of Florida, 1996), ch. 2 "First European Contacts," 17.
8. L.D. Scisco, "The Track of Ponce de Leon in 1513," *Bulletin of the American Geographical Society* 45, no. 10 (1913): 721–35.
9. Robert H. Fuson, *Juan Ponce de Leon and the Spanish Discovery of Puerto Rico and Florida* (Blacksburg, VA: McDonald and Woodward Publishing Co., 2000), 70.
10. Charles Gallagher, PhD, *Cross and Crozier: The History of the Diocese of Saint Augustine* (Strasbourg, France: Editions de Signe, 1999), 8.
11. Fuson, *Juan Ponce de Leon*, 225.

12. Chelle Delaney, *Rewriting American History*. St. Augustine Catholic (St. Augustine, FL: Allied Graphics, Inc., 2005). In 2005, a Boston newspaper complained that he (Dr. Gannon) was the Grinch who stole Thanksgiving.
13. Michael Gannon, PhD, "We Gather Together," *St. Augustine Magazine* (November 2002).
14. Patricia C. Griffin, "Life on the Plantations of East Florida 1763–1848," *Florida Anthropologist* 56, no. 3 (September 2003): 163–88.

SPAIN'S CONTROL OF AND CONTRIBUTIONS TO NORTH FLORIDA, 1565–1763

15. Paul L. Weaver, *Historic Properties Survey of St. Johns County Florida* (St. Augustine, FL: Historic St. Augustine Preservation Board, September 1985), ref. 207.17.
16. Kathleen Deagan, *The Spanish Missions of La Florida* (Gainesville: University Press of Florida, 1993), see preface by Bonnie G.

SETTLEMENT OF DIEGO PLAINS (PALM VALLEY), 1700

17. WPA (Work Progress Administration), *Spanish Land Grants in Florida* 5, 43 (1940), St. Augustine Historical Society copies; Historical Records Survey, Division of Community Service Programs, Work Projects Administration, *Spanish Land Grants in Florida* xxxii (November 1940). By Article VIII of the Adams-Onis treaty of February 22, 1819, whereby Spain ceded the Floridas to the United States, all Spanish grants of land made prior to January 24, 1818, the date on which the king of Spain definitely expressed his willingness to negotiate, were to be "ratified and confirmed to the persons in possession of the lands, to the same extent that the said grants would be valid if the territories had remained under the domain of his Catholic Majesty."
18. Greg C. Smith, *A Cultural Assessment Survey of the Sanchez Grant Tracts and Plantation Annex, St. Johns County, Florida* (Jacksonville, FL: Environmental Services, Inc., 1962).
19. Fort San Diego, *El Escribano* 8, 4 (October 1971): 139–48.

ARRIVAL AND INFLUENCE OF THE BRITISH IN FLORIDA, 1763–1783

20. Brent Handley, Greg Smith and Susan Parker, *An Intensive Cultural Resource Assessment Survey of the Nocatee Tract, Duval and St. Johns Counties, Florida* (unpublished ms., Jacksonville, FL, 2000), 37.
21. Michael Gannon, *Florida: A Short History* (Gainesville: University Press of Florida, 1993), 24.

22. Sidney P. Johnson, "Historic Properties Survey St Johns County, Florida," *Environmental Services, Inc. Report of Investigations* 245 (June 1, 2001): 15.
23. Daniel L. Schafer, *The Oldest City: St Augustine Saga of Survival* (St. Augustine, FL: St Augustine Historical Society, 1983), 100.
24. J. Leitch Wright, *British St. Augustine* (St. Augustine, FL: Historic St. Augustine Preservation Board, 1975).
25. Daniel L. Schafer, "Governor James Grant's Villa: A British East Florida Indigo Plantation," *St. Augustine Journal of History* (2000): 58.
26. Daniel L. Schafer, "'Yellow Silk Ferret Tied Round their Wrists': African Americans in British East Florida, 1763–1784," in David R. Colburn and Jane L. Landers, *The African American Heritage of Florida* (Gainesville: University Press of Florida, 1995).
27. Schafer, "'Yellow Silk Ferret."
28. Johnson, "Historic Properties Survey," 15.
29. Ibid., 85, 87–88.
30. Dr. William R. Adams et al., *The King's Road, Florida's First Highway* (unpublished report of City of New Smyrna and Volusia County Board of Commissioners, Florida State Library, 1997).
31. William P. Ryan, *Tracing Old Kings Road: Flagler County's Historic Heritage Link* (Bunnell, FL: Friends of the Library, Inc., 2006).
32. Adams et al., *King's Road*, 11.

Three Spanish Citizens Remained Through the British Period

33. Jane G. Landers, ed., *Colonial Plantations and Economy in Florida* (Gainesville: University Press of Florida, 2000), 84, 93.
34. Dena Snodgrass, *Dee-Dot Ranch and Twenty Mile House: A History* (Jacksonville, FL: privately published, 1973). This work can be found at Jacksonville Archives, Jacksonville University.
35. Bruce S. Chappell, *A Report on Documentation Relating to the History of the Diego Plains Region in Second Spanish Period Florida (1784–1821)* (Jacksonville Beach, FL: Beaches Area Historical Society, Inc., n.d.), 8.
36. Daniel L. Shafer, "St. Augustine's British Years, 1763–1784," *El Escribano* (2001): 266.
37. Landers, *Colonial Plantations*, 83.
38. Ibid.
39. Jane G. Landers, *Black Society in Spanish Florida* (Urbana: University of Illinois Press, 1999), 173.
40. Ibid., 343; Benjamin Guerard to Luis de Unzaga, August 2, 1783, manuscript box 45, PKY.
41. Landers, *Black Society*, 173.
42. Landers, *Colonial Plantations*, 87.
43. Ibid., 87–88.

44. Chappell, *Report on Documentation*, 12.
45. Ibid., 8; also see chapter on McGirtt.
46. Landers, *Colonial Plantations*, 86.
47. Thomas J. Kirkland and Robert M. Kennedy, *Historic Camden* (Columbia, SC: State Co., 1905), 297–305.
48. Helen Hornbeck Tanner, "The Second Spanish Period Begins" in Jacqueline K. Fretwell and Susan R. Parker, eds., *Clash Between Cultures: Spanish East Florida, 1784–1821* (St. Augustine, FL: St. Augustine Historical Society, 1988).
49. Snodgrass, *Dee-Dot Ranch.*
50. Kirkland and Kennedy, *Historic Camden.*
51. Landers, *Colonial Plantations*, 89.
52. Ibid., 90.
53. Chappell, *Report on Documentation*, 10–11.
54. Jane G. Landers, "Francisco Xavier Sanchez, Floridano Planter," in Ann L. Henderson and Gary R. Mormino, eds., *Spanish Pathways in Florida, 1492–1992* (Sarasota, FL: Pineapple Press, 1991), 168–87; also included in David R. Colburn and Jane L. Landers, *The African American Heritage of Florida* (Gainesville: University Press of Florida, c1995), 92.
55. Mario Hugas, *Francisco Xavier Sanchez* (St. Augustine, FL: Los Floridanos Society Publication, 2000), 2.
56. Chappell, *Report on Documentation*, 15.
57. Hugas, *Francisco Xavier Sanchez*, 2.
58. Light T. Cummins, "Luciano de Herrera and Spanish Espionage in British St. Augustine," *El Escribano* (1979), 43. A genealogical sketch of Herrera has been prepared by Mrs. Eleanor Phillips Barnes based on the St. Augustine Parish Registers. See Luciano de Herrera file, St. Augustine Historical Society Library. Although this is the only study that deals exclusively with Herrera, it is not complete in scope.
59. Katherine S. Lawson, "Luciano de Herrera, Spanish Spy in British St. Augustine," *Florida Historical Quarterly* 23, no. 3 (January 1945). The others were: mounted Dragoons Antonio de Leon, Sebastian Espinosa and Manuel Solana; infantrymen Francisco Canto and Pablo de Aguilar; and militiaman Francisco Salgado. The interpreter was Josef de Almo.
60. Daniel Schafer, "Out of the Wreck," *El Escribano* 38 (1979, 2001), 256; Cummins, "Luciano de Herrera," 43–57.
61. Handley et al., *Cultural Resource Assessment*, 38.

From Diego to Palm Valley, 1800s–1900s

62. William M. Jones, 1993, University of North Florida Archives, Jacksonville, FL. The tract of land that has been referred to in the Spanish land grants as "Fort San Diego" is identified today as "Section 422, Township 4 South, Range 29 East," and is located immediately west of the present Palm Valley Road, at a point one-half mile south of the Palm Valley Landing Road.

63. Myrtle Staley, "A View of the Valley," *Ponte Vedra Recorder*, December 17, 1976, 10.
64. Snodgrass, *Dee-Dot Ranch.*
65. Staley, "View of the Valley," 10.
66. "The Micklers," *Ponte Vedra Recorder*, August 26, 1988.
67. *Jacksonville Beach Florida*, February 25, 2000.
68. Baynard Kendrick, *The Site of Twenty-Mile Station—Palm Valley* (St. Augustine, FL: St. Augustine Historical Society, 1962), Reference 975.918. Kendrick also wrote a historical novel, *Flames of Time*.
69. Ibid.
70. Johnson, "Historic Properties Survey," 16.
71. Weaver, *Historic Properties Survey.*
72. Snodgrass, *Dee-Dot Ranch.*
73. "Spanish Dragoons Barracks," *El Escribano* 8 (1971): 149–57.
74. Kelly Hartman, "Valley Couples Share Common Ground," *Ponte Vedra Leader*, October 8 2003; "A Mickler recalls Palm Valley Bridge," *Ponte Vedra Leader*, September 11, 2002; Flavian Mickler, former bridge tender, personal communication, 1992.
75. Marsha A. Chance and Greg C. Smith, *A Brief History of the Mickler Palm Valley Bridge* (Jacksonville, FL: Environmental Services Inc., 1992).
76. Grahl Barkoskie Neitz, *Cabbageberries, Duck Feathers and the Tides: A Collection of Palm Valley Memories* (Flagler Beach, FL: Ocean Publishing, 2006), 39.
77. Rull Tolle, U.S. Army Corps of Engineers (USACE), North Florida Engineer, Jacksonville District office, 701 San Marco Boulevard, Jacksonville, Florida.
78. Dr. Wayne W. Wood, *Jacksonville's Architectural Heritage: Landmarks for the Future* (Gainesville: University Press of Florida, 1989).
79. Staley, "View of the Valley."
80. Neitz, *Cabbageberries*, 31.
81. James L. Miller, *An Environmental History of Northeast Florida* (Gainesville: University Press of Florida, 1998), 176.
82. Snodgrass, *Dee-Dot Ranch.*
83. April 29, 2003, BAHS.
84. Patricia Ferguson Mickler, *The Micklers of Florida* (Chuluota, FL: Mickler House, Pub. 1991).
85. Dennie Carter, "Ponte Vedra Pioneers: Flavian Mickler," *Ponte Vedra Recorder* 14, no. 18, July 29, 1983.
86. Staley, "View of the Valley."
87. Ibid.
88. Carter, "Ponte Vedra Pioneers."
89. *Beaches Leader*, June 30, 1999.
90. A small structure used as a refreshment stand.
91. Neitz, *Cabbageberries*, 269.
92. Carter, "Ponte Vedra Pioneers," 7.
93. *Ponte Vedra Recorder*, November 24, 1972.

94. Michel Oesterreicher, *Pioneer Family: Life on Florida's Twentieth Century Frontier* (Tuscaloosa: University of Alabama Press, 1996).
95. Myrtle E. Stanley, "History of Palm Valley Community Club," *Ocean Beach Reporter*, March 5, 1954.
96. Neitz, *Cabbageberries*, 321.

Town of Mineral City—Mining for Minerals, 1914–1928

97. Scott Madry, Greg C. Smith and Carrie Whitehall, *Archaeological Survey and Development of a GIS-based Site Probability Model* (Jacksonville, FL: Environmental Services, Inc., 2001).
98. "Newcomer's Guide," *Ponte Vedra Recorder*, 1999.
99. Dick Bussard, ed., "How Mineral City Helped Win the War," *Jacksonville Journal*, March 1977.
100. *Ponte Vedra Recorder*.
101. Patricia Pritchard Finley was the oldest daughter of George Pritchard. *Ponte Vedra Recorder*.
102. *Ponte Vedra Recorder.*
103. Richard Stalder, "Serene Ponte Vedra Beach was a Bustling Mining Town," *Times-Union*, March 11, 1956, Jacksonville Public Library Archives.
104. *Ponte Vedra Recorder*.
105. *Ponte Vedra Recorder*.
106. *Times-Union*, 1956, Jacksonville Public Library Archives.
107. "How Mineral City Helped Win the War," *Beaches Leader/Ponte Vedra Leader*, October 1998.
108. Dick Bussard, "Mineral City: A Local Boom Town," *Journal City*, March 3, 1977, Jacksonville Public Library.
109 Neitz, *Cabbageberries*, 313.
110. "How Mineral City Helped," *Beaches Leader/Ponte Vedra Leader.*
111. Bussard, "Mineral City."

First Church in Palm Valley and Ponte Vedra

112. *Jacksonville Times-Union*, February 13, 1977.
113. Staley, "View of the Valley."
114. Betty Sheetz, "Our History," May 20, 1995, Beaches Area Historical Society, Jacksonville Beach Florida.
115. Staley, "View of the Valley."

116. Palm Valley Baptist Church brochure celebrating one hundred years in 2002; Jim Witt, pastor's personal interview, 2003.
117. "Christmas Church Schedules: History of Christ Church." *Ponte Vedra Recorder*, December 17, 1976, 3.
118. "Genesis 28:18 The Lord is in This Place," *Ponte Vedra Recorder*, December 17, 1976, 11.
119 Laurie Wizemann and Kim Durbin, communications; Reverend Joan Bryan, associate pastor; Reverend Jo Hoskins and longtime member, Henry Newcomer; personal interviews.
120. Jacksonville Historical Society Archives, August 20 1966. Copper installed on the roof's steeple. Ed Smith, *Them Good Ole Days: In Mayport and the Beaches* (n.p., 1974), 93, 94.
121. Fred Woolverton, personal conversation in Jacksonville.
122. Alice Juhan, wife of Reverend Juhan, personal conversation at Vicar's Landing, 2006.
123. Dennie Carter, "Spotlight People," *Ponte Vedra Recorder*, March 22, 1985, 21.
124. *Ponte Vedra Recorder*, 1976.
125. Randy Brown, personal interview, 2006. Brown is the son of one of the founders of Ponte Vedra Beach.
126. Henrietta (Hinkey) Gilliard, beginning member of the church, personal interview, 2006.
127. "Christmas Church Schedules: History of Christ Church," *Ponte Vedra Recorder*, December 17, 1976, 3.

GERMAN SABOTEURS—*OPERATION PASTORIUS*, 1942

128. *Florida Historical Quarterly* (October 1970): 129. Leon O. Prior is a professor of history at Miami-Dade Junior College, North Campus, and a retired special agent of the Federal Bureau of Investigation.
129. Micheal Dobbs, *Saboteurs: The Nazi Raid on America* (New York: Alfred A. Knopf, 2006), 129–31.
130. Eugene Rachlis, *They Came To Kill: The Story of Eight Nazi Sabotirs in America* (New York: Random House, 1961). This book tells, for the first time, the complete story of *Operation Pastorius*.

PONTE VEDRA INN AND CLUB HISTORY

131. Elaine B. Koehl, *Ponte Vedra Club: The First Fifty-five Years, 1927–1982* (Ponte Vedra: Ponte Vedra Club, 1982), 1.
132. Koehl, *Ponte Vedra Club*, 5.

133. "The Rebirth of a Grand Florida Tradition," *Florida Times-Union*, February 10, 2002, 6.
134. Koehl, *Ponte Vedra Club*, 6.
135. This was included in an article in the Ponte Vedra Club news by Louis Kurz, 1956.
136. Koehl, *Ponte Vedra Club*, 21–22.
137. Ibid., 19.
138. Ibid., 81.
139. Ibid., 19.
140. Richard Vach, "Jax-Tennis Magazine," *Florida Times-Union*, March 2007.
141. Koehl, *Ponte Vedra Club*, 55.
142. Neitz, *Cabbageberries*, 313.
143. Koehl, *Ponte Vedra Club*, 85.
144. Ibid., 82.
145. Ibid., 85.
146. Herbert Hill Peyton, *Newboy: The Autobiography of Herbert Hill Peyton* (Lillington, NC: Edwards Brother, Ind., 1997), 165–181.
147. Phil and Julianna Howe, personal interviews, 2007.
148. "A Super-Super Person," *Ponte Vedra Recorder*, March 4, 1977, 10.
149. "The Rebirth of a Grand Florida Tradition," *Ponte Vedra Recorder*, March 4, 1977, 6.

PONTE VEDRA BEACH VOLUNTEER FIRE DEPARTMENT

150. Fred Woolverton, Ponte Vedra chief (1959–74), personal conversation.
151. Murle Harrison, volunteer fire chief at Ponte Vedra Club and Ponte Vedra Club manager (1978–83), interview, 2004. Related stories about Harry Johnson, founder.
152. "Ponte Vedra Fire Chiefs Honored," *Ponte Vedra Recorder*, March 15 1985, 15.

THE PONTE VEDRA BRANCH LIBRARY

153. Jack Morgan, *A Brief History of the Ponte Vedra Beach Branch Library and the Friends of the Library* (Ponte Vedra, FL: Ponte Vedra Printing, 1995).
154. "Palm Valley Library Open to all Ponte Vedrans," *Ponte Vedra Recorder*, July 13, 1984, 15.
155. Morgan, *Brief History*.
156. "Ponte Vedra Beach Library hits Links," *Jacksonville Business Journal*, August 6, 2002.

Beginning of the First Elementary and High School

157. Margaret Clark, "Generous Gift Benefits Community School," *Ponte Vedra Recorder*, November 30, 1984, 1,5.
158. St. Johns County School District, 40 Orange Street, St. Augustine, Florida 32084, School Board member District 2, Tommy Allen.
159. Maggie FitzRoy, "Nease Players Meet Widow of Man School is Named For," *Ponte Vedra Shoreline*, December 17, 2005.
160. Tommy Allen, Chairman St. Johns County School Board, 2004, a presentation to graduating class of Allen D. Nease High School; Margo Nease Stevens, daughter of Allen Nease, living in St. Augustine Florida; and Nancy Powell, staff writer, 1975, article in the *Florida Times-Union*, 1998; Lee Goddard, "The Name Game: Area Athletes Get Educated on School Namesakes," *Times-Union*.

Post Office History

161. Staley, "View of the Valley."
162. Neitz, *Cabbageberries*.
163. Recollections of Dwight Wilson, Neptune Beach, who delivered newspapers to the homes along Roscoe Boulevard.
164. Myrtle Staley, *Ocean Beach Reporter*, March 11, 1955.
165. *Beaches Leader/Ponte Vedra Leader*, June 27, 2003. Special edition, fortieth anniversary.

Beaches Area Historical Society

166. Beaches and Museum and History Center's Grand Opening Brochure, March 4, 2006, Jacksonville Beach, FL.
167. "Beaches Area Historical Society," *Ponte Vedra Recorder*, April 7, 1978.
168. Ibid., August 10, 1979.
169. Ibid., August 26, 1983. Requesting memorabilia for railroad museum.
170. "McCormick Founded BAHS in '78," *Ponte Vedra Recorder*, March, 2006.
171. Ibid.
172. Beaches Museum and History Center, "A Glimpse of the People & Events that have shaped the First Coast Beaches," *Arbus Magazine* (July/August 2007).
173. "Beaches Museum Prepares for Visitors," *Times-Union Shorelines*, March 4, 2006.
174. "A Rich Beaches History," *Ponte Vedra Shorelines*, September 1, 2004.
175. *Arbus Magazine*, 22–23.

PRESERVING THE GUANA TRACT

176. Andrew E. Douglas, "A Find of Ceremonial Axes in a Florida Mound," *American Antiquarian* 4, no. 100–09 (1885); "Some Characteristics of the Indian Earth and Shell Mounds on the Atlantic Coast of Florida," *American Antiquarian* 7, no. 74–82 (1882): 140–147.
177. Peyton, *Newboy*, 183–93.

THE FLETCHER LEGACY

178. Fletcher, *Brief History*.
179. Jerome S. Fletcher, personal interview, April, 2007.
180. "History of the Marsh: at Home with Jerome Fletcher," *Jacksonville Home & Hospitality* (February/March 2007): 24.
181. Randy Noles, "Mr. Outside and Mr. Inside," *Jacksonville Magazine* (2007): 56.
182. Kevin M. McCarthy, *Thirty Florida Shipwrecks* (Sarasota, FL: Pineapple Press, Inc., 1992).
183. "Fire Guts Local Landmark," *Ponte Vedra Recorder*, September 13, 1974.
184. Susanna Barton, "Condo Sales clipping along in South Ponte Vedra Beach," *Jacksonville Business Journal*, July 16, 2001.
185. Ibid.
186. Ryan Geddes, "Solving a Land Puzzle Sets Up Ritzy New Suburb," *Jacksonville Business Journal*, January 26, 2004; Kirstin Dorsch, "Found Forest," July 31, 2006.
187. Fletcher, *Brief History*, 8.

PGA HEADQUARTERS' BEGINNING AND THE TPC

188. "What it was like Then—What It's like Now," *Ponte Vedra Recorder*, March 23, 1984, 46–47.
189. Jean Batchelder, *The Record*, February 16, 2007.
190. Sally Peterson, "The Dollar Deal That Shaped Ponte Vedra Beach," *Ponte Vedra Recorder*, 1990; also printed in *Jacksonville Today*, April, 1991.
191. Erica Opisso, "Storytellers to Relate 'Once Upon a Time' at TPC," *Ponte Vedra Recorder*, May 11, 2007, 1.
192. Opisso, "Storytellers to Relate."
193. Joy Batteh-Freiha, "The Dawning of a New Era: The New TPC Sawgrass," *Florida Times-Union*, June 2007, 2,4,10.

ATP (Association of Tennis Professionals) International Headquarters

194. Richard Evans, *Open Tennis 1968–1988; The Players, the Politics, the Pressures, the Passions, and the Great Matches* (Lexington, MA: Stephen Greene Press, 1989).
195. Ibid.
196. Ibid.
197. Jerome Fletcher, personal interview at Marsh Landing, March 2007.
198. "*Tennis* Ranks Inn & Club Among Top Resorts," *Jacksonville Business Journal*, November 14, 2002.

Chronological History of Ponte Vedra Beach

199. Florida Coast Line Canal & Transportation Company (FCLC & TC 1880–1927).
200. Jacksonville, St. Augustine and Halifax River Railway (JSTAHRR).
201. Florida Coast Line Canal & Transportation Company (1880–1927).
202. The name *serenata* was given by Italian composers in the time of Handel, and by Handel himself, to a cantata of a pastoral of dramatic character, to a secular ode, etc.; also by Mozart and others to an orchestral composition, in several movements, midway between the suite of an earlier period and the modern symphony.

About the Author and Artist

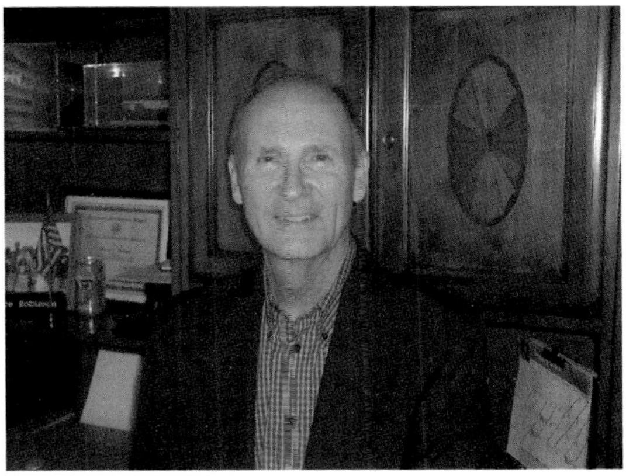

Maurice Robinson was transferred from Richmond, Virginia, to Ponte Vedra Beach, Florida, in 1993, as an accountant with CSX Corporation. He retired in 2003 after thirty-five years. Born in Virginia, he holds a bachelor's degree from Virginia Commonwealth University and has completed classes at the University of North Florida. His interests focus on North Florida and especially the First Coast topics in St. Johns County, Florida. He now resides with his wife in historic Midlothian, Virginia.

Ellen Diamond, whose painting appears on the cover, is a resident of Ponte Vedra Beach. She is an internationally acclaimed contemporary impressionist whose subjects range from the local beaches and marshes of northern Florida to the landscapes of Tuscany and Provence, both of which she visits regularly..